THE GEIST ATLAS OF CANADA

THE GEIST ATLAS OF CANADA

Meat Maps and Other Strange Cartographies

by Melissa Edwards

Introduction by Stephen Osborne

ARSENAL
PULP PRESS

VANCOUVER

The Geist Atlas of Canada
Copyright © 2006 by Melissa Edwards and the Geist Foundation

ARSENAL PULP PRESS
341 Water Street, Suite 200
Vancouver, BC
Canada V6B 1B8
arsenalpulp.com

The publisher gratefully acknowledges the support of the Government of Canada
through the Book Publishing Industry Development Program and the Government
of British Columbia through the Book Publishing Tax Credit Program for its
publishing activities.

Text, cover design, and interior illustrations by Diane Yee, Electra Design Group
Creative direction by Lisa Eng-Lodge, Electra Design Group
Editing by Derek Fairbridge
Cover illustration by Bernie Lyon
Cover map used with permission from Bibliothèque nationale de France
   (with thanks to Derek Hayes)

Printed and Bound in Canada

Library and Archives Canada Cataloguing in Publication

Edwards, Melissa, 1970–
      The Geist atlas of Canada : meat maps and other strange
cartographies / Melissa Edwards.

Includes bibliographical references and index.
ISBN 1-55152-216-0

      1. Canada—Maps. 2. Names, Geographical—Canada—Humor. I. Title.

FC36.E49 2006   912.7102'07   C2006-903532-6

ISBN13: 978-155152-216-6

TABLE OF CONTENTS

PREFACE

One of my first tasks as a *Geist* volunteer was to help create the Canadian Map of Heaven and Hell & Mortality of the Flesh, which at the time was the current installment in the magazine's Caught Mapping series of Canadian maps. I was handed a massive atlas and instructed to dig through its index for relevant place names. Not everyone would have enjoyed this job, but for me the discovery of a surprising, funny, and apt name hidden among all the various Lakeviews and Rosedales was as thrilling as finding a loonie in a penny jar.

Over the years, I took on a good share of the mapping work but the maps remain very much a collaborative effort. Some of the themes are chance discoveries, such as the Map of Loudmouths & Outbursts, which came about when I saw a sign for Saint-Louis-du-Ha!-Ha! on a road trip through eastern Canada. Some are part of a strategy, as with the Stan Rogers Map, which we did in connection with a Stan-Rogers-for-Hall-of-Fame campaign. Some are serendipity, such as the Beer Map, which began when a Geist volunteer spotted the return address of Molson, MB, on an envelope. Other maps are milestones on the *Geist* quest to define a Canadian identity: the Hockey Map, the CBC Map, the Map of Peggy's Canada, and the Original Map are obvious examples, but cartographies of Angst, Joe Jobs, Doughnuts, and Malls are just as reflective of our modern nation. The idea for some maps just seemed fun (Happy, Fairy Tales, Nicknames); for others, the reasoning just can't be explained (Impolite, Haircuts, Kitchen Implements). Each one of them grew out of our true affection for this country, even if some of them poke a

little fun. And really, what is more Canadian than making fun of ourselves?

Most of us at *Geist* have been questioned at various times about places that appear on these maps—how they got their names, whether a town really was named after a sex act or a doughnut. And sometimes we are asked whether they are simply all made up. We have seized the opportunity with this *Geist Atlas of Canada* to illuminate a few of these places through stories about who named them and why. Though this book could present only a few of the thousands of toponymic histories in Canada, even this small handful helps bring home that, yes, these places are real, they are all fascinating to discover, and—weird map topics aside—most of them are not named after beer, condiments, or sex. To address the themes, and because some of these factoids were too interesting not to include, we've also thrown in a bit of relevant Canadian trivia with each map.

It has been a great stroke of fortune for me to land such strange and enjoyable work for such a unique publication, and to be involved in the creation of this atlas. I hope that readers will find these maps, stories, and facts as enjoyable to browse through as they were to research. And, though it is in no way meant to be used for navigation, I hope the atlas inspires at least a few readers to get out and explore some Meat Coves, Pink Mountains, Weeping Walls, Top-of-the-Worlds, Dildos, and other singular points tucked away in this vast and undiscovered country.

MELISSA EDWARDS

ACKNOWLEDGEMENTS

This book, like the *Geist* maps themselves, is the result of a collaborative process. A special salute must first go to the original *Geist* mappers: Kevin Barefoot, Billeh Nickerson, and Neil MacDonald, as well as to Kris Rothstein, Pamela Priebe, Jill Mandrake, Gwen Fosse, Chris Conway, Gary Whiteford, and everyone who has been a part of the *Geist* mapping team, and to Paul Davies for creating the original Geistonic Projection. A special thanks to Barbara Zatyko for her smart titles, her great eye for a funny name, and for her whip-quick skill with the pun, and to Patty Osborne for her own unique touches and for taking a bunch of scribbles and turning them into proper cartography.

Thanks to Nicole Marteinsson and Bethanne Grabham at Arsenal Pulp Press, who contributed invaluable research to this book, and to Shyla Seller, who worked hard to see it into print. Thanks to Li Eng-Lodge and Diane Yee for their designs and their beautiful re-envisioning of the *Geist* maps, to Bernie Lyon for her illustration, to Derek Hayes for his help with the cover map (which appears in his book *The Historical Atlas of Canada*), and to the rest of the Arsenal Pulp team: Brian Lam, Robert Ballantyne, Tessa Vanderkop, and Janice Beley. Thanks also to all the staff and volunteers at *Geist*, including Carla Elm Clement, Carra Simpson, C.E. Coughlan, Trevor Battye, Mindy Abramowitz, and especially those who were conscripted to the map production line: Michal Kozlowski, Michael Jenner, Lina Jung, Katrina Rahardja, Carrie Villeneuve, Kathy Vito, André Cormier, and Michelle van de Merwe.

Thanks to all of the people who gave us advice and helped us to develop this book, including John Ng and the good people at the Geomatics Association of Nova Scotia and the New Brunswick chapter of the Canadian Institute of Geomatics. Thanks also to the people who gave their time to tell us stories about their home towns, to the many toponymic researchers who published histories of Canadian place names and made it so easy for us to research this book, and to Geomatics Canada and Natural Resources Canada for their excellent, publicly accessible database of Canadian geographical names.

Finally, thanks to Stephen Osborne and Mary Schendlinger, who began the *Geist* mapping empire and who worked to make every aspect of this book as good as it could be. And a big thanks to Derek Fairbridge, for his fine editing and for setting the Atlas in motion.

INTRODUCTION
Entirely Unafraid ~ *Stephen Osborne*

It's not easy to imagine a world without maps. Indeed, a world without maps would barely be a world at all—when we hear someone say "there's Canada," we know that they are pointing not out the window but at a piece of paper. We consult maps every day. We stand on subway trains hypnotized by the schematics posted above the door; we search desperately through shopping malls for the map to lead us out; we consult "mind maps" when at a loss for ideas.

To get somewhere you haven't been before, you consult a map—to find the opera house in Moncton, for example, or the nearest liquor store in Swift Current; perhaps a passing citizen will draw a map for you on the back of that envelope you've been carrying around in your hip pocket. If you want to get from Lac Salami in Quebec to, say, Veal Lake in Manitoba, you consult a map before you set foot out the door, and when the fishing at Veal Lake turns out to be not so good, you might carry on overland to Eatlots Lake, for the pickerel. Or if you want to go from Brimstone to Black Hole to Yum Yum Point, or even from Coffee Rocks to Breakfast Cove (a short hop, but a tricky passage), you need to find the right map for the job.

One of the earliest uses of maps in modern Canada was to show European farmers how pleasant it would be to get out to and travel around in the vast, possibly endless western plains. The Canadian Pacific Railway and the federal government, often mistaken for each other in that epoch, sent out hundreds of thousands of colourful maps inset with bucolic scenes and dotted with the names of cities linked by a dense network of railway lines; many thousands of immigrants poured into Canada and across the treeless plain, where they learned that the cities on the maps were tent cities and the railways purely hallucinatory. Even the average mean temperatures printed in the margins were hypothetical—today these maps are classified as early science fiction.

Maps conceal as much as they seem to reveal. The map that John Cabot took with him when he sailed for China contained no trace of Newfoundland; by the time Captain Cook got to the mouth of the Northwest Passage, as delineated in Maldonado's famous map of 1588, the Northwest Passage had disappeared from the face of the earth. Maps can be paradoxical in these and other ways, and one can be led to a suspicion of maps in general. Hence the well-known wariness of Canadians setting out for Treasure Island, say, or Giant's Castle: they remain skeptical until they see the place with their own eyes. This native skepticism is what led the *Geist* mapping team, whose motto from the beginning has been

"Entirely Unafraid of Canadian Place Names," to engage in such close scrutiny of the Canadian cartographic record. We were convinced that something more than meets the eye was there to be found, and this volume is the result.

The maps collected here offer glimpses of imaginary nations that call themselves Canada—like parallel universes, they oscillate in and out of consciousness. Names lose their meanings quickly when repeated again and again, so that putting a name on a map is a way of memorializing and at the same time obliterating it. Who, for instance, when thinking of British Columbia, thinks of the Admiral of the Ocean Sea, or while pondering the scenic aspects of Lake Louise is put in mind of Queen Victoria's offspring? The *Geist Atlas of Canada* demonstrates how promiscuously new meaning attaches to old names. The Old Testament roots of Jericho Beach, for example, go back no further than to a nineteenth-century logger named Jerry who floated his logs in a cove named for him by friends or possibly by himself; the village of Ganges has no connection with the holy river of India—it was named for a British ship of the line authorized to frighten Americans during the (now forgotten) War of Griffin's Pig. Chesterfield Inlet, associated in the popular mind with images of sofas abandoned on icebergs, was named for an English

lord denigrated in 1755 by Samuel Johnson. And throughout the landscapes of the nation, echoes of autobiography reverberate through the ages. Desolation Sound, Fear Lake, Drunken Dick, Pain Court, Anger Island, Sigh Lake—such are the anguished traces of those who have gone before, many of them drawn to this country by the early maps produced by the CPR and the government. Immigrants always bring new mappings to new terrain, and as new mappings are laid down, older mappings created by those who were already here are erased, hence the work of First Nations to reclaim the memory and the fact of traditional territories.

Implicit in the concept of the *Geist Atlas* are the itineraries proposed in its pages. As the world's destination points lose their lustre, as the catchphrase "world class" loses its magic, whole expeditions into new worlds begin to emerge from the maps in this collection. Soon we will be booking reservations for Erotic Tours of a Nation, Kitchen Implement Pilgrimages, National Beer Crawls, Journeys to Places That Sound Impolite, and for Sojourns along Philosopher's Walk or Junkets into Angst. These are a few of the adventure tours of the future that promise to draw the whole world once again to our doorstep.

GAME GUARDIAN SWAMP, MB: A wetland area on the west side of Mantagao Lake. It may be so named because park officials frequently hid in the swamp in attempts to catch poachers.

JERSEY TICKLE, NL: A tickle is a hazardous ocean channel, usually peppered with submerged rocks and beset by a strong tidal pull. The term is native to Newfoundland—Jersey is one of about 250 official tickles on the island and in Labrador. Others include Pinchgut Tickle, Blind Mugford Tickle, and Leading Tickles (see Erotic Map, p. 98).

STICK PINGO, NT: A pingo is a conical land feature that forms on the tundra when underground water reserves freeze and swell, then push the land upwards. Pingos can reach up to fifty metres (165 feet) high. Most of them erode quite quickly, but some are more than 1,000 years old. More than 1,400 pingos are clustered around the Mackenzie Delta near Tuktoyaktuk, NT. Other pockets of pingos are scattered along the Alaska–Yukon border and in Vuntut National Park. The word "pingo" comes from the Inuit for "small hill."

ELBOW, SK: This community sits on an elbow-shaped bend in the South Saskatchewan River. In 1804 a North West Company employee named John McDonald wrote in his log:

"There is an elbow in the river parallel to that of the north branch, a most beautiful place. I crossed the neck of land... with my interpreter, while the canoes, always in sight, had to go around ten miles at least."

MONEY MAKERS ROCK, BC: A submerged rock in Ganges Harbour, Saltspring Island.

HULL, QC: Hull is a district of Gatineau and is often referred to as *vieux secteur* Hull (it was an independent city before the amalgamation of several towns in 2002). Some say the name comes from Kingston-upon-Hull, the British hometown of Philemon Wright ("the King of Gatineau"), who established a logging camp here in 1800. Others claim that it comes from "hyll," an old English word for "hill," and that Wright was actually born in Massachusetts. Before 1800 the area was known as Portage des Chaudières (which evolved from the Algonquin name for Boiler or Kettle Rapids), then as Columbia Farm for a while (supposedly from Wright's mispronunciation of "Chaudières"). Hull is directly across the Ottawa River from Ottawa and, as part of the National Capital Region, it has enough office space for more than 20,000 *fonctionnaires* (civil servants).

LORD STANLEY'S MUG

The silver bowl atop the Stanley Cup was made by G.R. Collis and Co. Silversmiths (now Boodles and Dunthorne Jewellers) in London, England. Lord Stanley, then Governor General of Canada, purchased the bowl for $50, called it the Dominion Hockey Challenge Cup, and donated it to the Amateur Hockey Association to use as a prize. The first team to win the Cup was the Montreal AAA, in 1893.

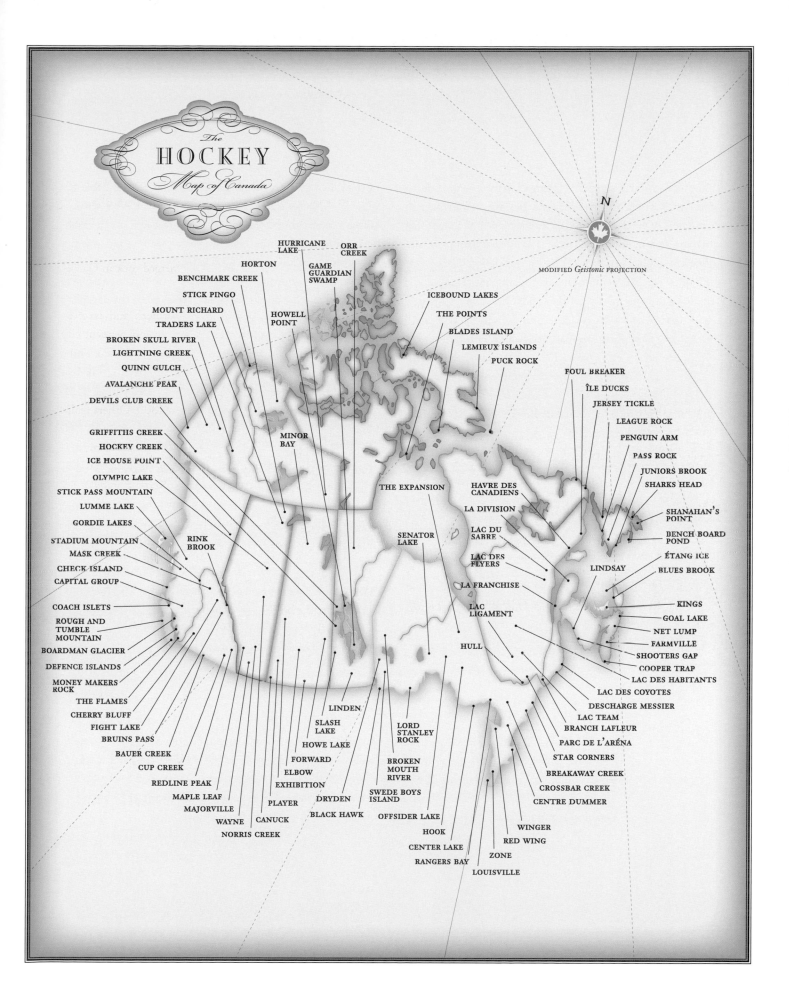

The
HOCKEY
Map of Canada

N

MODIFIED *Geistonic* PROJECTION

HURRICANE LAKE
ORR CREEK
HORTON
GAME GUARDIAN SWAMP
BENCHMARK CREEK
STICK PINGO
MOUNT RICHARD
HOWELL POINT
TRADERS LAKE
BROKEN SKULL RIVER
LIGHTNING CREEK
QUINN GULCH
AVALANCHE PEAK
DEVILS CLUB CREEK

ICEBOUND LAKES
THE POINTS
BLADES ISLAND
LEMIEUX ISLANDS
PUCK ROCK

FOUL BREAKER
ÎLE DUCKS
JERSEY TICKLE
LEAGUE ROCK
PENGUIN ARM
PASS ROCK
JUNIORS BROOK
SHARKS HEAD

GRIFFITHS CREEK
HOCKEY CREEK
ICE HOUSE POINT
OLYMPIC LAKE
STICK PASS MOUNTAIN
LUMME LAKE
GORDIE LAKES
STADIUM MOUNTAIN
MASK CREEK
CHECK ISLAND
CAPITAL GROUP

MINOR BAY

RINK BROOK

THE EXPANSION

HAVRE DES CANADIENS
LA DIVISION

SENATOR LAKE

LAC DU SABRE

LAC DES FLYERS

LA FRANCHISE

LAC LIGAMENT

SHANAHAN'S POINT
BENCH BOARD POND
ÉTANG ICE
BLUES BROOK

LINDSAY

KINGS
GOAL LAKE
NET LUMP
FARMVILLE
SHOOTERS GAP
COOPER TRAP
LAC DES HABITANTS
LAC DES COYOTES

COACH ISLETS
ROUGH AND TUMBLE MOUNTAIN
BOARDMAN GLACIER
DEFENCE ISLANDS
MONEY MAKERS ROCK
THE FLAMES
CHERRY BLUFF
FIGHT LAKE
BRUINS PASS
BAUER CREEK
CUP CREEK
REDLINE PEAK
MAPLE LEAF
MAJORVILLE
WAYNE
NORRIS CREEK

LINDEN
SLASH LAKE
HOWE LAKE
FORWARD
ELBOW
EXHIBITION
DRYDEN
PLAYER
CANUCK
BLACK HAWK

LORD STANLEY ROCK

BROKEN MOUTH RIVER

SWEDE BOYS ISLAND

OFFSIDER LAKE

HOOK

CENTER LAKE

RANGERS BAY

HULL

WINGER
RED WING
ZONE
LOUISVILLE

DESCHARGE MESSIER
LAC TEAM
BRANCH LAFLEUR
PARC DE L'ARÉNA
STAR CORNERS
BREAKAWAY CREEK
CROSSBAR CREEK
CENTRE DUMMER

BELCHER ISLANDS, NU: Attempts have been made to connect this name to Sir Edward Belcher, commander of a mission to find the Franklin Expedition, but a map that predates that mission lists the area as Île de Roteur ("island of belch"). That handle was likely a translation of the name of James Belcher, a Hudson's Bay Company captain. The archipelago consists of 1,500 islands in a unique squiggly shape that from the air resembles oil on water. The islands' only town, Sanikiluaq on Flaherty Island, is the southernmost community in Nunavut. Henry Hudson, who explored the bay, is said to be buried somewhere on the Belcher Islands, though most believe his body was never found after his mutinous crew set him adrift in a small boat with his son and a few loyal crew members (see notes on Hudson Bay, Retail Map, p. 88).

KEG RIVER, AB: A hamlet on a river that was noted as "Keg of Rum" in some early records. The rum part came later: "Keg River" comes from the original name, *markak seepee*, which translators understood to mean "something narrow and deep," such as a keg.

CAP-SEIZE, QC: A cape whose name translates as "Cape Sixteen," which evolved from a French transliteration of the English word "capsize."

FOAM LAKE, SK: So named, according to the *Macmillan Book of Canadian Place Names*, because "after a blow there is always foam around the edges." A nearby sign on the highway, calling it "the best place in the world to live," was put up after Foam Lake won a CBC call-in vote on the best place in Saskatchewan to live. That was in 1996, the same year that the United Nations declared Canada to be the best place in the world to live, and a research company determined Saskatchewan to be the best place in Canada to live.

MOLSON, MB: A team of volunteers for *Geist* magazine spotted this name while they were stuffing envelopes in the office. Molson started as a railway stop called Monmouth, but in the late 1800s it was founded as a town and renamed for F.W. Molson, a former director of the CPR.

FLAT LAKES, NT: Paleontologists named this area Trilobite Lakes, but in 1968 the Department of Indian Affairs and Northern Development noted that miners and aircraft pilots in the region knew it as Flat Lakes, and the name was changed.

PITCHERS FARM, NS: A community on the Sunrise Trail in Antigonish County, named for Moses Pitcher, its first rightsholder. In the 1970s the name was changed from Pitcher Farm to Pitchers Farm. (Why not "Pitcher's Farm"? See notes on Clarke's Head, Map of Haircuts, p. 84.)

FAREWELL TO THE STUBBIE

Canadian breweries discontinued the iconic squat, brown "stubbie" beer bottle in favour of American-style longnecks in the early 1980s, even though the stubbie was stronger (and so had a longer life) and it was more economical to pack and ship. It was also more difficult to hit someone over the head with a stubbie in a bar fight. In 1983 the William Lyon Mackenzie Appreciation Society initiated a boycott of beers that came in longnecks, in an attempt to hang on to a Canadian symbol, but to no avail.

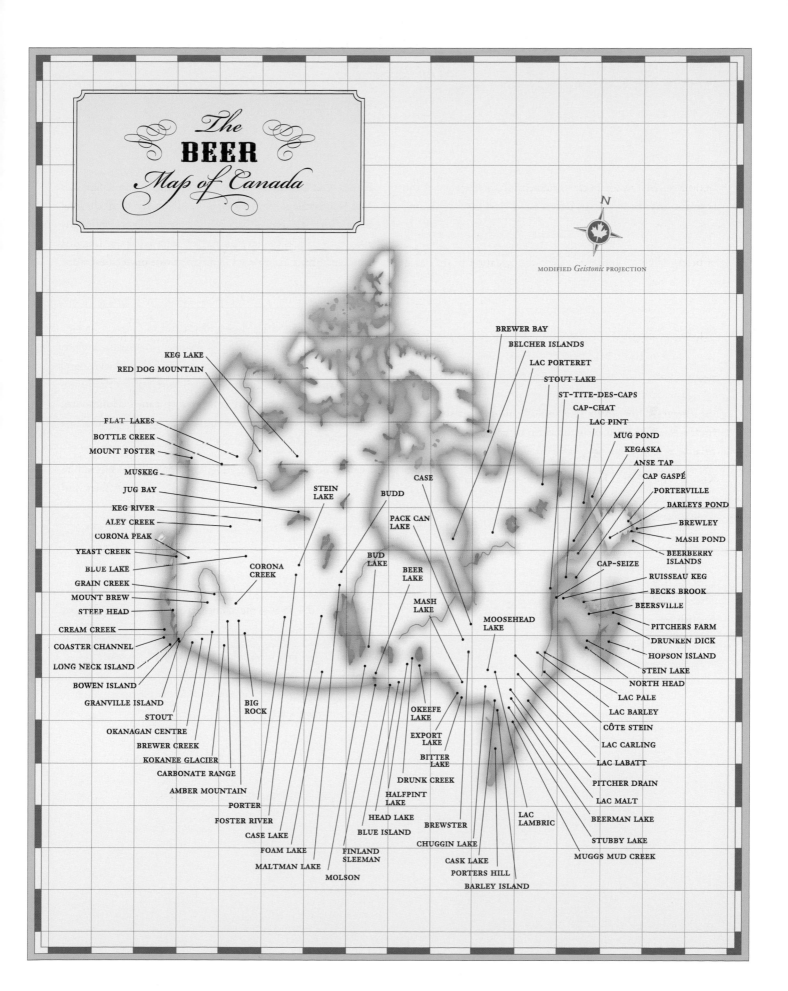

The
BEER
Map of Canada

N

MODIFIED *Geistonic* PROJECTION

KEG LAKE
RED DOG MOUNTAIN

BREWER BAY
BELCHER ISLANDS
LAC PORTERET
STOUT LAKE
ST-TITE-DES-CAPS
CAP-CHAT
LAC PINT
MUG POND
KEGASKA
ANSE TAP
CAP GASPÉ
PORTERVILLE
BARLEYS POND
BREWLEY
MASH POND
BEERBERRY ISLANDS

FLAT LAKES
BOTTLE CREEK
MOUNT FOSTER
MUSKEG
JUG BAY
KEG RIVER
ALEY CREEK
CORONA PEAK
YEAST CREEK
BLUE LAKE
GRAIN CREEK
MOUNT BREW
STEEP HEAD
CREAM CREEK
COASTER CHANNEL
LONG NECK ISLAND
BOWEN ISLAND
GRANVILLE ISLAND
STOUT
OKANAGAN CENTRE
BREWER CREEK
KOKANEE GLACIER
CARBONATE RANGE
AMBER MOUNTAIN
PORTER
FOSTER RIVER
CASE LAKE
FOAM LAKE
MALTMAN LAKE

STEIN LAKE
BUDD
PACK CAN LAKE
CASE
BUD LAKE
BEER LAKE
MASH LAKE
CORONA CREEK

MOOSEHEAD LAKE

CAP-SEIZE
RUISSEAU KEG
BECKS BROOK
BEERSVILLE
PITCHERS FARM
DRUNKEN DICK
HOPSON ISLAND
STEIN LAKE
NORTH HEAD
LAC PALE
LAC BARLEY
CÔTE STEIN
LAC CARLING
LAC LABATT
PITCHER DRAIN
LAC MALT
BEERMAN LAKE
STUBBY LAKE
MUGGS MUD CREEK

BIG ROCK

OKEEFE LAKE
EXPORT LAKE
BITTER LAKE
DRUNK CREEK
HALFPINT LAKE
HEAD LAKE
BLUE ISLAND
FINLAND SLEEMAN
MOLSON

BREWSTER
CHUGGIN LAKE
CASK LAKE
PORTERS HILL
BARLEY ISLAND

LAC LAMBRIC

PORTERS HILL

—15—

MILLION, MB: Once a town named for the fertility of the region, now listed in the gazetteers as a "locality."

SAWBACK, AB: Another "locality." Sawback is situated beneath a mountain range of the same name. The range was named by Sir James Hector (1834–1907), a Scottish geologist and explorer whose own name was given to many mountains and lakes in Alberta (and also to a rare breed of dolphin native to New Zealand).

BUTTERFLY BAY, NU: In 1944 the explorer Diamond Jenness renamed this spot after its original name, Tukelik, which he believed was a short form of "*tarkalikitark*," meaning "butterfly" or "moth." Several species of butterfly occur in the Arctic, at least six of them—including the Dingy Fritillary, Hecla Sulphur and American Copper—above the 75th parallel. Arctic breeds have developed special methods of making the most of solar energy. They are smaller than other butterflies, for example. Arctic butterflies also build up a kind of natural antifreeze in the fall, and then go into dormancy in the winter.

ROACHVILLE, NB: *Geographic Place Names of New Brunswick* says that Roachville is the Canadian headquarters of Black Flag brand insecticide, but *Place Names of Atlantic Canada* claims the town was named for its first settler, John Roach, a Loyalist and a member of the Royal Fencible American Regiment.

OFF THE MAP

Claimants to the title Mosquito Capital of Canada include Winnipeg and Churchill, MB. Foreign claimants include towns in Minnesota, Mississippi, Louisiana, Florida, and Arkansas. Ottawa could be in the running, too: approximately 500 workers died of malaria (then called swamp fever) during the building of the Rideau Canal (see Chaffeys Locks, Map of Haircuts, p. 84).

BATTLE OF THE BUGS

In 2005 Winnipeg seeded ponds and other standing-water sources with dragonfly eggs in the hope that the larvae would eat up a good portion of the mosquito eggs that infest such areas. Until then, the standard mosquito-control tactic in Winnipeg was chemical fogging, but residents made such a fuss that the city turned to more natural methods and launched an awareness campaign to remind people not to keep birdbaths, koi ponds, rain traps, or other puddly spots in their backyards.

The
ENTOMOLOGICAL
MAP *of* CANADA

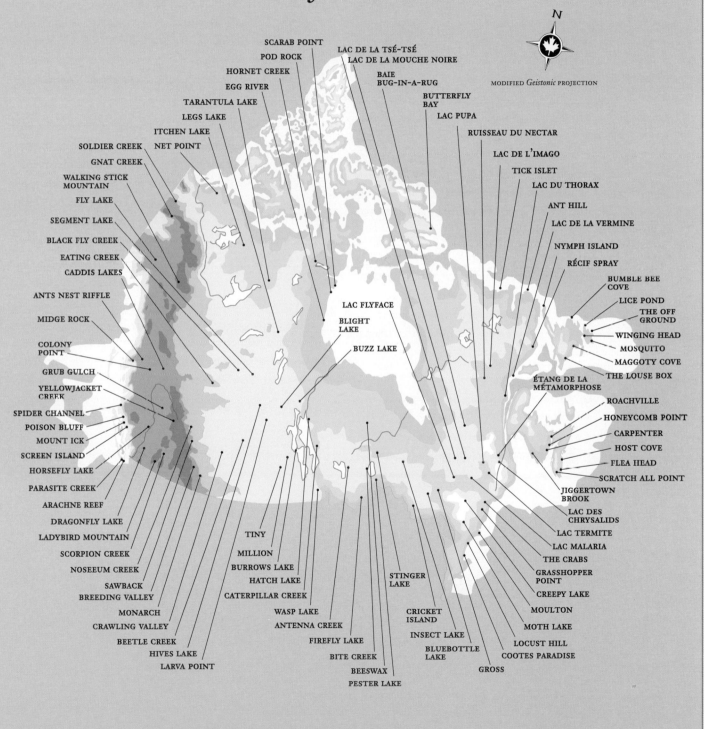

MODIFIED *Geistonic* PROJECTION

SCARAB POINT
POD ROCK
HORNET CREEK
EGG RIVER
TARANTULA LAKE
LEGS LAKE
ITCHEN LAKE
SOLDIER CREEK
NET POINT
GNAT CREEK
WALKING STICK MOUNTAIN
FLY LAKE
SEGMENT LAKE
BLACK FLY CREEK
EATING CREEK
CADDIS LAKES
ANTS NEST RIFFLE
MIDGE ROCK
COLONY POINT
GRUB GULCH
YELLOWJACKET CREEK
SPIDER CHANNEL
POISON BLUFF
MOUNT ICK
SCREEN ISLAND
HORSEFLY LAKE
PARASITE CREEK
ARACHNE REEF
DRAGONFLY LAKE
LADYBIRD MOUNTAIN
SCORPION CREEK
NOSEEUM CREEK
SAWBACK
BREEDING VALLEY
MONARCH
CRAWLING VALLEY
BEETLE CREEK
HIVES LAKE
LARVA POINT

LAC DE LA TSÉ-TSÉ
LAC DE LA MOUCHE NOIRE
BAIE BUG-IN-A-RUG
BUTTERFLY BAY
LAC PUPA
RUISSEAU DU NECTAR
LAC DE L'IMAGO
TICK ISLET
LAC DU THORAX
ANT HILL
LAC DE LA VERMINE
NYMPH ISLAND
RÉCIF SPRAY
BUMBLE BEE COVE
LICE POND
THE OFF GROUND
WINGING HEAD
MOSQUITO
MAGGOTY COVE
THE LOUSE BOX
ÉTANG DE LA MÉTAMORPHOSE
ROACHVILLE
HONEYCOMB POINT
CARPENTER
HOST COVE
FLEA HEAD
SCRATCH ALL POINT
JIGGERTOWN BROOK
LAC DES CHRYSALIDS
LAC TERMITE
LAC MALARIA
THE CRABS
GRASSHOPPER POINT
CREEPY LAKE
MOULTON
MOTH LAKE
LOCUST HILL
COOTES PARADISE

LAC FLYFACE
BLIGHT LAKE
BUZZ LAKE

TINY
MILLION
BURROWS LAKE
HATCH LAKE
CATERPILLAR CREEK
WASP LAKE
ANTENNA CREEK
FIREFLY LAKE
BITE CREEK
BEESWAX
PESTER LAKE

STINGER LAKE
CRICKET ISLAND
INSECT LAKE
BLUEBOTTLE LAKE
GROSS

MT. MISERY, NL: William Epps Cormack, an explorer, named this mountain after spending an "unpleasant night" there during a snowstorm on October 16, 1822. Cormack made two expeditions to Newfoundland, during which he collected information about the Beothuk First Nation, which was wiped out by European settlers. In 1827 Cormack founded the Beothuk Institution, an organization that tried—and failed—to locate survivors. The last-known Beothuk, a woman named Shanawdithit who worked as a maid in St. John's, died of tuberculosis in 1829. Cormack later took her skull to the Royal College of Physicians in London, England, where it stayed until it was destroyed during the Blitz in World War II.

DEATHDEALER ISLAND, ON: Part of the Thousand Islands chain (see Number I Map, p. 24, and Map of Toppings, p. 32) that Captain William Fitzwilliam Owen named after British gunboats operating on the Great Lakes during the War of 1812. The subgroup called the Lake Fleet Islands includes Axeman Island, Endymion Island, Dumfounder Island, and Bloodletter Island.

BURDEN COVE, NB: There was once a small village on this cove that was reputed to have suffered a long string of setbacks, including a mayor who drowned in Mactaquac Lake. The village no longer exists, but its original schoolhouse is still on display at the University of New Brunswick in Fredericton.

SUICIDE HILL, MB: Named for the treacherous road that leads to its peak. The location—or one named for it—is immortalized in Miriam Toews' 2004 novel *A Complicated Kindness*. Nomi, the 16-year-old protagonist, hangs out on Suicide Hill to escape the confines of a small, strict, no-fun Mennonite town in Manitoba.

DESTRUCTION BAY, YT: A settlement (population: about 50) on the western shore of Kluane Lake. One local story says it was named for a Klondike-era storm that smashed all the boats in the harbour and drowned a group of prospectors, but the actual namesake storm occurred during World War II and destroyed a set of military barracks.

OFF THE MAP

Bay d'Espoir, NL, is a pretty inlet that didn't make it onto the Angst Map because its name means "bay of hope." It was originally called Baie d'Esprit, or "spirit bay," and English settlers later pronounced and mapped it as Bay Despair. Newfoundland changed it to Bay d'Espoir, but everyone continues to say "Bay Despair."

YOUNG ANGST

Teen angst didn't originate in Canada, but official young-adult angst did. In his novel *Generation X: Tales for an Accelerated Culture* (1991), the Canadian author Douglas Coupland describes the detached, undefined, culturally destitute group of people born between 1960 and 1965. The book hit a nerve and went to the top of the bestseller lists. The titular term was later appropriated by a younger group, leaving the real Gen-Xers undefined yet again.

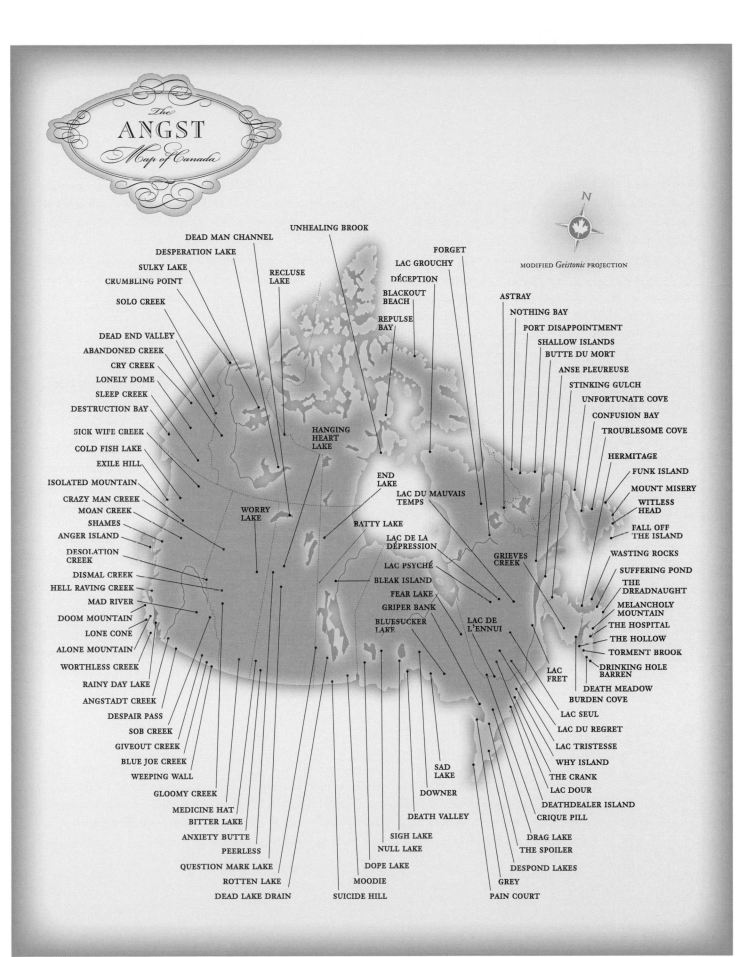

The ANGST Map of Canada

MODIFIED *Geistonic* PROJECTION

UNHEALING BROOK
DEAD MAN CHANNEL
DESPERATION LAKE
SULKY LAKE
CRUMBLING POINT
SOLO CREEK
RECLUSE LAKE
FORGET
LAC GROUCHY
DÉCEPTION
BLACKOUT BEACH
REPULSE BAY
ASTRAY
NOTHING BAY
PORT DISAPPOINTMENT
SHALLOW ISLANDS
BUTTE DU MORT
ANSE PLEUREUSE
STINKING GULCH
UNFORTUNATE COVE
CONFUSION BAY
TROUBLESOME COVE
DEAD END VALLEY
ABANDONED CREEK
CRY CREEK
LONELY DOME
SLEEP CREEK
DESTRUCTION BAY
SICK WIFE CREEK
COLD FISH LAKE
EXILE HILL
ISOLATED MOUNTAIN
CRAZY MAN CREEK
MOAN CREEK
SHAMES
ANGER ISLAND
DESOLATION CREEK
DISMAL CREEK
HELL RAVING CREEK
MAD RIVER
DOOM MOUNTAIN
LONE CONE
ALONE MOUNTAIN
WORTHLESS CREEK
RAINY DAY LAKE
ANGSTADT CREEK
DESPAIR PASS
SOB CREEK
GIVEOUT CREEK
BLUE JOE CREEK
WEEPING WALL
GLOOMY CREEK
MEDICINE HAT
BITTER LAKE
ANXIETY BUTTE
PEERLESS
QUESTION MARK LAKE
ROTTEN LAKE
DEAD LAKE DRAIN
HANGING HEART LAKE
WORRY LAKE
END LAKE
LAC DU MAUVAIS TEMPS
BATTY LAKE
LAC DE LA DÉPRESSION
LAC PSYCHÉ
BLEAK ISLAND
FEAR LAKE
GRIPER BANK
BLUESUCKER LAKE
LAC DE L'ENNUI
GRIEVES CREEK
HERMITAGE
FUNK ISLAND
MOUNT MISERY
WITLESS HEAD
FALL OFF THE ISLAND
WASTING ROCKS
SUFFERING POND
THE DREADNAUGHT
MELANCHOLY MOUNTAIN
THE HOSPITAL
THE HOLLOW
TORMENT BROOK
DRINKING HOLE BARREN
DEATH MEADOW
BURDEN COVE
LAC SEUL
LAC DU REGRET
LAC TRISTESSE
WHY ISLAND
THE CRANK
LAC DOUR
DEATHDEALER ISLAND
CRIQUE PILL
DRAG LAKE
THE SPOILER
DESPOND LAKES
GREY
PAIN COURT
LAC FRET
SAD LAKE
DOWNER
DEATH VALLEY
SIGH LAKE
NULL LAKE
DOPE LAKE
MOODIE
SUICIDE HILL

BOSTON BAR, BC: During the Fraser River gold rush of the mid-1800s, First Nations people frequently referred to American gold prospectors as "Boston men" and the British as "King George men," and panners working the area picked up the slang. When white prospectors came to outnumber Native people in the area around the village of Koia'um, it became known as Boston Bar. Relations between the Americans and the First Nations were tense, and skirmishes broke out frequently. Hostilities came to a peak in 1858 at "the Battle of Boston Bar" (some say it actually happened near Spuzzum), when 150 American prospectors fought for three hours with a smaller group of local villagers. One American was wounded and at least seven Natives were killed.

PERSIAN LAKE, MB: *Geist* received many letters about this map, many of them debating the existence of a doughnut called a Persian, since confirmed to be a flattish white cake doughnut with icing that contains strawberries or raspberries. Unique to Thunder Bay, it was supposedly named for John Pershing, an American World War I general. Persian Lake's name honours Arthur T. Persian, a Manitoba pilot shot down during World War II (the geographical boards of both Manitoba and Saskatchewan have programs in place to name features after fallen soldiers). Persian Lake is also locally known as Cleaver Lake because of its shape. It also appears on the Map of House Pets (p. 50).

BISMARCK, ON: Another contested doughnut, although better known than the Persian. The Bismarck is a fruit-filled pastry also known as a "Berlin doughnut" or "Berliner." The town of Bismarck was named for Prince Otto von Bismarck, a nineteenth-century Prussian statesman who also lent his name to the capital of North Dakota, a town in Arkansas, and a sea north of New Guinea. Before it was called Bismarck, the Ontario town was called Ball's Corner after a local shopkeeper, and before that it was Sunday's Settlement, named for Christian Sunday, an early settler from Germany.

DUTCH CREEK, AB: A Dutch prospector was supposedly murdered here by his greedy partner after they found a valuable strike of minerals.

BAKER LAKE, NU: Named for Sir William Baker and his brother Richard, both Hudson's Bay Company employees. The Inuktitut name for the community is Qamani'tuaq, which was translated in early records as "far inland" but actually means "where the river widens." Before the HBC opened a post in 1916, there were nine Inuit communities in the area: the Illuiliqmiut, the Kihlirnirmiut, the Hanningayuqmiut, the Ukkuhiksalingmiut, the Qairnirmiut, the Hauniqturmiut, the Akilinirmiut, the Harvaqtuurmiut, and the Paalirmiut. A residential school built here in the 1950s drew in even more Inuit people, from a wider area. Parents came to Baker Lake to be closer to their children, who had been taken to the school by the government. Today, the population is about 1,500.

HOLY DOUGHNUT!

In September 1998, a strange image that many believed to be a likeness of Jesus appeared under the floodlights on the exterior wall of a Tim Hortons in Bras D'Or, NS. Hundreds of people came to pray outside the store. Staff at the outlet said the vision was caused by faulty light bulbs, but even after they were replaced, a few faithful said they could still see the image farther down the wall.

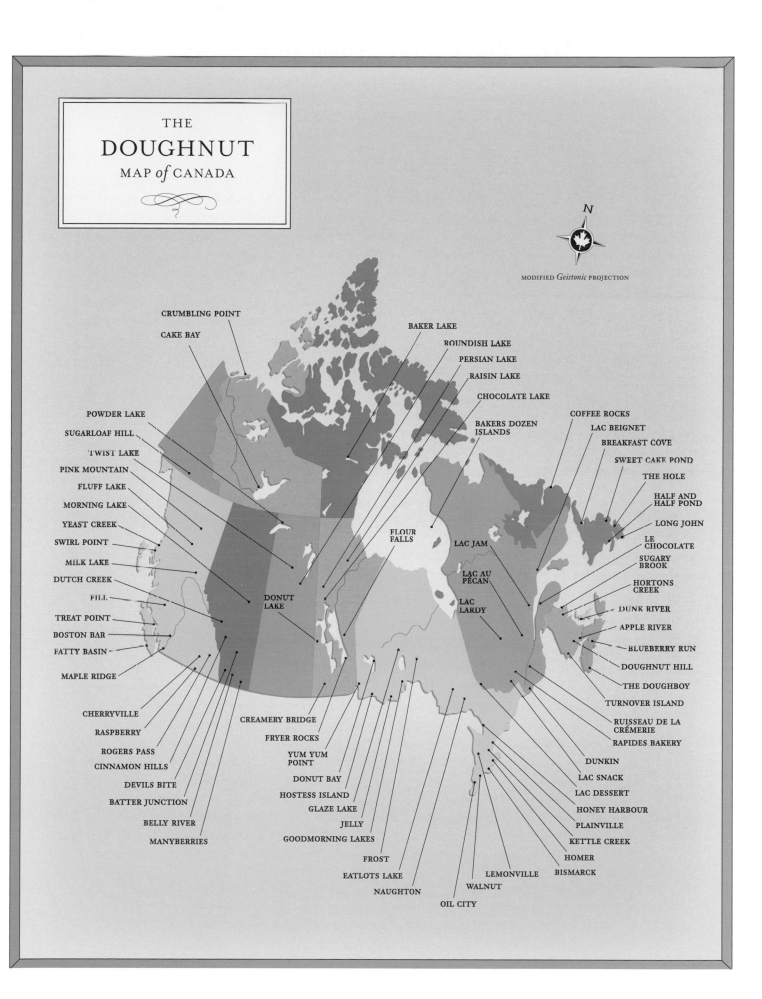

THE
DOUGHNUT
MAP *of* CANADA

N

MODIFIED *Geistonic* PROJECTION

CRUMBLING POINT
CAKE BAY
BAKER LAKE
ROUNDISH LAKE
PERSIAN LAKE
RAISIN LAKE
CHOCOLATE LAKE
COFFEE ROCKS
POWDER LAKE
LAC BEIGNET
BAKERS DOZEN
ISLANDS
SUGARLOAF HILL
BREAKFAST COVE
TWIST LAKE
SWEET CAKE POND
PINK MOUNTAIN
THE HOLE
FLUFF LAKE
HALF AND
HALF POND
MORNING LAKE
YEAST CREEK
LONG JOHN
SWIRL POINT
FLOUR
FALLS
LAC JAM
LE
CHOCOLATE
MILK LAKE
SUGARY
BROOK
DUTCH CREEK
LAC AU
PÉCAN
HORTONS
CREEK
FILL
DONUT
LAKE
LAC
LARDY
DUNK RIVER
TREAT POINT
APPLE RIVER
BOSTON BAR
BLUEBERRY RUN
FATTY BASIN
DOUGHNUT HILL
MAPLE RIDGE
THE DOUGHBOY
TURNOVER ISLAND
CHERRYVILLE
CREAMERY BRIDGE
RUISSEAU DE LA
CRÉMERIE
RASPBERRY
FRYER ROCKS
RAPIDES BAKERY
ROGERS PASS
YUM YUM
POINT
CINNAMON HILLS
DUNKIN
DEVILS BITE
DONUT BAY
LAC SNACK
BATTER JUNCTION
HOSTESS ISLAND
LAC DESSERT
GLAZE LAKE
HONEY HARBOUR
BELLY RIVER
JELLY
PLAINVILLE
MANYBERRIES
GOODMORNING LAKES
KETTLE CREEK
HOMER
FROST
LEMONVILLE
BISMARCK
EATLOTS LAKE
NAUGHTON
WALNUT
OIL CITY

— 21 —

STAR CITY, SK: In 1900, when Walter Starkey founded Star City, the trend in western settlement was to add the word "City" to a town's name, to encourage development. But in fact, according to *Naming Canada*, no town in Canada with "City" in its official name has achieved the population necessary to incorporate as an actual city. Many towns have dropped the appellation (see notes on Golden, Fairy Tale Map, p. 72).

VEGA, AB: Alberta is Big Sky Country, but this Vega was named in 1928 after a Vega-brand cream-separating appliance that was sitting in the shed where the town leaders met to pick a name (they wanted Viewpoint, but a nearby district had taken that name). Vega Peak, in the Starlight Mountain Range near Jasper, was, in fact, named for Vega, the brightest star in the northern hemisphere.

SATELLITE BAY, NT: Sir Francis Leopold McClintock (1819–1907) named this bay for either his sled, an early form of secondary tow-sled called a satellite sled, or HMS *Satellite*, a vessel that sailed with HMS *Gorgon*, on which McClintock served. McClintock led the search party that finally discovered the remains of the Franklin Expedition.

COPERNICUS HILL, MB: Located in Duck Mountain Provincial Park, it is locally known as Glad Hill, but was officially renamed in 1973 to honour the 500th birthday of Copernicus, the Polish astronomer who calculated that the earth went around the sun.

PARC GARNEAU, QC: No literal connection to Marc Garneau, Canada's first astronaut, who flew aboard the Space Shuttle *Challenger* in 1984. The park was founded in 1924 and named for François-Xavier Garneau (1809–1866), a notable poet, historian, and newspaper publisher.

OFF THE MAP

The Malcolm Knapp Research Forest, about sixty kilometres (thirty-seven miles) east of Vancouver, BC, is the current home of the Large Zenith Telescope, the third-largest optical telescope in North America, which is not quite as big as— and these are their real names—the Very Large Telescope in Cerro Paranal, Chile, and the still-in-development Overwhelmingly Large Telescope (location to be determined).

ASTEROIDS: THE CANADIAN CONNECTIONS

Dominiona, named to honour Canada; *Klondike*, named by Y. Väisälä to salute Finnish prospectors who brought home a fortune; *Underhill*, for Anne Underhill, a Canadian astrophysicist; *Anngower*, for Ann C. Gower, an astronomy teacher in Victoria; *Millman*, for Peter Millman, former president of the Royal Astronomical Society of Canada; *Siyueguo*, for Si Yue Guo, a gifted physics student from Montreal; *Plaskett*, for John Plaskett, founding director of the Dominion Astrophysical Observatory in Victoria; *Albertacentenary*, to celebrate Alberta's 100th anniversary; *Peterpatricia*, for the parents of A. Lowe, the Canadian who discovered it; *Reginaldglenice*, for Lowe's parents-in-law.

THE CELESTIAL
MAP *of* CANADA

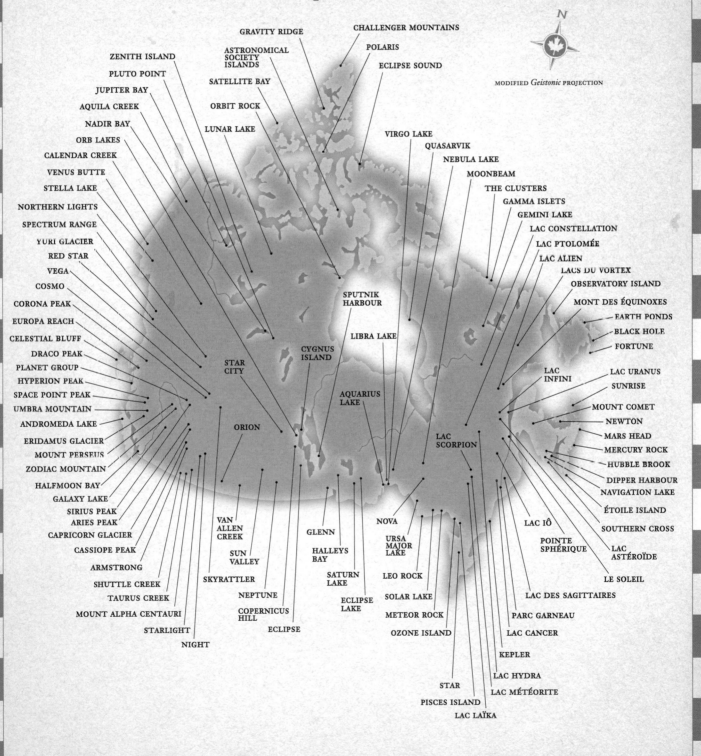

MODIFIED *Geistonic* PROJECTION

GRAVITY RIDGE

ASTRONOMICAL SOCIETY ISLANDS

SATELLITE BAY

ORBIT ROCK

LUNAR LAKE

ZENITH ISLAND

PLUTO POINT

JUPITER BAY

AQUILA CREEK

NADIR BAY

ORB LAKES

CALENDAR CREEK

VENUS BUTTE

STELLA LAKE

NORTHERN LIGHTS

SPECTRUM RANGE

YURI GLACIER

RED STAR

VEGA

COSMO

CORONA PEAK

EUROPA REACH

CELESTIAL BLUFF

DRACO PEAK

PLANET GROUP

HYPERION PEAK

SPACE POINT PEAK

UMBRA MOUNTAIN

ANDROMEDA LAKE

ERIDAMUS GLACIER

MOUNT PERSEUS

ZODIAC MOUNTAIN

HALFMOON BAY

GALAXY LAKE

SIRIUS PEAK

ARIES PEAK

CAPRICORN GLACIER

CASSIOPE PEAK

ARMSTRONG

SHUTTLE CREEK

TAURUS CREEK

MOUNT ALPHA CENTAURI

STARLIGHT

NIGHT

STAR CITY

ORION

VAN ALLEN CREEK

SUN VALLEY

SKYRATTLER

NEPTUNE

COPERNICUS HILL

ECLIPSE

CYGNUS ISLAND

GLENN

HALLEYS BAY

SATURN LAKE

ECLIPSE LAKE

CHALLENGER MOUNTAINS

POLARIS

ECLIPSE SOUND

VIRGO LAKE

QUASARVIK

NEBULA LAKE

MOONBEAM

THE CLUSTERS

GAMMA ISLETS

GEMINI LAKE

LAC CONSTELLATION

LAC PTOLOMÉE

LAC ALIEN

LACS DU VORTEX

OBSERVATORY ISLAND

MONT DES ÉQUINOXES

EARTH PONDS

BLACK HOLE

FORTUNE

LAC URANUS

SUNRISE

MOUNT COMET

NEWTON

MARS HEAD

MERCURY ROCK

HUBBLE BROOK

DIPPER HARBOUR

NAVIGATION LAKE

ÉTOILE ISLAND

SOUTHERN CROSS

LAC ASTÉROÏDE

LE SOLEIL

SPUTNIK HARBOUR

LIBRA LAKE

AQUARIUS LAKE

LAC INFINI

LAC SCORPION

NOVA

URSA MAJOR LAKE

LEO ROCK

SOLAR LAKE

METEOR ROCK

OZONE ISLAND

STAR

PISCES ISLAND

LAC LAÏKA

LAC IÔ

POINTE SPHÉRIQUE

LAC DES SAGITTAIRES

PARC GARNEAU

LAC CANCER

KEPLER

LAC HYDRA

LAC MÉTÉORITE

THOUSAND ISLANDS, ON: This vacation region along the St. Lawrence River actually consists of 1,149 islands. Earlier surveyors counted 1,692, but the official criteria for an island (as opposed to a rock) have become stricter since then. Ontario shares the islands with New York State: 662 are Canadian and 484 are American (and only 367 have names), and the Thousand Islands Bridge connects the two countries. Originally the islands were populated mainly by the Iroquois First Nation, whose legend says that they were created when the Garden of the Great Spirit fell out of a blanket and broke into many pieces.

THIRTY THOUSAND ISLANDS, ON: Thousand Islands? That's nothing. The Thirty Thousand Islands on the east side of Georgian Bay comprises 34,560 islands and islets.

FIVE FINGER RAPIDS, YT: Four basalt columns divide the Yukon River into five streams of rapids at this point on the Klondike Highway. During the gold rush, the rapids were formidable obstacles for riverboats taking people and cargo to Dawson City. Larger sternwheelers had to be pulled up the easternmost rapids with winches, until the government blasted out part of the eastern rock column in 1900. Today the spot is popular with kayakers, and it has a boardwalk and rest stop for highway tourists.

LA VINGT-SEPTIEME LETTRE, QC: One of 101 islands in the Caniapiscau Reservoir named for literary works (see notes on La Fragilité des Choses, Cheap Map, p. 92). This one named is for a poem by Stephen Morrissey, later translated into French by Pierre DesRuisseaux and published in *Contre-taille*: *Poèmes Choisis de Vingt-Cinq Auteurs Canadiens-Anglais*. The poem begins, "Je ne dois rien au monde" ("I owe the world nothing").

100 MILE HOUSE, BC: The largest in a series of number-named towns and landmarks that count off the miles of the Cariboo Road, a trail that took prospectors north during the Cariboo Gold Rush (1862–1865). Mile zero of the Cariboo Road is on Main Street in the town of Lillooet, BC.

THIRTY-TWO ISLAND, MB: Most of the land and water features on this map were numbered as a route-marking tool (first creek, second creek, etc.), by their gold-discovery claims number (49 gulch), or because there are too many features to be named individually. But this island on Cormorant Lake got its name after a fisherman's boat slipped off the beach and drifted away, leaving him stranded here for thirty-two days.

CANADA BY THE NUMBERS

People: 32,555,061; dogs: 5,104,800; cats: 7,274,300; cars: 18,500,000; population density (people): 3.5 per square kilometre (1.3 square miles); area: 9,984,670 square kilometres (3,855,102 square miles); water area: 891,163 square kilometres (334,080 square miles); coastline: 202,080 kilometres (78,023 square miles); saltwater shoreline: 243,042 square kilometres (98,839 square miles); highest point: 5,959 metres (19,550 feet); highest settled latitude: 82.5°; percentage of world's lakes: 60; birth rate: 10.8/1,000; infant mortality rate: 4.7/1,000; life expectancy: 80.2; literacy: 97 percent; arable land: 5 percent; GDP: $1,371,425,000,000; per capita GDP: $42,298; exports: $453,600,200,000; imports: $386,906,900,000; Tim Hortons outlets: 2,611; mass transit rides per day: 110,100,000; prime ministers from Quebec: 5; from Ontario: 7; from the Atlantic provinces: 4; from Alberta: 1; from BC: 1; from the United Kingdom: 4.

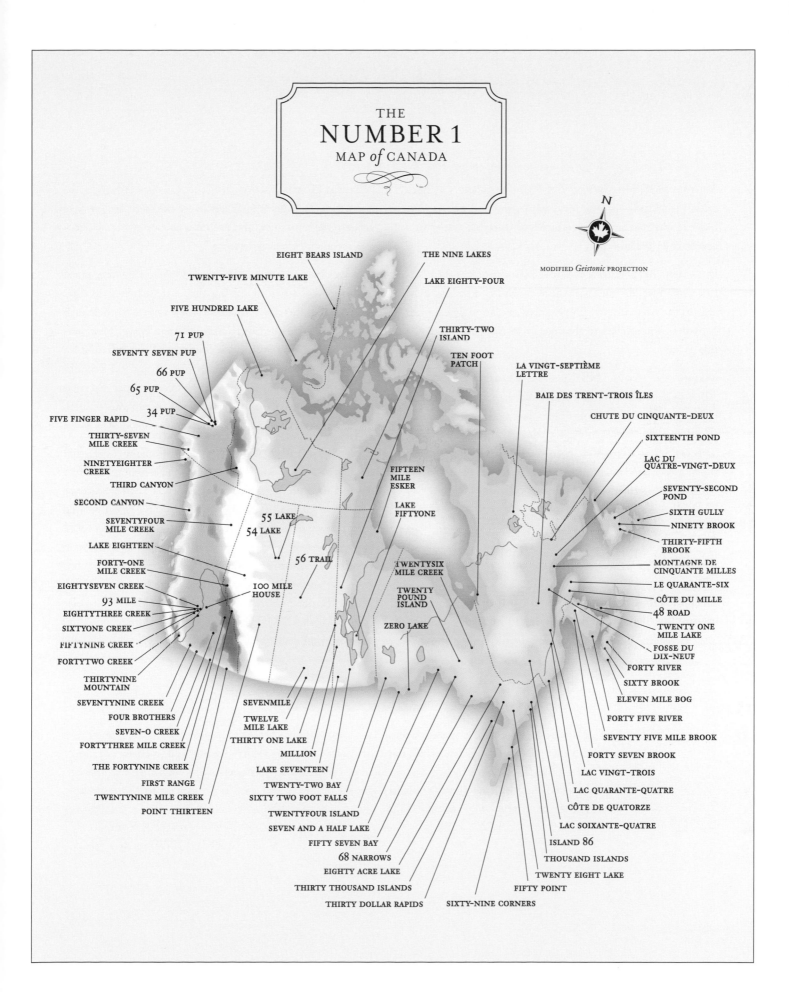

THE
NUMBER 1
MAP *of* CANADA

N

MODIFIED *Geistonic* PROJECTION

EIGHT BEARS ISLAND

THE NINE LAKES

TWENTY-FIVE MINUTE LAKE

LAKE EIGHTY-FOUR

FIVE HUNDRED LAKE

71 PUP

THIRTY-TWO ISLAND

SEVENTY SEVEN PUP

TEN FOOT PATCH

66 PUP

LA VINGT-SEPTIÈME LETTRE

65 PUP

BAIE DES TRENT-TROIS ÎLES

34 PUP

CHUTE DU CINQUANTE-DEUX

FIVE FINGER RAPID

SIXTEENTH POND

THIRTY-SEVEN MILE CREEK

LAC DU QUATRE-VINGT-DEUX

NINETYEIGHTER CREEK

SEVENTY-SECOND POND

THIRD CANYON

FIFTEEN MILE ESKER

SIXTH GULLY

SECOND CANYON

NINETY BROOK

SEVENTYFOUR MILE CREEK

LAKE FIFTYONE

THIRTY-FIFTH BROOK

55 LAKE

LAKE EIGHTEEN

54 LAKE

MONTAGNE DE CINQUANTE MILLES

FORTY-ONE MILE CREEK

56 TRAIL

LE QUARANTE-SIX

EIGHTYSEVEN CREEK

TWENTYSIX MILE CREEK

CÔTE DU MILLE

93 MILE

100 MILE HOUSE

TWENTY POUND ISLAND

48 ROAD

EIGHTYTHREE CREEK

TWENTY ONE MILE LAKE

SIXTYONE CREEK

ZERO LAKE

FOSSE DU DIX-NEUF

FIFTYNINE CREEK

FORTY RIVER

FORTYTWO CREEK

SIXTY BROOK

THIRTYNINE MOUNTAIN

ELEVEN MILE BOG

SEVENTYNINE CREEK

FORTY FIVE RIVER

FOUR BROTHERS

SEVENMILE

SEVEN-O CREEK

SEVENTY FIVE MILE BROOK

TWELVE MILE LAKE

FORTYTHREE MILE CREEK

FORTY SEVEN BROOK

THIRTY ONE LAKE

THE FORTYNINE CREEK

LAC VINGT-TROIS

MILLION

FIRST RANGE

LAC QUARANTE-QUATRE

LAKE SEVENTEEN

TWENTYNINE MILE CREEK

CÔTE DE QUATORZE

TWENTY-TWO BAY

POINT THIRTEEN

LAC SOIXANTE-QUATRE

SIXTY TWO FOOT FALLS

TWENTYFOUR ISLAND

ISLAND 86

SEVEN AND A HALF LAKE

THOUSAND ISLANDS

FIFTY SEVEN BAY

TWENTY EIGHT LAKE

68 NARROWS

FIFTY POINT

EIGHTY ACRE LAKE

THIRTY THOUSAND ISLANDS

THIRTY DOLLAR RAPIDS

SIXTY-NINE CORNERS

ARGUE, MB: This former CN Railway station was once called Trackend—it was, for a while, the end of the line. Later it was renamed for James Argue, the first settler in a nearby town called Elgin.

PUSH AND BE DAMNED RAPIDS, NB: Enshrines the experience of travellers on this waterway who had to row hard against the river current. There is also a Pull and Be Damned Narrows, which refers to the equally taxing pull of the ebb tide.

MALIGNANT COVE, NS: In 1774, when HMS *Malignant*, a British warship, sank in a storm off the Northumberland Coast of Nova Scotia, most of her crew made it to shore and found help and shelter in Pictou, but many died of exposure. Two official attempts have been made to change the name: the first to Barradale, but the campaign failed; the second to Milburn, which made it onto the official books but never was adopted in common usage.

NITRO, QC: Founded during World War II to house the workers of Dominion Industries Ltd., a munitions manufacturer.

LAKE OF THE ENEMY, NT: The original Chipewyan name means "Cree Lake," but the Chipewyan words for "enemy" and "Cree" are the same. According to the Prince of Wales Northern Heritage Centre, the lake was once thought to be home to an evil spirit; people who see the spirit are "at once afflicted with insanity, and are incapable of giving an accurate account of their experience."

NORTH BATTLEFORD, SK: In 1885 Metis fighters razed the town of Battleford during the Riel Rebellion. Rather than rebuild, the CNR founded a new service town, North Battleford, across the North Saskatchewan River. There was a brief outcry from both sides: residents of North Battleford would have preferred the name Fairview, and the remaining residents of old Battleford complained that the new town would hurt their business. They were right—North Battleford is now the predominant city.

CAPE SPEAR, NF: Canada's oldest surviving lighthouse stands at this National Historic Site. The military added a fortress and gun house during World War II to protect the coast from German U-boats. The name Cape Spear evolved from one given by early Portuguese settlers: Cauo de la spera, or "waiting cape." Cape Spear is the easternmost point in Canada. (Demarcation Point on the Yukon–Alaska boundary is the westernmost, Cape Columbia on Ellesmere Island, NU, is the northernmost, and Middle Island in Point Pelee National Park, ON, is the southernmost—although in 2006, a windstorm knocked its point off.)

FIVE-MINUTE MAJOR

During the course of the 1,230 games of the 2003–2004 National Hockey League season, there were 789 fights, involving 340 players. The best-known incident of the year occurred when Todd Bertuzzi of the Vancouver Canucks sucker-punched Steve Moore of the Colorado Avalanche. The following year there was only one fight, involving all of the players, plus the managers and owners—a lockout that shut down the entire season of play.

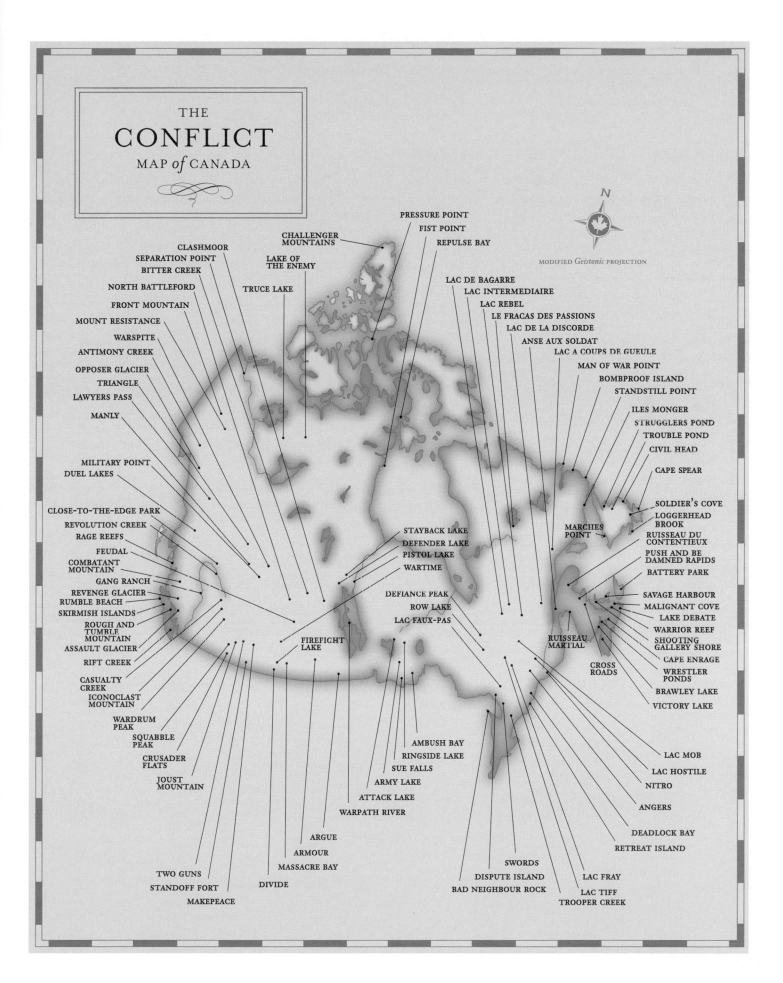

THE
CONFLICT
MAP *of* CANADA

N

MODIFIED *Geistonic* PROJECTION

PRESSURE POINT
FIST POINT
REPULSE BAY

CHALLENGER
MOUNTAINS

CLASHMOOR
SEPARATION POINT
BITTER CREEK
LAKE OF
THE ENEMY

NORTH BATTLEFORD
FRONT MOUNTAIN
TRUCE LAKE

LAC DE BAGARRE
LAC INTERMEDIAIRE
LAC REBEL
LE FRACAS DES PASSIONS
LAC DE LA DISCORDE
ANSE AUX SOLDAT
LAC A COUPS DE GUEULE

MOUNT RESISTANCE
WARSPITE
ANTIMONY CREEK
OPPOSER GLACIER
TRIANGLE
LAWYERS PASS

MAN OF WAR POINT
BOMBPROOF ISLAND
STANDSTILL POINT

MANLY

ILES MONGER
STRUGGLERS POND
TROUBLE POND
CIVIL HEAD

CAPE SPEAR

MILITARY POINT
DUEL LAKES

SOLDIER'S COVE
LOGGERHEAD
BROOK
RUISSEAU DU
CONTENTIEUX
PUSH AND BE
DAMNED RAPIDS
BATTERY PARK

CLOSE-TO-THE-EDGE PARK
REVOLUTION CREEK
RAGE REEFS
FEUDAL
COMBATANT
MOUNTAIN
GANG RANCH
REVENGE GLACIER
RUMBLE BEACH
SKIRMISH ISLANDS
ROUGH AND
TUMBLE
MOUNTAIN
ASSAULT GLACIER
RIFT CREEK
CASUALTY
CREEK
ICONOCLAST
MOUNTAIN
WARDRUM
PEAK
SQUABBLE
PEAK
CRUSADER
FLATS
JOUST
MOUNTAIN

STAYBACK LAKE
DEFENDER LAKE
PISTOL LAKE
WARTIME

MARCHES
POINT

DEFIANCE PEAK
ROW LAKE
LAC FAUX-PAS

SAVAGE HARBOUR
MALIGNANT COVE
LAKE DEBATE
WARRIOR REEF
SHOOTING
GALLERY SHORE
CAPE ENRAGE
WRESTLER
PONDS
BRAWLEY LAKE
VICTORY LAKE

FIREFIGHT
LAKE

RUISSEAU
MARTIAL

CROSS
ROADS

AMBUSH BAY
RINGSIDE LAKE
SUE FALLS
ARMY LAKE
ATTACK LAKE
WARPATH RIVER

LAC MOB
LAC HOSTILE
NITRO
ANGERS

DEADLOCK BAY
RETREAT ISLAND

ARGUE
ARMOUR
MASSACRE BAY

TWO GUNS
STANDOFF FORT
MAKEPEACE

DIVIDE

SWORDS
DISPUTE ISLAND
BAD NEIGHBOUR ROCK

LAC FRAY
LAC TIFF
TROOPER CREEK

FARO, YT: One of the Yukon's youngest towns, founded in 1969, named for an ancient gambling game that uses a deck of cards showing portraits of Egyptian pharaohs. Faro is a game of pure luck—a single turn of a card takes the pot. Like the game, the town has a long history of booms and busts. Temperatures in Faro, located at 62°N at an elevation of 717 metres (2,352 feet), can drop as low as −55°C (−67°F). (Keno City, population 20, was also named for a game of chance.)

HEARTS HILL, SK: Formed in 1912, Hearts Hill got a boost in 1930, when the rail line was extended through the town and out to Brodo, AB. The name comes from the system of hills beyond it, which look heart-shaped when seen from the top of the range.

PONT DU CHEMIN DE FER, QC: In English, "railway bridge," which is what this place is. *Chemin de fer* is also a French variant of Baccarat.

CHANCE HARBOUR, NB: The Bingo capital of New Brunswick, according to *Geographical Place Names of New Brunswick* (but see notes on Roachville, Entomological Map, p. 16). The original name, Harbour by Chance, referred to the entrance to the harbour, which is full of reefs and rock ledges and is very hazardous to larger vessels. The better-known Come by Chance Harbour in Newfoundland is supposedly named for the surprise attacks of French pirates preying on English ships.

DRAGON, QC: A dragon was featured on the logo of Northern Explosive, a World War I munitions company that had a factory here. A massive explosion levelled the plant in 1917.

CARDSTON, AB: Named for Charles Ora Card, the son-in-law of Brigham Young. Young was a disciple of Joseph Smith, founder of the Church of Latter Day Saints (the Mormons). Charles Card brought ten families up from Logan, Utah, in 1886 and settled them on the banks of Lees Creek, which eventually became Cardston. It still has a large Mormon population and is home to a remarkable 8,222-square-metre (88,500-square-foot) temple with Greek and Aztec architectural influences.

CHESS ISLAND, MB: This island in Shannon Lake was named for James B. Chess, a pilot officer from Winnipeg who died in World War II. Chess had served in the 419th Halifax Squadron. The lake was named in the 1970s as part of a program to honour Manitobans who died in battle (see also notes on Persian Lake, Doughnut Map, p. 20).

AMONG QUESTIONS NOT ASKED IN TRIVIAL PURSUIT (WHICH WAS INVENTED IN CANADA IN 1979, BY THE WAY)

a) Who was Canada's second prime minister?
b) Who wrote the Deptford Trilogy and the Salterton Trilogy?
c) What is Canada's official motto?
d) To what country did FLQ terrorists flee in 1970?
e) Performer Frank Mills is most recognized for what song?
f) What university developed the world's first anti-gravity suit?

f) University of Toronto

a) Alexander Mackenzie; b) Robertson Davies; c) a mari usque ad mare ("from sea to sea"); d) Cuba; e) "Music Box Dancer";

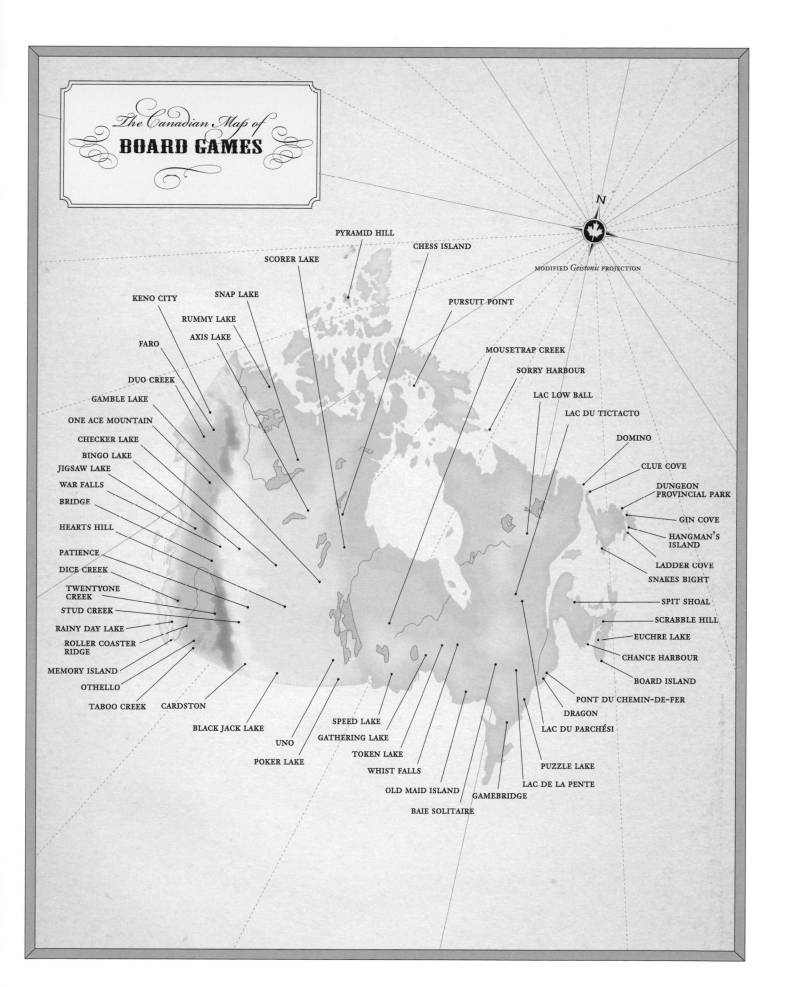

The Canadian Map of
BOARD GAMES

N

MODIFIED *Geistonic* PROJECTION

PYRAMID HILL

CHESS ISLAND

SCORER LAKE

PURSUIT POINT

KENO CITY

SNAP LAKE

RUMMY LAKE

MOUSETRAP CREEK

FARO

AXIS LAKE

SORRY HARBOUR

DUO CREEK

LAC LOW BALL

GAMBLE LAKE

LAC DU TICTACTO

ONE ACE MOUNTAIN

DOMINO

CHECKER LAKE

CLUE COVE

BINGO LAKE

DUNGEON
PROVINCIAL PARK

JIGSAW LAKE

WAR FALLS

GIN COVE

BRIDGE

HANGMAN'S
ISLAND

HEARTS HILL

LADDER COVE

PATIENCE

SNAKES BIGHT

DICE CREEK

SPIT SHOAL

TWENTYONE
CREEK

SCRABBLE HILL

STUD CREEK

EUCHRE LAKE

RAINY DAY LAKE

CHANCE HARBOUR

ROLLER COASTER
RIDGE

BOARD ISLAND

MEMORY ISLAND

PONT DU CHEMIN-DE-FER

OTHELLO

DRAGON

TABOO CREEK

CARDSTON

LAC DU PARCHÉSI

BLACK JACK LAKE

SPEED LAKE

UNO

GATHERING LAKE

PUZZLE LAKE

TOKEN LAKE

POKER LAKE

WHIST FALLS

LAC DE LA PENTE

OLD MAID ISLAND

GAMEBRIDGE

BAIE SOLITAIRE

— 29 —

GRAND FORKS, BC: The eponymous fork is the confluence of the Granby and Kettle rivers, making this a doubly kitchen-named town. It was originally called Grande Prairie, but the name was changed to Grand Forks in 1897. (Grande Prairie, AB, is actually on the prairie.)

MT. COOK, YT: The Yukon has two Mt. Cooks: one located in a cartographically convenient spot and the other (better known) on the BC–Alaska border, in the St. Elias Mountain Range (see notes on Mt. Beelzebub, Spooky Map, p. 34). The latter Mt. Cook was named for Captain James Cook, who explored the coastline from California to Alaska in the 1770s. Cook has been honoured with a number of capes, points, inlets, and channels in BC and the Yukon (not to mention along the US west coast). He was killed during an altercation with Hawaiian warriors in 1779.

YELLOWKNIFE, NT: Named in honour of the First Nations in the Athapaskan language group, who used tools made from yellow copper. The settlement was founded in 1934 after a gold discovery, and was incorporated as a city in 1970.

AJAX, ON: Founded as a munitions factory during World War II which filled 40 million shells over the course of the war. In the 1950s Ajax was expanded and redeveloped by city planners as a model of an ideal industrial urban centre.

KITCHENER, ON: The childhood home of William Lyon Mackenzie King, Kitchener was founded in 1807 as Sand Hills, then renamed Ebytown for a Mennonite Bishop. In 1833 it was renamed again, this time to Berlin to honour the town's large German population. During World War I, a time of anti-German sentiment in Canada, it was renamed yet again, for Lord Kitchener, who died in 1916. Around the same time, New Germany, ON changed its name to Rottenbury, then, on second thought, to Maryhill, after a nearby hill where a statue of the Virgin Mary had been installed. Swastika, ON was named in 1906 after a good-luck charm worn by a local woman (*svasti* means "fortune" in Sanskrit). Residents resisted pressure during World War II to change its name to Winston (for Winston Churchill) and posted a sign that read: "To hell with Hitler, we had it first." Swastikans still have to defend the name, though the district is now a division of Kirkland Lake.

AN ELECTRIFYING MEAL

The world's first-ever meal cooked with electricity was prepared by Thomas Ahearn, a man whom the CBC called "Canada's Thomas Edison" and who invented the electric range, among other things. It was served at the Windsor Hotel in Ottawa on August 29, 1892.

THE
CANADIAN MAP *of*
KITCHEN
IMPLEMENTS

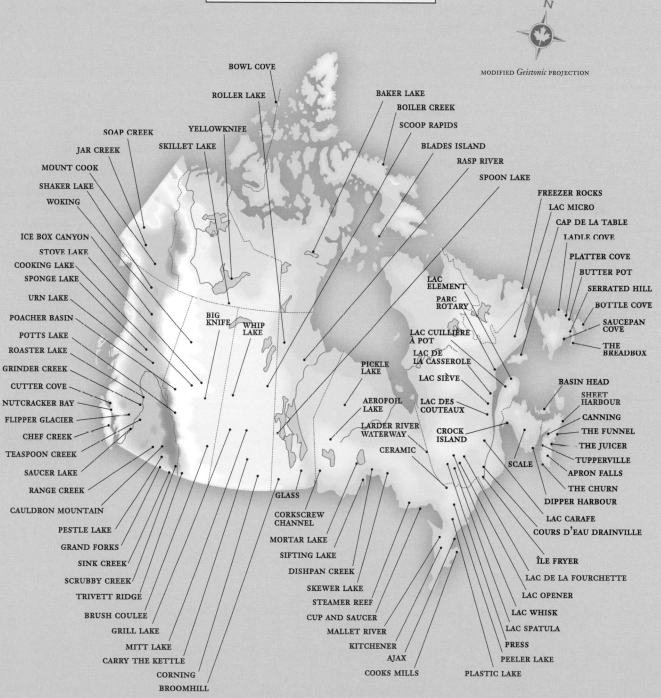

MODIFIED *Geistonic* PROJECTION

BOWL COVE

ROLLER LAKE

BAKER LAKE

BOILER CREEK

SCOOP RAPIDS

SOAP CREEK

YELLOWKNIFE

BLADES ISLAND

JAR CREEK

SKILLET LAKE

RASP RIVER

MOUNT COOK

SPOON LAKE

SHAKER LAKE

FREEZER ROCKS

WOKING

LAC MICRO

CAP DE LA TABLE

LADLE COVE

ICE BOX CANYON

STOVE LAKE

PLATTER COVE

COOKING LAKE

BUTTER POT

SPONGE LAKE

LAC
ELEMENT

SERRATED HILL

URN LAKE

PARC
ROTARY

BOTTLE COVE

POACHER BASIN

SAUCEPAN
COVE

POTTS LAKE

BIG
KNIFE

WHIP
LAKE

LAC CUILLIÈRE
À POT

THE
BREADBOX

ROASTER LAKE

LAC DE
LA CASSEROLE

GRINDER CREEK

LAC SIÈVE

BASIN HEAD

CUTTER COVE

SHEET
HARBOUR

NUTCRACKER BAY

PICKLE
LAKE

LAC DES
COUTEAUX

CANNING

FLIPPER GLACIER

AEROFOIL
LAKE

THE FUNNEL

CHEF CREEK

LARDER RIVER
WATERWAY

CROCK
ISLAND

THE JUICER

TEASPOON CREEK

CERAMIC

TUPPERVILLE

SAUCER LAKE

SCALE

APRON FALLS

RANGE CREEK

THE CHURN

CAULDRON MOUNTAIN

DIPPER HARBOUR

GLASS

PESTLE LAKE

LAC CARAFE

CORKSCREW
CHANNEL

GRAND FORKS

COURS D'EAU DRAINVILLE

MORTAR LAKE

SINK CREEK

SIFTING LAKE

ÎLE FRYER

SCRUBBY CREEK

DISHPAN CREEK

LAC DE LA FOURCHETTE

TRIVETT RIDGE

SKEWER LAKE

LAC OPENER

BRUSH COULEE

STEAMER REEF

LAC WHISK

GRILL LAKE

CUP AND SAUCER

LAC SPATULA

MITT LAKE

MALLET RIVER

PRESS

CARRY THE KETTLE

KITCHENER

PEELER LAKE

CORNING

AJAX

PLASTIC LAKE

BROOMHILL

COOKS MILLS

MAYO, YT: Originally Mayo Landing, named for Captain Alfred S. Mayo—entrepreneur, trader, steamboat captain, former circus acrobat, and business partner of Leroy Napoleon "Jack" McQuesten, once known as "the father of the Yukon." Mayo thrived during the Klondike Gold Rush, then declined, then boomed again when more mineral deposits were found in the 1960s. The town holds the record for the greatest temperature range from warmest month to coldest: 98.2°C (208.9° F) [the average range in the Yukon is 40°C (104°F)]. Mayo once had a cold spell in which temperatures remained below −40°C (−40°F) for 24 consecutive days.

TABASCO LAKE, NT: Named in 1974 (the heyday of the Bloody Caesar, a uniquely Canadian cocktail) for the reddish-brown colour of its water.

MANGO LAKE, MB: This "mango" may have evolved from a transliteration of the Saulteaux word for "loon."

CHILI TOWER, BC: Some sources say that members of an unnamed party consumed chili while climbing this mountain in 1961, but the *Canadian Mountain Encyclopedia* says that the name comes from "Chilli-cootin," an old slang word for the Chilcotin region of BC.

DRIEDMEAT CREEK, AB: According to a Cree and Blackfoot story, there was once such a big haul of buffalo that the entire hill above this creek was covered with strips of drying meat. Driedmeat is a translation: the hill's original names were *ka-ke-wuk* in Cree and *kyé-tomo* in Blackfoot.

ÎLE AU BEURRE, QC: This unofficial name (the official one is Île Demers) was given at the beginning of the twentieth century, when the island was covered with butter-yellow wildflowers. Butter has always been close to Quebec's heart: in 2005 the Quebec government upheld the contentious Oleomargarine Act, which protects local dairy producers by forbidding the sale of artificially coloured margarine in the province. Ontario had a similar law, but it wasn't enforced and was repealed in 1995.

CRANBERRY COULEE, SK: A coulee is a steep-sided gully, often pinched at either end, that cuts through high, flat prairie land. Most coulees were made by fast-running meltwater during the time of glacial retreat. The word is common in Alberta, Saskatchewan, and the northwestern US and has taken on a real cowboy flavour, though the term originated in Quebec and comes from the French word *couler*, to "flow" or "run." Coulees are usually dry but can be subject to seasonal flooding, and evaporated floodwater occasionally leaves white salt streaks along their floors. Cranberry Coulee is in southern Saskatchewan, which has the highest concentration of coulees in Canada.

ACCORDING TO OUR SOURCES

Statistics Canada reports that the average Canadian spends about $2.56 per week on condiments; Canada is the world's largest exporter of mustard seed, according to Agriculture & Agri-Food Canada, and Canada is the only country in the world where ketchup chips are readily available.

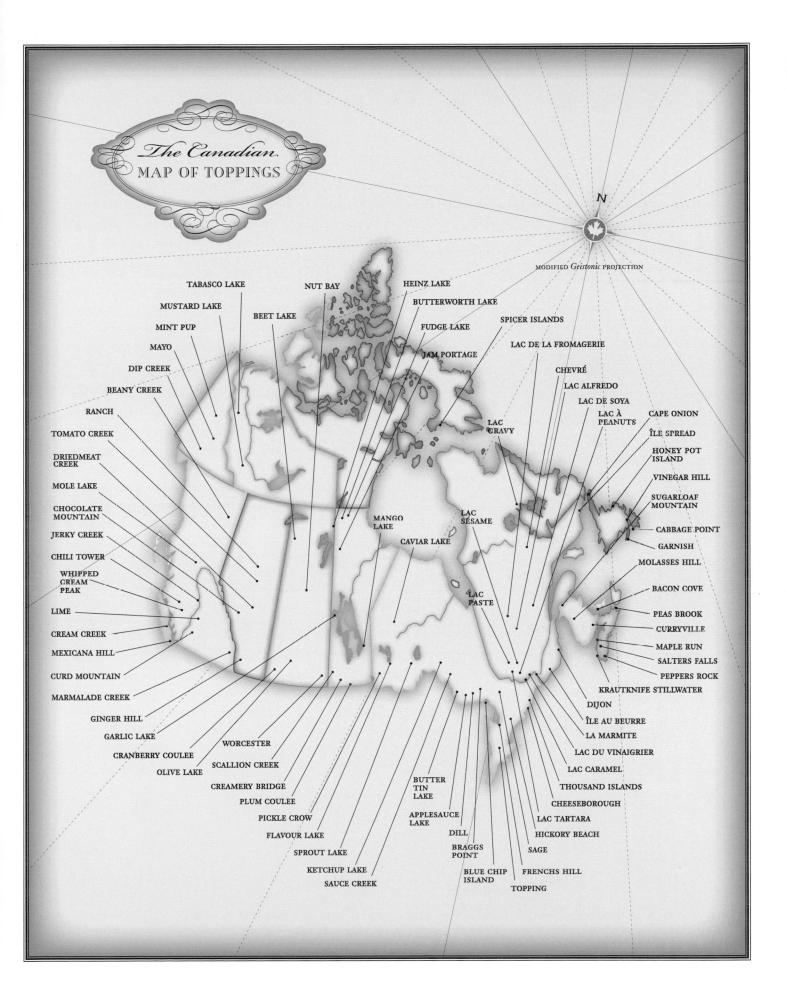

The Canadian
MAP OF TOPPINGS

N

MODIFIED *Geistonic* PROJECTION

TABASCO LAKE
MUSTARD LAKE
MINT PUP
MAYO
DIP CREEK
BEANY CREEK
RANCH
TOMATO CREEK
DRIEDMEAT CREEK
MOLE LAKE
CHOCOLATE MOUNTAIN
JERKY CREEK
CHILI TOWER
WHIPPED CREAM PEAK
LIME
CREAM CREEK
MEXICANA HILL
CURD MOUNTAIN
MARMALADE CREEK
GINGER HILL
GARLIC LAKE
CRANBERRY COULEE
OLIVE LAKE

NUT BAY
BEET LAKE

HEINZ LAKE
BUTTERWORTH LAKE
FUDGE LAKE
JAM PORTAGE

SPICER ISLANDS
LAC DE LA FROMAGERIE
CHEVRÉ
LAC ALFREDO
LAC DE SOYA
LAC À PEANUTS

LAC GRAVY

MANGO LAKE
CAVIAR LAKE

LAC SÉSAME

LAC PASTE

CAPE ONION
ÎLE SPREAD
HONEY POT ISLAND
VINEGAR HILL
SUGARLOAF MOUNTAIN
CABBAGE POINT
GARNISH
MOLASSES HILL
BACON COVE
PEAS BROOK
CURRYVILLE
MAPLE RUN
SALTERS FALLS
PEPPERS ROCK
KRAUTKNIFE STILLWATER
DIJON
ÎLE AU BEURRE
LA MARMITE
LAC DU VINAIGRIER
LAC CARAMEL
THOUSAND ISLANDS
CHEESEBOROUGH
LAC TARTARA
HICKORY BEACH
SAGE
FRENCHS HILL
TOPPING

WORCESTER
SCALLION CREEK
CREAMERY BRIDGE
PLUM COULEE
PICKLE CROW
FLAVOUR LAKE
SPROUT LAKE
KETCHUP LAKE
SAUCE CREEK

BUTTER TIN LAKE
APPLESAUCE LAKE
DILL
BRAGGS POINT
BLUE CHIP ISLAND

BURY HEAD, PE: Listed on eighteenth-century maps as Barry Head; later shown as Berry Head; in 1966 officially re-renamed to honour a nearby historic graveyard.

MT. BEELZEBUB, BC: A whole series of mountains in this region were named for generals in the army of darkness, including Mt. Azazel, Mt. Moloch, Mt. Dagon, Mt. Belial, Mt. Rimmon, and the red guy himself, Mt. Satan. Perhaps because BC's features were surveyed and named more recently than others in North America, many names depart from the standard of honouring people, industry, or regional functions and instead reflect literary, biblical, or emotional themes. Mt. Baal, BC, for example, is one of a set of features named along Brimstone-and-Gideon lines. Mt. Baal could be the geological enemy of Mt. St. Elias in the Yukon, which was named by early Danish explorers for the saint who punished the worship of Baal by calling a drought upon the kingdom of Jezebel.

WENDIGO BEACH, MB: In Ojibwa mythology, a *windigo* (or *wendigo*, or *wetigo*) is an evil flesh-eating spirit. Many places in central and eastern Canada are named for this creature, including Windigo, QC, Windego, ON, Wetigo Hills, MB, Windigo Bay Provincial Park, ON, and dozens of lakes, rivers, and bays. Cannibal Island, MB, on the Meat Map (p. 96), is a translated name that originated as *windigo*.

CRYPT FALLS, AB: These beautiful falls in Waterton Lakes National Park were named for being hidden. (Some etymologically alert mountaineer must have reached back to the Greek *krupto*, for "hide.") To find the falls, a hiker must follow a very steep trail and then crawl through a low rock tunnel.

BUGABOO PROVINCIAL PARK, BC: A Scottish prospector is believed to have named the Bugaboos, a chain of glacier-carved alpine peaks, many of which have eerie, dramatic spires. The glacial icefields in the region are the largest in the Purcell Mountain Range, and the region is popular with experienced climbers and mountaineers. The Bugaboos are not to be confused with the eerie sandstone formations in Alberta called Hoodoos, which in turn are not to be confused with Hoodoo Mountain, a peak in northern BC considered to be the inactive Canadian volcano most likely to reawaken.

GHOST RIDER

Scugog Island, ON, is reputedly inhabited by the ghost of a young man who was hot-dogging on his motorcycle in 1968 when he lost control, skidded across the road into a field, and was decapitated on an old barbed-wire fence. People walking down this road at night sometimes see a large white light that charges toward them, whizzes by, then becomes a small red light fading into the night, as if a motorcycle had driven by. Ghost researchers have observed a light hovering above the road facing south, but not moving.

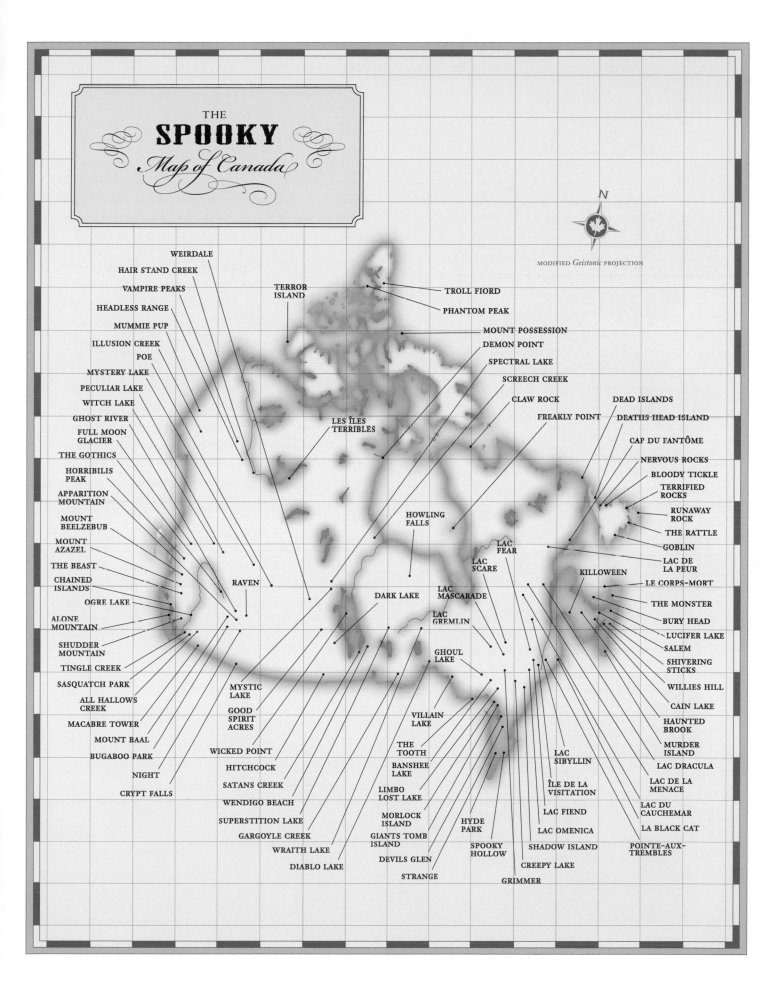

THE
SPOOKY
Map of Canada

N

MODIFIED *Geistonic* PROJECTION

WEIRDALE

HAIR STAND CREEK

VAMPIRE PEAKS

HEADLESS RANGE

MUMMIE PUP

ILLUSION CREEK

POE

MYSTERY LAKE

PECULIAR LAKE

WITCH LAKE

GHOST RIVER

FULL MOON GLACIER

THE GOTHICS

HORRIBILIS PEAK

APPARITION MOUNTAIN

MOUNT BEELZEBUB

MOUNT AZAZEL

THE BEAST

CHAINED ISLANDS

OGRE LAKE

ALONE MOUNTAIN

SHUDDER MOUNTAIN

TINGLE CREEK

SASQUATCH PARK

ALL HALLOWS CREEK

MACABRE TOWER

MOUNT BAAL

BUGABOO PARK

NIGHT

CRYPT FALLS

RAVEN

MYSTIC LAKE

GOOD SPIRIT ACRES

WICKED POINT

HITCHCOCK

SATANS CREEK

WENDIGO BEACH

SUPERSTITION LAKE

GARGOYLE CREEK

WRAITH LAKE

DIABLO LAKE

TERROR ISLAND

LES ÎLES TERRIBLES

DARK LAKE

HOWLING FALLS

GHOUL LAKE

VILLAIN LAKE

THE TOOTH

BANSHEE LAKE

LIMBO LOST LAKE

MORLOCK ISLAND

GIANTS TOMB ISLAND

DEVILS GLEN

STRANGE

HYDE PARK

SPOOKY HOLLOW

GRIMMER

TROLL FIORD

PHANTOM PEAK

MOUNT POSSESSION

DEMON POINT

SPECTRAL LAKE

SCREECH CREEK

CLAW ROCK

FREAKLY POINT

LAC FEAR

LAC SCARE

LAC MASCARADE

LAC GREMLIN

CREEPY LAKE

SHADOW ISLAND

LAC OMENICA

LAC FIEND

ÎLE DE LA VISITATION

LAC SIBYLLIN

KILLOWEEN

DEAD ISLANDS

DEATHS HEAD ISLAND

CAP DU FANTÔME

NERVOUS ROCKS

BLOODY TICKLE

TERRIFIED ROCKS

RUNAWAY ROCK

THE RATTLE

GOBLIN

LAC DE LA PEUR

LE CORPS-MORT

THE MONSTER

BURY HEAD

LUCIFER LAKE

SALEM

SHIVERING STICKS

WILLIES HILL

CAIN LAKE

HAUNTED BROOK

MURDER ISLAND

LAC DRACULA

LAC DE LA MENACE

LAC DU CAUCHEMAR

LA BLACK CAT

POINTE-AUX-TREMBLES

— 35 —

MOOSE JAW, SK: A much-discredited story tells of a travelling nobleman who awed the local Native population by repairing the broken wheel of his cart with the jawbone of a moose. More likely, "Moose Jaw" is either a translation of the original name for a jawbone-shaped creek nearby, or a transliteration of the first two syllables of *moscāstani-sīiy*, an earlier Cree name referring to warm breezes or a warm place by the river. One of the best-known local features is a network of underground bootlegging tunnels built by American gangsters during the Prohibition era. The little community was a hotbed of gang activity and liquor transport at that time, complete with a corrupt police force and a thriving brothel scene. It is rumoured that Al Capone frequently visited the town between 1929 and 1933.

CHESTERFIELD INLET, NU: The original Inuktitut name was Igluligaarjuk, or "place with few houses." In 1749 it was renamed for Philip Dormer Stanhope, the 4th Earl of Chesterfield, known for his witty writings. According to the Prince of Wales Northern Heritage Centre, "when a blow comes up anywhere from the south through southeast to east, a ship has to get out and seek shelter up Chesterfield Inlet or else ride out the storm in Hudson Bay."

SALMON ARM, BC: A pretty town at the north end of the Okanagan Valley, in the Shuswap district. It is supported by logging and fruit orchards, and hosts an annual writers' conference.

The town takes its name from the once-salmon-rich branch of Shuswap Lake, on which it sits. Fish used to swarm up the creeks and springs of this arm in such numbers that settlers harvested them with pitchforks and used them as fertilizer.

NAIL POND, PE: The name may have evolved from Neal's Pond, Noil's Pond (for a Dutch family who once settled in the area), or even the original Mi'kmaq name for the pond, *Nioetjg* (meaning "dry"). But according to another bit of local lore, in about 1825 someone found a bunch of nails near the pond after a shipwreck, and the name came from that.

BLACKFOOT, AB: The Aboriginal word *"siksikauwa"* ("blackfoot") refers to the early tradition of blackening moccasins with prairie fire ash. The Blackfoot Hills near this community are named to commemorate a series of late nineteenth-century battles between Blackfoot raiders and a 400-man army of Cree defenders led by Chief Katchemut.

EAR FALLS, ON: The Ojibwa called this place Otak Powitik ("ear falls") for the rock lip of the waterfall that had been worn into the shape of an ear. Voyageurs translated the name to Portage de l'Oreille, and the town that was founded here took on the name in English. The region is now home to a massive 1920s-era dam and hydroelectric station.

DOWN THE HATCH!

The Downtown Hotel pub in Dawson City, YT, home of the elite Sourtoe Cocktail Club, keeps a collection of preserved human toes donated by their former owners (most were lost to frostbite). To join the club, you select a toe from the collection, place it in your beverage, then drink the whole thing, allowing the toe to touch your lips as you drain the glass.

Map: Kevin Barefoot and Pamela Priebe

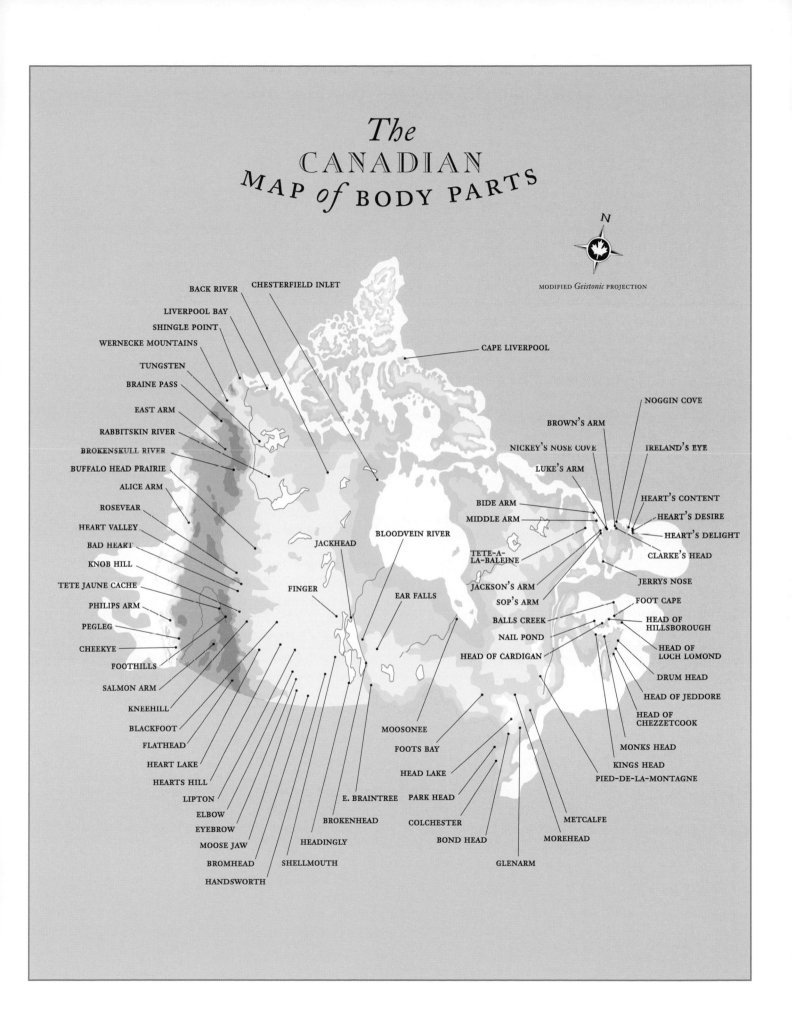

The
CANADIAN
MAP of BODY PARTS

N

MODIFIED *Geistonic* PROJECTION

BACK RIVER CHESTERFIELD INLET

LIVERPOOL BAY

SHINGLE POINT

WERNECKE MOUNTAINS

TUNGSTEN

BRAINE PASS

EAST ARM

RABBITSKIN RIVER

BROKENSKULL RIVER

BUFFALO HEAD PRAIRIE

ALICE ARM

ROSEVEAR

HEART VALLEY

BAD HEART

KNOB HILL

TETE JAUNE CACHE

PHILIPS ARM

PEGLEG

CHEEKYE

FOOTHILLS

SALMON ARM

KNEEHILL

BLACKFOOT

FLATHEAD

HEART LAKE

HEARTS HILL

LIPTON

ELBOW

EYEBROW

MOOSE JAW

BROMHEAD

HANDSWORTH

CAPE LIVERPOOL

NOGGIN COVE

BROWN'S ARM

NICKEY'S NOSE COVE

LUKE'S ARM

IRELAND'S EYE

HEART'S CONTENT

HEART'S DESIRE

HEART'S DELIGHT

CLARKE'S HEAD

JERRYS NOSE

BIDE ARM

MIDDLE ARM

JACKHEAD

BLOODVEIN RIVER

TETE-A-
LA-BALEINE

JACKSON'S ARM

SOP'S ARM

BALLS CREEK

NAIL POND

HEAD OF CARDIGAN

FINGER

EAR FALLS

FOOT CAPE

HEAD OF
HILLSBOROUGH

HEAD OF
LOCH LOMOND

DRUM HEAD

HEAD OF JEDDORE

HEAD OF
CHEZZETCOOK

MONKS HEAD

KINGS HEAD

PIED-DE-LA-MONTAGNE

MOOSONEE

FOOTS BAY

HEAD LAKE

PARK HEAD

E. BRAINTREE

BROKENHEAD

HEADINGLY

SHELLMOUTH

COLCHESTER

BOND HEAD

GLENARM

METCALFE

MOREHEAD

BARKERVILLE, BC: Once the northern terminus of the Cariboo Road, which led gold prospectors north from Yale, BC. Barkerville boomed in the 1860s—$20–30 million in gold was taken from the region during that decade. It burned to the ground and was rebuilt in 1868, then busted flat in the early 1870s when the Cariboo Gold Rush came to a close. Barkerville spent a century as a ghost town, interrupted briefly by a mini-gold rush in the 1930s, until 1958 when it was declared a historic site and was fully restored. Today it is a tourist attraction, with a saloon, a pan-your-own-gold setup, a souvenir shop, cowboy shows, and a summer staff of actors playing Wild West characters. Barkerville was originally named for William Barker, a Cornish sailor who gave up the seafaring life to go and hunt for gold. He struck it rich with a claim worth $600,000, but managed it badly and died poor.

BLOW ME DOWN, NL: A park, but Newfoundland also has a village, a mountain range, and at least thirty other places that bear this name, or its variant, Blomidon. "Blow Me Down" describes areas where sudden gusts of wind rush over the headlands and capsize small boats. One legend says that the term originated with a Captain Messervey, who looked up at high mountains that loomed over his anchorage and said, "I hope they don't blow me down!"

THUNDER BAY, ON: The name was adopted in 1970, after the amalgamation of Fort William, Port Arthur, McIntyre, and Neebing. "Thunder Bay" is a translation of the Ojibwe Animikie Wekwed, the first name for the bay. Fort William, the original settlement, was a critical post for the North West Company. Today the port of Thunder Bay is a massive grain-shipping operation—the largest port in Ontario and the sixth largest in Canada.

GASCONS, QC: It may have been named for a shipwrecked sailor from Gascogne, France, who washed ashore and settled here. The region eventually developed the name Sainte-Germaine-de-l'Anse-aux-Gascons, of which the village of Gascons is a part. "*Gascon*" is also French slang for "braggart."

BAIE DU HA! HA!, QC: In the common naming tale for this inlet, early voyageurs exploring the Saguenay thought it was the mouth of a river. When they discovered a dead end, they shouted "ha ha!"—the joke was on them. More likely the name comes from "*haha*," anantiquated French term meaning "dead end" that dates back to the fifteenth century. (The exclamation points were added later by surveyors.) The village of Saint-Louis-du-Ha!-Ha! was named for the inlet, and several other places in central and northern Quebec are also called Haha or Ha! Ha! (the northern region of the province, along with much of Labrador, comprises a territory once known as the Silent Places).

HOMEMADE MOOSE CALL

Punch a small hole in middle of the bottom of a coffee can. Push a shoelace through the hole and tie it off on the inside. Place a few wet leaves in the can, and wet the free end of the shoelace. Hold the can under one arm with the open end facing forward and pull the shoelace through the hole, hard. Wait for moose.

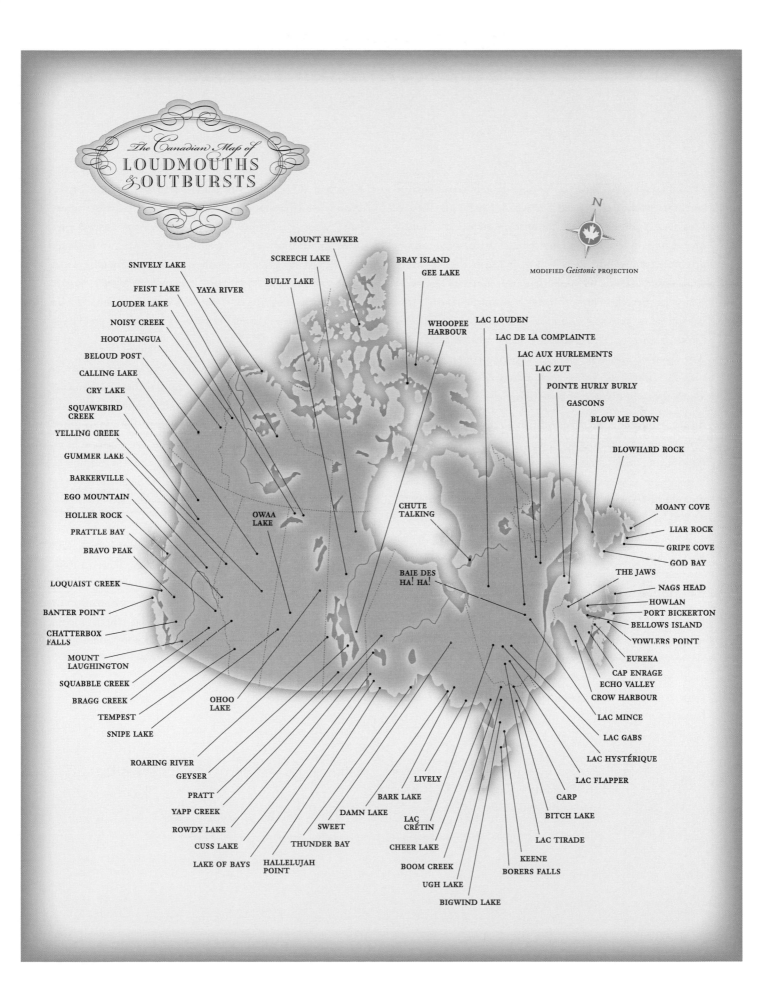

The Canadian Map of
LOUDMOUTHS
& OUTBURSTS

N

MODIFIED *Geistonic* PROJECTION

MOUNT HAWKER
SCREECH LAKE
BRAY ISLAND
GEE LAKE
SNIVELY LAKE
BULLY LAKE
FEIST LAKE
YAYA RIVER
LOUDER LAKE
NOISY CREEK
WHOOPEE
HARBOUR
LAC LOUDEN
HOOTALINGUA
LAC DE LA COMPLAINTE
BELOUD POST
LAC AUX HURLEMENTS
CALLING LAKE
LAC ZUT
CRY LAKE
POINTE HURLY BURLY
SQUAWKBIRD
CREEK
GASCONS
YELLING CREEK
BLOW ME DOWN
GUMMER LAKE
BLOWHARD ROCK
BARKERVILLE
EGO MOUNTAIN
HOLLER ROCK
CHUTE
TALKING
MOANY COVE
OWAA
LAKE
LIAR ROCK
PRATTLE BAY
GRIPE COVE
BRAVO PEAK
GOD BAY
LOQUAIST CREEK
BAIE DES
HA! HA!
THE JAWS
NAGS HEAD
BANTER POINT
HOWLAN
CHATTERBOX
FALLS
PORT BICKERTON
BELLOWS ISLAND
MOUNT
LAUGHINGTON
YOWLERS POINT
SQUABBLE CREEK
EUREKA
BRAGG CREEK
CAP ENRAGE
OHOO
LAKE
ECHO VALLEY
TEMPEST
CROW HARBOUR
SNIPE LAKE
LAC MINCE
LAC GABS
ROARING RIVER
LAC HYSTÉRIQUE
GEYSER
LAC FLAPPER
PRATT
LIVELY
CARP
YAPP CREEK
BARK LAKE
DAMN LAKE
BITCH LAKE
ROWDY LAKE
SWEET
LAC
CRÉTIN
CUSS LAKE
THUNDER BAY
LAC TIRADE
CHEER LAKE
KEENE
LAKE OF BAYS
HALLELUJAH
POINT
BOOM CREEK
BORERS FALLS
UGH LAKE
BIGWIND LAKE

FLIN FLON, MB: Short for Josiah Flintabbatey Flonatin, a character in a novel called *The Sunless City* by J.E. Preston Muddock, published in 1905. Flonatin travels to the bottom of a mountain lake in a submarine and discovers an underground city made of gold. When he learns that the city's women rule over the men, Flonatin flees in horror and eventually reaches the surface through a volcano vent. Tom Creighton, a prospector, supposedly named the site for Flonatin when his friend found a deep hole with gold in it. The town of Flin Flon put up a statue of Flonatin (nicknamed "Flinty") in 1962; Creighton's name was conferred on another town southwest of Flin Flon.

SWIFT CURRENT, SK: Named for the river it lies on, Swift Current Creek—an English translation of the original Cree meaning of "Saskatchewan" (see Original Map, p. 64). There is a rumour that Swift Current achieved the population of 550 needed to reach official town status by including dogs in its 1907 census. The town was once the home of Ira E. Argue, a sort of Prairie Robin Hood, who stole a CPR train car full of coal during a cold winter. Today Swift Current is an agricultural hub and the home of Canada's largest government-run experimental farm.

FORT McMURRAY, AB: Once a trading post and then a fish-processing centre, now the whole town is hard at work at extracting black gold from the Athabasca Tar Sands. One of its nicknames is "Little Newfoundland," because of the large population of Newfoundlanders who came for the lucrative jobs.

KENORA, ON: Kenora is at the north end of Lake of the Woods, which is a remnant of Lake Agassiz, an extinct "great lake." The town used to be called Rat Portage and was part of Manitoba until the Ontario border was redrawn in 1892. In 1905 it was given the more development-friendly name of Kenora (see notes on Snafu Creek, Cheap Map, p. 92). A twelve-metre (forty-foot) statue of a musky (walleye) stands here, and a "Kenora dinner jacket" is a fleece-lined plaid flannel work shirt.

SACKVILLE, NB: Named for George Sackville Germain, a late-1800s colonial secretary, by the Loyalists who moved in after the Acadians were ejected (see notes on Falmouth, Impolite Map, p. 42). Sackville later became a large shipbuilding centre and finally a university town—its school, Mount Allison University, was the first in the Commonwealth to grant a degree to a woman. This Sackville is not to be confused with the Sackvilles, a conglomeration of suburbs around Halifax, NS.

SHAWINIGAN, QC: The term "Shawinigan handshake," slang for grabbing someone by the throat, was coined in 1996 after then Prime Minister Jean Chrétien grabbed a protestor by the throat to push him out of his way. (Shawinigan is Chrétien's hometown.) The city's name may originate from Azawanigan, the Abénaquis name. The transliteration was first used in 1800 by the Shawinigan Water and Power Co.

THE POSSIBLE ORIGINS OF "CANUCK"

A Chinook Jargon word for Canadian; Canada + "uc," an Algonquian suffix; Canada + "iuk," an Inuit suffix; or "Connaught," an obscure term for Irish French Canadians.

THE CANADIAN
MAP of
NICKNAMES

MODIFIED *Geistonic* PROJECTION

Mayo:
MAYONNAISE

Whitehorse:
THE HORSE

Fort Liard:
THE BANANA BELT

Dawson Creek:
THE CRIK

Dawson City:
DODGE

Grande Prairie:
TOWN, GP

Lloydminster:
LLOYD,
BORDER CITY

Edmonton:
ED, E-TOWN,
THE CAPITAL,
DEADMONTON,
EDMONCHUCK

Prince George:
PRINCE, PG

Prince Rupert:
RINSE RUPERT

Port Clements:
POURED CEMENT

Kitimat:
OLD SNOWY

Cumberland:
DODGE

Port Alberni:
THE DITCH

Nanaimo:
'NAM, HUB CITY,
NANAIMOCHUCK

Victoria:
LITTLE ENGLAND,
VIC, CULT CAPITAL

Vancouver:
VAN, GVRD,
HOLLYWOOD NORTH,
LOTUSLAND,
RAINCOUVER,
TERMINAL CITY,
VANGROOVY,
VANSTERDAM

Chilliwack:
THE WACK

Kamloops:
CAMEL LIPS, THE LOOPS

Penticton:
THE TICKER, TEN PICNICS

Kelowna: K-TOWN

Revelstoke:
THE STOKE, REVELBUSH

Calgary:
C-TOWN, COWTOWN,
COWGARY

Lethbridge:
WINDY CITY, L.A.

Drumheller:
THE DRUM

Medicine Hat:
THE HAT

Swift Current:
SPEEDY CREEK

Saskatoon:
SASKABUSH,
TOON TOWN,
CITY OF BRIDGES

Moose Jaw:
THE JAW, MOOSE LIPS,
45 MINUTES

Regina:
QUEEN CITY

Brandon:
WHEAT CITY

Kenora:
RAT PORTAGE

Fort Simpson:
DEVIL'S ISLAND

Yellowknife:
YK, THE KNIFE

Norman Wells:
THE WELLS

Hay River:
THE HUB

Fairview:
FAIRROCK

Gladstone:
HAPPY ROCK

Waskesiu Lake:
WHISKEY SLOUGH

Port Hardy:
PARTY HARDY

Red Deer:
DEAD BEER,
DEAD REAR

Cambridge Bay:
CAMBAY

Fort McMurray:
WATERWAYS,
OIL SANDS CITY

Baker Lake:
MOSQUITO CAPITAL

Churchill:
POLAR BEAR
CAPITAL

Pangnirtung:
PANG

Portage la Prairie:
PLAP

Winnipeg:
THE PEG,
WINTERPEG,
WEINERPIG

Thunder Bay:
SLEEPING GIANT,
LAKEHEAD

Kapuskasing:
THE KAP

Sault Ste. Marie:
THE SOO

Peterborough:
PETERPATCH,
THE PATCH,
PETER PO'

Guelph:
G-SPOT, MOO-U

Toronto: GTA, T.O., T-DOT,
TRAWNA, THE BIG SMOKE,
HOGTOWN, TORONTO
THE GOOD, CENTRE OF
THE UNIVERSE

Fermont:
LA VILLE
AVEC LE MUR

North West River:
STRIVER

Happy Valley:
SKUNK HOLLOW

Paradise:
DONOVAN'S

St. John's:
TOWN, SIN JOHN'S
TWIN CITIES
(WITH MOUNT PEARL)

Sackville:
BAGTOWN

Fredericton:
FREDDY BEACH,
FREDDIVILLE

Québec:
LA VIEILLE
CAPITALE

Chicoutimi:
BLEUET,
BLUEBERRY

Moncton:
MONKEY
TOWN

Charlottetown:
IN TOWN

Sydney:
SKIDNEY

Port Hawkesbury:
THE HAWK

Antigonish:
ANTAGONISH,
ANTIGONOWHERE

Truro:
THE HUB

Sherbrooke:
LA CITÉ
ÉTUDIANTE,
STUDENT CITY

Halifax:
HRM, HALI,
THE FAX,
HAFILAX,
SUPERCITY,
HALIGONIA,
HALIWOOD

Shawinigan:
SHAGGIN WAGON

Montréal:
MTL, LA MÉTROPOLE, SIN CITY

Ottawa:
'TWA, BYTOWN

Kingston:
K-TOWN

Port Hope:
PORT HOPELESS

Oshawa:
THE SCHWA

St. Catharines:
ST. KITTS

Hamilton:
THE HAMMER

Windsor:
TIJUANA NORTH, DETROIT JR.

BARTIBOG RIVER, NB: Named for a Mi'kmaq chief, Bartholomew La Bogue, who was called Balt Bogue by the Mi'kmaq and Bartabogue by the French and English. The moose population of Newfoundland was supposedly given a boost by John Connell, a Bartibog man. He had a tame moose named Tommy, whose saddle can be seen at the Miramichi Natural History Museum. The story goes that in the winter of 1904, the government of Newfoundland put out a request for live moose. Connell got together with a group of friends, captured six Miramichi moose with lassoes, strapped them to sleds, and sent them off to the island by train and ferry—quite a feat, even though moose are thinner, weaker, and antler-free in winter. Connell was paid $50 a head for the four moose that survived. Later, those moose multiplied; today there is a dense population of moose on the island. In 1964 an unsuccessful attempt was made to introduce bison to an island off Newfoundland.

FALMOUTH, NS: Once Saint-Famille, a settlement of Acadian farmers. But the mid-1700s brought the Great Expulsion, in which 12,000 Acadians were deported, often violently, by the British government, which suspected them (wrongly) of allying with France. Many were killed, some were sent to France, and most resettled in the US (where they became known as Cajuns). Loyalist settlers from New England took over Saint-Famille and at their first town meeting, on July 8, 1760, they renamed the village after the Viscount of Falmouth.

QUOICH RIVER, NU: In 1853 a Hudson's Bay Company employee used the word *"quoich,"* Gaelic for "drinking cup," to describe the river here. The word "quaff" comes from the same root.

MONCHY, SK: Named to honour H.G. Richards, a soldier from Saskatchewan who was killed during World War I. His brother suggested that the town be named for the Battle of Hooge, in which his brother had died, but officials went with Monchy, a different but nearby battle. The victory at Monchy was important in the breaking of the Hindenburg Line.

DIXVILLE, QC: Pronounced in the anglo way—"Dicksville." Most likely named for Richard "Dick" Baldwin, an early mill owner and postmaster.

LOWER NIMPKISH, BC: Nimpkish was a mythical monster that in Kwakwaka'wakw legend pulled canoes underwater and caused the strong tide rip at the mouth of the Nimpkish River. The name survived a trend on Vancouver Island to rename places that sounded rude to English ears. Examples: Kokshittle Arm (changed to Kashutl Inlet), Kowshet Cove (Cullite Cove), and Foul Bay (Gonzales Bay). Viking, AB, was once called Meighen, but it was changed because people pronounced it "mean," or possibly because of Arthur Meighen, an unpopular Prime Minister who brought in conscription during World War I. A series of places in Ontario named for the Cree word *"paska"* were also changed when the Finnish community complained that the word means "shit" in Finnish (see also notes on Belly River, Map of Body Parts, p. 36, and Pugwash, Map of House Pets, p. 50).

TRAILER-PARK TALK

An average of eighty-four censorable (but uncensored, at least in Canada) swear words are spoken during a single twenty-two-minute episode of the Canadian television comedy series *Trailer Park Boys*. The record during the show's first five seasons was 146 profanities in one episode—between six and seven per minute of airtime. The "cleanest" episode contained thirty-six profanities.

The
IMPOLITE
MAP *of* CANADA

N

MODIFIED *Geistonic* PROJECTION

KUKLOK

HUMPY LAKE

DAGGITT LAKE

MOUNT KLOTZ

TSEEPANTEE LAKE

MOUNT PITTS

BALDOCK LAKE

BISTCHO LAKE

NEEB

LAC LA BICHE

NUTTLUDE LAKE

CHUCHI LAKE

BROWN PASSAGE

FOCH LAGOON

DEMMITT

MOUNT BAGG

KIMSQUIT

BICKERDIKE

NIMPO LAKE

GODS POCKET

LOWER NIMPKISH

KNUTSFORD

SQUITTY BAY

SPUZZUM

CRUMP

KOCH CREEK

YAHK

BAWLF

KILLAM

SPUTINOW

COUTTS

SNIPE LAKE

SMUTS

MONCHY

GRUND

PEPEEKISIS

QUOICH RIVER

COCKRAM STRAIT

GITCHIE RIVER

LAC BIGOT

LAC COXIPI

LAC DU GAS

MISTINIPPI LAKE

GRAND LAC SQUATEC

L'ANSE À FUGÈRE

MANFUL BIGHT

BARENEED

GOOBIES

ATHAPAP

WORBY

PÉRIBONKA

BARTIBOG

KOUCHIBOUGUAC

DINGWALL

PISQUID

ECUM SECUM

ATHOL

FALMOUTH

MINUDIE

POODIAC

GROSSE COQUES

BURPEE

DIXVILLE

BAGOTVILLE

LAC FAGUY

CUSHING

POCKNOCK

STITTSVILLE

SLABTOWN

EFFINGHAM

DORKING

COBOCONK

BUMMERS ROOST

WRIGGLY LAKE

KUKATUSH

LAC PFISTER

OBONGA LAKE

COUCHICHING

WILDE, MB: A point on the Canadian National Railway (CNR)'s Hudson Bay line, originally named Ellice for a man who helped merge the Hudson's Bay Company with the North West Company, but the name conflicted with Ellis, a Canadian Pacific Railway (CPR) point in Ontario. So Ellice was renamed in the 1920s for Sergeant W.B. Wilde, an RCMP officer killed in 1896. The town also appears on the Fairy Tale Map (p. 72) and the Gay Map (p. 94); all three inclusions are intended to honour Oscar Wilde.

JOLIETTE, QC: Founded by Barthélemy Joliette in 1823. He opened a sawmill, a granary, and an iron foundry, and he named it L'Industrie, hoping that it would become a major industrial centre. Town leaders later renamed it Joliette. The pulp, paper, steel, and textile industries are still mainstays of the local economy.

OFFICERS POND, PE: A lake formerly called Johnstons Pond, for a mill owner named Mark Johnston, and renamed in 1950 to honour the United Services Officers Fishing Club.

COURT, SK: One of a series of towns along the CPR line, all named to celebrate the Coronation of King George V in 1911. Some others in the series are Veteran, Throne, Fleet, Loyalist, Consort, and Coronation.

EXECUTIONER CLIFFS, NU: These sheer 914-metre (3,000-foot) cliffs resemble an axe head, hence the grim name, bestowed in 1938. Hangover Hill, not far away (in Arctic terms), is also named for its appearance—a hanging lip, not the aftermath of a midnight-sun party.

ANARCHIST MOUNTAIN, BC: Renamed (from Larch Tree Hill) in honour of Richard G. Sidley, an anarchist and Irish immigrant who became a customs officer and justice of the peace in Osoyoos in the late 1800s. His extreme political leanings cost him both jobs.

KILLOWEEN, NB: A (misspelled) tribute to Baron Russell of Killowen (1832–1900). Killoween had a haunted bridge until it was destroyed by fire in 2001 (arson is suspected). According to legend, the bridge was haunted by a woman whose headless body was found in 1890 in the river below (her head was discovered in 1927, when bridge builders were digging abutments in the riverbed). Some travellers have reported a woman dressed in black sitting next to them in their carriages as they crossed the bridge. Killoween also appears on the Spooky Map (p. 34).

CRIMINAL ACTS

In 2002, according to Statistics Canada, Quebec had the lowest crime rate in Canada at 5,700 incidents per 100,000 people, and Saskatchewan had the highest at 13,300 incidents per 100,000. Alberta and the Atlantic provinces have historically low crime rates, which have been rising in recent years.

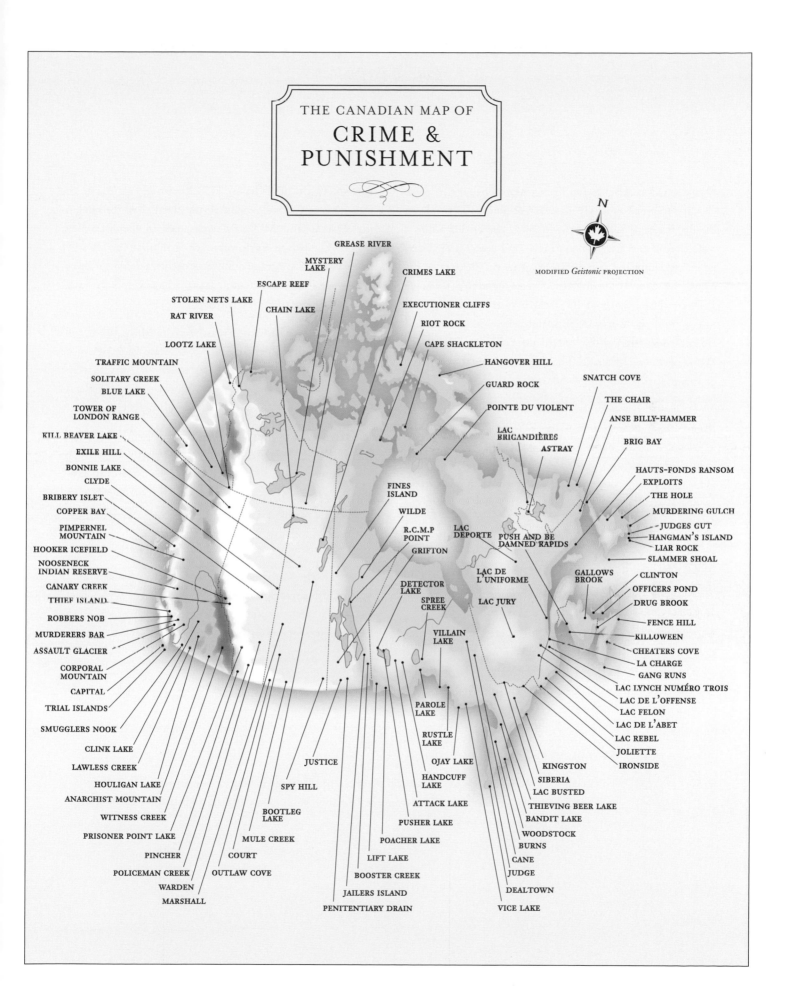

THE CANADIAN MAP OF
CRIME & PUNISHMENT

N

MODIFIED *Geistonic* PROJECTION

GREASE RIVER
MYSTERY LAKE
CRIMES LAKE
ESCAPE REEF
STOLEN NETS LAKE
CHAIN LAKE
EXECUTIONER CLIFFS
RAT RIVER
RIOT ROCK
LOOTZ LAKE
CAPE SHACKLETON
TRAFFIC MOUNTAIN
HANGOVER HILL
SNATCH COVE
SOLITARY CREEK
GUARD ROCK
BLUE LAKE
THE CHAIR
TOWER OF LONDON RANGE
POINTE DU VIOLENT
ANSE BILLY-HAMMER
KILL BEAVER LAKE
LAC BRIGANDIÈRES
BRIG BAY
EXILE HILL
ASTRAY
BONNIE LAKE
HAUTS-FONDS RANSOM
CLYDE
EXPLOITS
BRIBERY ISLET
FINES ISLAND
THE HOLE
COPPER BAY
MURDERING GULCH
PIMPERNEL MOUNTAIN
WILDE
JUDGES GUT
HOOKER ICEFIELD
R.C.M.P POINT
LAC DEPORTE
PUSH AND BE DAMNED RAPIDS
HANGMAN'S ISLAND
NOOSENECK INDIAN RESERVE
GRIFTON
LIAR ROCK
SLAMMER SHOAL
CANARY CREEK
LAC DE L'UNIFORME
GALLOWS BROOK
CLINTON
THIEF ISLAND
DETECTOR LAKE
OFFICERS POND
ROBBERS NOB
SPREE CREEK
LAC JURY
DRUG BROOK
MURDERERS BAR
VILLAIN LAKE
FENCE HILL
ASSAULT GLACIER
KILLOWEEN
CORPORAL MOUNTAIN
CHEATERS COVE
LA CHARGE
CAPITAL
GANG RUNS
TRIAL ISLANDS
LAC LYNCH NUMÉRO TROIS
SMUGGLERS NOOK
PAROLE LAKE
LAC DE L'OFFENSE
LAC FELON
CLINK LAKE
RUSTLE LAKE
LAC DE L'ABET
LAWLESS CREEK
LAC REBEL
JOLIETTE
OJAY LAKE
IRONSIDE
HOULIGAN LAKE
JUSTICE
HANDCUFF LAKE
KINGSTON
ANARCHIST MOUNTAIN
SPY HILL
SIBERIA
WITNESS CREEK
ATTACK LAKE
LAC BUSTED
BOOTLEG LAKE
THIEVING BEER LAKE
PRISONER POINT LAKE
PUSHER LAKE
BANDIT LAKE
MULE CREEK
WOODSTOCK
PINCHER
POACHER LAKE
BURNS
COURT
CANE
POLICEMAN CREEK
OUTLAW COVE
LIFT LAKE
JUDGE
WARDEN
BOOSTER CREEK
DEALTOWN
MARSHALL
JAILERS ISLAND
VICE LAKE
PENITENTIARY DRAIN

DRUMHELLER, AB: As you drive toward Drumheller from Calgary, the road signs say it's near but nothing is visible on the flat horizon. Suddenly the highway curves down into a wide canyon and the town appears—and you realize there's more happening on the prairie than meets the eye. It was named for Samuel Drumheller, a major landholder who in 1910 converted much of the local industry from ranching to coal mining. In the 1920s Drumheller was the site of a violent miners' strike that led to the creation of the Mine Workers Union of Canada. The valley was later discovered to be rich in fossils, and is now home to both the Royal Tyrrell Museum of Palaeontology and a lot of big dinosaur statues.

MERCY BAY, NT: Named by the explorer Robert McClure in honour of "the bounty and goodness of Him who had upheld them through such anxieties and dangers" so that "His mercy might never be effaced from their memories." In 1851 McClure and his crew abandoned his ship the *Investigator* to the ice in this bay and took what shelter they could; they didn't get out until 1853.

BIBLE HILL, NS: A pious family named Archibald once lived here; the name was chosen either to honour or to mock them.

BLOODVEIN RIVER, MB: The banks of this river, which flows into Bloodvein Bay on Lake Winnipeg, are streaked with red lines of granite. It was originally called Nekesepe ("goose river") in the Saulteaux dialect.

BURNT CHURCH, NB: In 1758 British troops under the leadership of Colonel James Murray razed all of the remaining Acadian and Mi'kmaq settlements in the Miramichi region. The village, Eskinwobudich (Mi'kmaq for "lookout place"), was later renamed for the scorched remains of a mission—one that even Murray admitted had been "very handsome"—destroyed during the raids.

MILTON, ON: Once known as Martin's Mills, for a gristmill owned by Jasper and Sarah Martin. Eighteen more mills were eventually built here, which suggests that the name is a variation of Mill-town, but town records indicate it was named for John Milton, the English poet.

PARADISE, NS: In the mid-1600s the French were calling what is now the Annapolis Valley, Paradis Terrestre, or "heaven on earth." When the English took the area in 1760, they applied the French name to a single creek, and the community of Paradise grew up on the banks of Paradise Brook.

PARADISE HILL, SK: Two prospectors, Alphonse and Ernest Beliveau, came upon this wide, beautiful plateau on their way back from the Klondike. Thinking it was a promising place to establish a farm, Ernest yelled out, "This is paradise!" He stayed, started a ranch, and suggested the name when the municipality formed in 1913.

AFTERLIVES

A 2003 *Reader's Digest* survey found that 55 percent of Canadians believe in life after death, 7 percent believe they will be reincarnated, 11 percent believe they will cease to exist, and 27 percent of those surveyed said they just don't know. Or care.

Map: A collaboration by the *Geist* mapping team

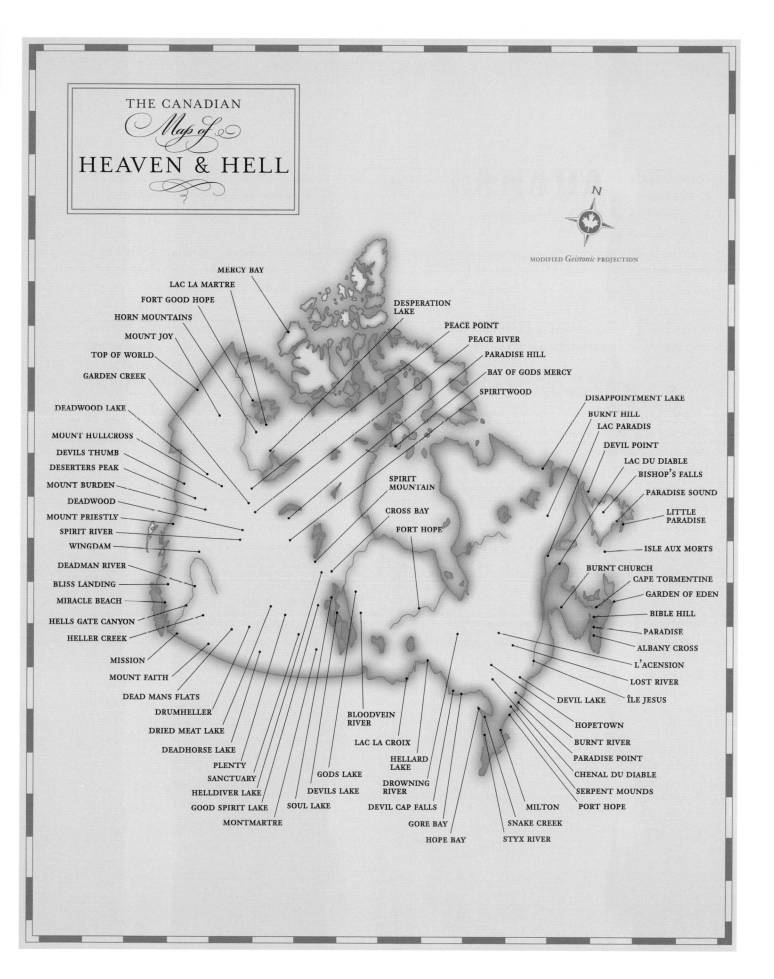

THE CANADIAN
Map of
HEAVEN & HELL

N

MODIFIED *Geistonic* PROJECTION

MERCY BAY
LAC LA MARTRE
FORT GOOD HOPE
HORN MOUNTAINS
MOUNT JOY
TOP OF WORLD
GARDEN CREEK

DESPERATION LAKE
PEACE POINT
PEACE RIVER
PARADISE HILL
BAY OF GODS MERCY
SPIRITWOOD

DISAPPOINTMENT LAKE
BURNT HILL
LAC PARADIS
DEVIL POINT
LAC DU DIABLE
BISHOP'S FALLS
PARADISE SOUND
LITTLE PARADISE

DEADWOOD LAKE

MOUNT HULLCROSS
DEVILS THUMB
DESERTERS PEAK
MOUNT BURDEN
DEADWOOD
MOUNT PRIESTLY
SPIRIT RIVER
WINGDAM
DEADMAN RIVER
BLISS LANDING
MIRACLE BEACH
HELLS GATE CANYON
HELLER CREEK

SPIRIT MOUNTAIN

CROSS BAY
FORT HOPE

ISLE AUX MORTS

BURNT CHURCH
CAPE TORMENTINE
GARDEN OF EDEN
BIBLE HILL
PARADISE
ALBANY CROSS
L'ACENSION
LOST RIVER
ÎLE JESUS

MISSION
MOUNT FAITH
DEAD MANS FLATS
DRUMHELLER
DRIED MEAT LAKE
DEADHORSE LAKE
PLENTY
SANCTUARY
HELLDIVER LAKE
GOOD SPIRIT LAKE
MONTMARTRE

BLOODVEIN RIVER

LAC LA CROIX

HELLARD LAKE

GODS LAKE
DEVILS LAKE
SOUL LAKE

DROWNING RIVER

DEVIL CAP FALLS
GORE BAY
HOPE BAY

DEVIL LAKE

MILTON
SNAKE CREEK
STYX RIVER

HOPETOWN
BURNT RIVER
PARADISE POINT
CHENAL DU DIABLE
SERPENT MOUNDS
PORT HOPE

MEDICINE HAT, AB: Most experts agree that "Medicine Hat" is a translation of *"saamis,"* the Blackfoot word for a shaman's headdress. In the early 1900s there was a movement to change the name to something more staid, such as Smithville or Gasburg (the latter referred to natural gas deposits under the townsite, and would surely have ended up on the Impolite Map, p. 42). The debate was settled after the local postmaster wrote to Rudyard Kipling, who had recently visited Medicine Hat; Kipling responded by imploring the residents to keep the name, which made "men ask questions" and had a mysterious quality that drew people to the town. The *Calgary Herald* then published an editorial saying that if Medicine Hat changed its name, it should be rechristened Judasville.

BUTTON, MB: A railway point named for Sir Thomas Button, who led sailing expeditions along the western shore of the Hudson Bay in the early 1600s and was the first person to raise the British flag on what is now Manitoban soil. Among other things, Button hoped to discover a northern passage to India and to find Henry Hudson, who had been abandoned by his crew somewhere along the icy bay that would bear his name. Button didn't find Hudson or the passage to India, but he did chart and name the Nelson River and other features.

TWEEDSMUIR PARK, BC: A remote and rugged provincial park used mainly by experienced outdoor adventurers. Its best-known feature is a group of ancient pictographs near Two Rock, a giant glacial erratic that used to be called Big Rock until it snapped in half during a cold spell in the early 1990s. The park was formed in 1936 and named for then Governor General John Buchan Tweedsmuir. Lord Tweedsmuir was the founder of the Governor General's Literary Awards and was himself a prolific author; he published poetry, historical works, and even suspense novels—one of which, *The 39 Steps*, was made into a film by Alfred Hitchcock. Lady Susan Charlotte Tweedsmuir was also a writer: she undertook several literacy projects and sent some 40,000 books from Rideau Hall to prairie libraries.

TINCAP, ON: First known as Spring Valley, but when a schoolhouse with a prominent tin peak was constructed in the late 1800s, people started calling it Tincap. In 1905 the town postmaster reported that the unofficial name was much better known than the official one, and letters from all over the British Empire and the US came addressed to Tincap, not Spring Valley. The new name was made official in 1912, and another town a couple of kilometres away grabbed the Spring Valley name.

THERE'S A BEAVER ON MY HEAD

The famed Canadian beaver hat was not made from the whole beaver pelt, but from the hairs, which were mashed together with adhesive to form a kind of waterproof felt. Beaver hats were a fad during the reign of King Charles I, but they slipped out of fashion during Queen Victoria's time, when her consort, Prince Albert, adopted a silk top hat.

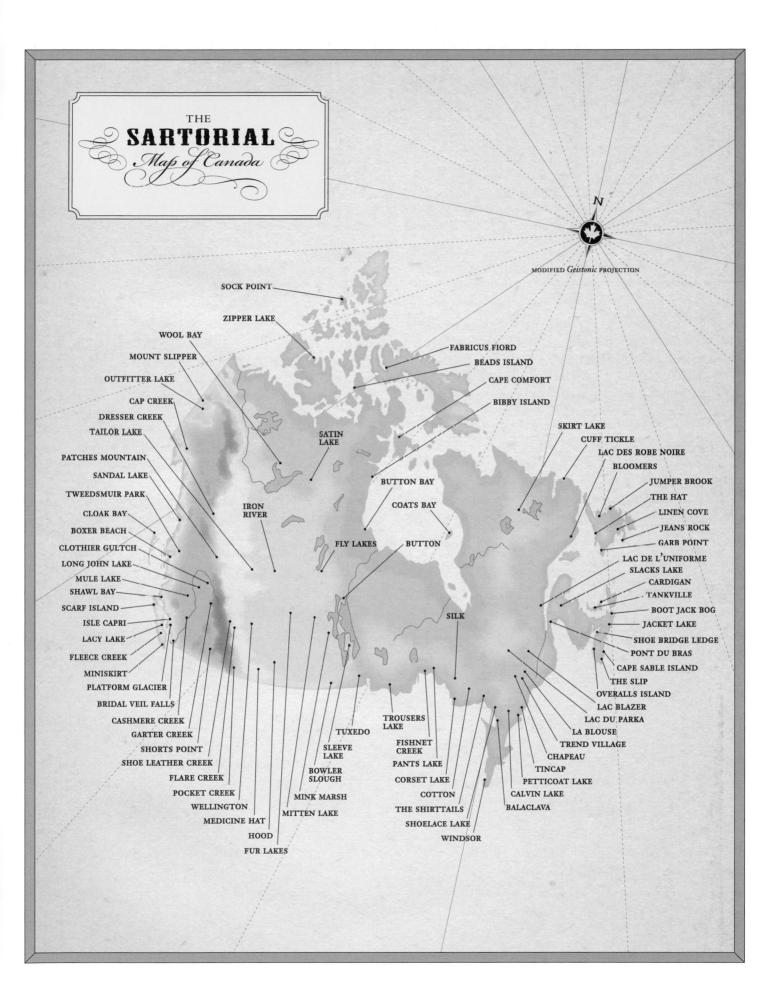

THE
SARTORIAL
Map of Canada

N

MODIFIED *Geistonic* PROJECTION

SOCK POINT

ZIPPER LAKE

WOOL BAY

MOUNT SLIPPER

OUTFITTER LAKE

CAP CREEK

DRESSER CREEK

TAILOR LAKE

PATCHES MOUNTAIN

SANDAL LAKE

TWEEDSMUIR PARK

CLOAK BAY

BOXER BEACH

CLOTHIER GULTCH

LONG JOHN LAKE

MULE LAKE

SHAWL BAY

SCARF ISLAND

ISLE CAPRI

LACY LAKE

FLEECE CREEK

MINISKIRT

PLATFORM GLACIER

BRIDAL VEIL FALLS

CASHMERE CREEK

GARTER CREEK

SHORTS POINT

SHOE LEATHER CREEK

FLARE CREEK

POCKET CREEK

WELLINGTON

MEDICINE HAT

HOOD

FUR LAKES

FABRICUS FIORD

BEADS ISLAND

CAPE COMFORT

BIBBY ISLAND

SATIN LAKE

BUTTON BAY

COATS BAY

IRON RIVER

FLY LAKES

BUTTON

SILK

TUXEDO

SLEEVE LAKE

BOWLER SLOUGH

MINK MARSH

MITTEN LAKE

TROUSERS LAKE

FISHNET CREEK

PANTS LAKE

CORSET LAKE

COTTON

THE SHIRTTAILS

SHOELACE LAKE

WINDSOR

SKIRT LAKE

CUFF TICKLE

LAC DES ROBE NOIRE

BLOOMERS

JUMPER BROOK

THE HAT

LINEN COVE

JEANS ROCK

GARB POINT

LAC DE L'UNIFORME

SLACKS LAKE

CARDIGAN

TANKVILLE

BOOT JACK BOG

JACKET LAKE

SHOE BRIDGE LEDGE

PONT DU BRAS

CAPE SABLE ISLAND

THE SLIP

OVERALLS ISLAND

LAC BLAZER

LAC DU PARKA

LA BLOUSE

TREND VILLAGE

CHAPEAU

TINCAP

PETTICOAT LAKE

CALVIN LAKE

BALACLAVA

PUGWASH, NS: From the Mi'kmaq word *"pagweak,"* which means "shoal." In 1826 a movement got underway to change this "uncouth" name to the more civilized Waterford, but residents remained loyal and the town kept the name. Pugwash is the namesake and birthplace of a global "thinker's conference" on science and world affairs, conceived and launched in 1957 by Cyrus Eaton, a Pugwashian scientist. Albert Einstein and Bertrand Russell attended the original Pugwash Conference and issued a manifesto calling for scientists everywhere to become activists against nuclear proliferation. Joseph Rotblat, a nuclear scientist, accepted the Nobel Peace Prize on behalf of the Pugwash movement in 1995.

DOG RIVER, ON: A portage at Denison Falls on Dog River that has been listed as one of the "ten worst portages on the planet" by a paddling magazine. Despite this—or perhaps because of it—the river is listed in the *The Book of Lists, The Canadian Edition* as a favourite site for advanced canoeists. Dog River, SK (no relation) is the fictional setting for *Corner Gas*, the Canadian sitcom whose theme song refers to an old joke: Saskatchewan is so flat that when your dog runs away, you can watch it go for three days.

REX, SK: An unincorporated area named for Rex L. Jones, an early settler who immigrated from Nottinghamshire, England, with his friend Edward Greenstreet, who also had an unincorporated area named for him.

TOODOGGONE RIVER, BC: An English-speaker's transliteration of the Sekani word for "water's arms."

ADOPTION POINT, NT: Adopted in 1962 to celebrate the adoption of another name: HMCS *Mackenzie*, named to honour the Mackenzie River. A cairn at this point marks the occasion. The *Mackenzie*, an anti-sub destroyer escort, protected the north and west coasts until her retirement in 1993. In 1995 she was sunk off Gooch Island (near Sidney, BC) to make an artificial reef.

CAP CHAT, QC: The most likely story is that the explorer Samuel de Champlain named this place in honour of Commander Aymar de Chaste, but sixteenth-century mapmakers misspelled the name. Another story mentions a nearby rock shaped like a cat, and yet another refers to an old myth about a she-lion that went on a killing spree until a *Fée-Chat* (Fairy Cat) locked her away. Another cat place name with non-feline origins is Cat Lake, MB, so named because a Caterpillar tractor sank in it.

THE LABRADOR OF NEWFOUNDLAND

Strange but true dog fact: the Labrador retriever was originally bred in Newfoundland, not Labrador. Early forms of the dog, which were mixes of small swimming dogs and larger, shaggy Newfoundlands, were first called St. John's Water Dogs, but the Duke of Malmesbury was the first to refer to them as Labradors. A steep dog tax and strict British quarantine laws caused the Lab population to drop in its original province, but the breed was eventually rescued by dog fanciers who wrote up anti-interbreeding laws to preserve its characteristics. Today the Lab is the most popular breed for guide and rescue dogs.

THE CANADIAN MAP of
HOUSE PETS

N

MODIFIED *Geistonic* PROJECTION

SHEPHERD BAY
BIRD
CUR ISLAND
BOOTS CREEK
BAIE DU CHIEN
CUDDLE LAKE
HUSKY CHANNEL
PERSIAN LAKE
DOBIE
ADOPTION POINT
CLAW BAY
REPTILE CREEK
TROUBLESOME PUP
MASCOT CREEK
DOG ISLAND
MALAMUTE
MOUNTAIN
LAC PARROT
MONKEY CREEK
RABBIT RIVER
STRIPED ISLAND
TOODOGGONE
RIVER
LABRADOR
FERRET ISLANDS
HAIRY HILL
FLUFF LAKE
LAC DE L'AQUARIUM
BULLDOG CREEK
ÎLE AUX PERROQUETS
PAW CREEK
ÎLE PUPPY
COLLIE CREEK
PIG ISLAND
BOXER CLIFF
POINTER
LAKE
NEWFOUNDLAND
SPANIEL POINT
FLEA POND
MANX PEAK
CALICO
ISLAND
MOULTING POND
WHISKER LAKE
CAP-CHAT
TRAINER PASSAGE
LAC MUTT
KITTEN ISLAND
STRAY LAKE
GARFIELD
FELINE PEAK
DOG RIVER
TOMCAT
HILL
CAGE SHOAL
HOBO CREEK
RAT
PORTAGE
LAC
SPRAY
PUGWASH
TOY LAKE
COY BROOK
BOWSER
SHEEPDOG POINT
ANGORA LAKE
CAT CREEK
HAMSTERLY LAKE
DANE
HOUNDS LEDGES
FURRY CREEK
LA SHED
KATZ
SCRATCH ALL POINT
GREYHOUND CREEK
POODLE
LAKE
LAC CANINE
WEINER HILL
LASSIE LAKE
LAC SNOOPY
CAT HILLS
MOGGY
COMPANION CREEK
MICE CREEK
WHITE RAT
LAKE
ÉTANG
GOOFY
SAINT-BERNARD
OLD TOM MOUNTAIN
LAC DU TERRIER
POOPOO CREEK
TURTLE RIVER
PROVINCIAL
PARK
JUMPINGCAT
LAKE
LAC FUZZ
BEAGLE CREEK
SCRUFFY LAKE
LAC ZOO
DOGPOUND
BUNNYRABBIT
LAKE
LAC CHATON FEMELLE
WIREHAIR
LAKE
GOLDFISH LAKE
WHELP BROOK
KIBBLE CREEK
BITCH LAKE
BULLPOUND
SCOOPER
CREEK
BASSETT ISLAND
BRINDLE CROSSING
REX
FOXHOUND ROCK
CANARY ISLAND
WAGTAIL LAKE
BREED CREEK
PUSSY LAKE
MEW LAKE

MILLION DOLLAR BAY, MB: Winter winds push water into this corner of Lake Manitoba, bringing large stocks of fish in with it. The fish stay because of the abundant food in the bay and in turn attract a lot of professional fishers, who named the bay after the big money they pull out of it.

CINEMA, BC: In 1924 a local hobby farmer and entrepreneur named Dr. Lloyd Champlain sold $800 worth of vegetables to a passing work crew. He used the money to take his female "housekeeper" (BC Geographical Names Database describes her as such—with the quotation marks) to Hollywood. On their return, Dr. Champlain named his farm Cinema City, because, as he put it, "Cinema means action … and that is what we are, action."

YOUNG, SK: When the CPR built a northern line from Regina to Colonsay, the village of Young became the "diamond" point (it crossed with an existing east-west line). Other connecting lines were proposed, and the residents called Young the "Diamond of the Prairie," hoping it would become a major hub; Young still does well as a grain centre. It was named for F.G. Young, a local insurance, loans, and real estate agent.

HITCHCOCK, SK: A tiny hamlet that all but disappeared in the 1950s. A couple of decades later it was partially resettled as a commuter town for people working in Estevan and the surrounding coalfields. It took its name from Arthur Hitchcock, a businessman from Moose Jaw who had considered opening a Royal Bank branch in the region in the early 1900s. He decided against the venture and went back to Moose Jaw, but the town retained his name.

DISILLUSION PEAK, NU: A group of explorers climbed to the summit and found they could "visually" solve an "illusion" (they did not elaborate) caused by two steep glaciers on the north flank.

LIVELY, ON: A central neighbourhood of Walden that was once an independent municipality. It was likely founded in 1950 as a company town for a nickel mining concern. It was named for Charles Lively, an employee of the company. (For a livelier Lively, see Off the Map note, Philosopher's Map, p. 76.)

OFF THE MAP

The 49th parallel is the Canadian location that got the least amount of screen time in the famous World War II propaganda movie of the same name. In the film, a German U-boat sinks off the coast of Hudson Bay; its crew, during their efforts to reach neutral (at the time) US soil, meet—and, in turn, kill or are influenced by—a philosophical French Canadian trapper (played by Laurence Olivier), a village of Hutterites in Manitoba, a woodsy intellectual (Leslie Howard) in Banff, and a patriotic AWOL soldier (Raymond Massey) at Niagara Falls. *49th Parallel* won an Oscar for Best Screenplay and was England's highest-grossing film of 1941.

ACTING LIKE EXPORTS (POST-MARY PICKFORD)

Dan Ackroyd, Pamela Anderson, Raymond Burr, Neve Campbell, Jim Carrey, Kim Cattrall, Tommy Chong, Hayden Christensen, Hume Cronyn, Elisha Cuthbert, Dave Foley, Michael J. Fox, Brendan Fraser, Victor Garber, Ryan Gosling, Tom Green, Phil Hartman, Eugene Levy, Evangeline Lilly, Rachel McAdams, Eric McCormack, Andrea Martin, Raymond Massey, Carrie-Anne Moss, Mike Myers, Leslie Nielsen, Sandra Oh, Catherine O'Hara, Anna Paquin, Matthew Perry, Christopher Plummer, Sarah Polley, Keanu Reeves, William Shatner, Martin Short, Donald and Kiefer Sutherland, Alan Thicke, Meg and Jennifer Tilly.

Map: Jill Mandrake and Melissa Edwards

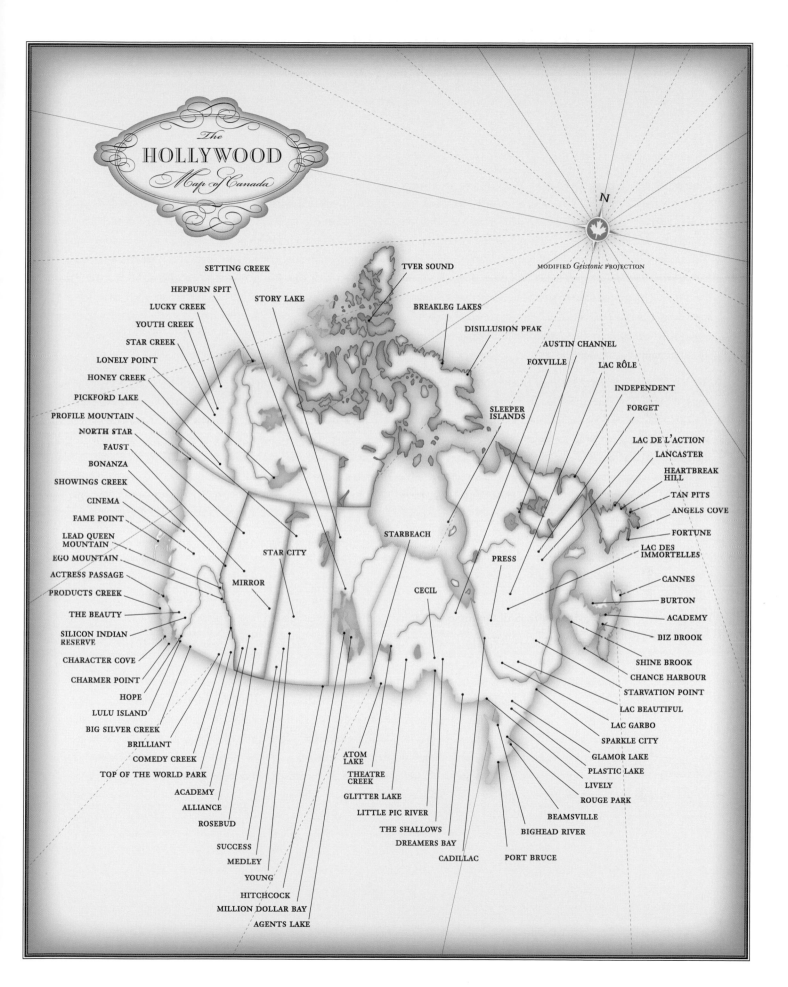

The HOLLYWOOD Map of Canada

MODIFIED *Geistonic* PROJECTION

N

SETTING CREEK
HEPBURN SPIT
LUCKY CREEK
YOUTH CREEK
STAR CREEK
LONELY POINT
HONEY CREEK
PICKFORD LAKE
PROFILE MOUNTAIN
NORTH STAR
FAUST
BONANZA
SHOWINGS CREEK
CINEMA
FAME POINT
LEAD QUEEN MOUNTAIN
EGO MOUNTAIN
ACTRESS PASSAGE
PRODUCTS CREEK
THE BEAUTY
SILICON INDIAN RESERVE
CHARACTER COVE
CHARMER POINT
HOPE
LULU ISLAND
BIG SILVER CREEK
BRILLIANT
COMEDY CREEK
TOP OF THE WORLD PARK
ACADEMY
ALLIANCE
ROSEBUD
SUCCESS
MEDLEY
YOUNG
HITCHCOCK
MILLION DOLLAR BAY
AGENTS LAKE

STORY LAKE

TVER SOUND
BREAKLEG LAKES
DISILLUSION PEAK
AUSTIN CHANNEL
FOXVILLE
LAC RÔLE
INDEPENDENT
FORGET
SLEEPER ISLANDS
LAC DE L'ACTION
LANCASTER
HEARTBREAK HILL
TAN PITS
ANGELS COVE
FORTUNE
LAC DES IMMORTELLES
CANNES
BURTON
ACADEMY
BIZ BROOK
SHINE BROOK
CHANCE HARBOUR
STARVATION POINT
LAC BEAUTIFUL
LAC GARBO
SPARKLE CITY
GLAMOR LAKE
PLASTIC LAKE
LIVELY
ROUGE PARK
BEAMSVILLE
BIGHEAD RIVER
PORT BRUCE

STARBEACH
PRESS
CECIL
STAR CITY
MIRROR

ATOM LAKE
THEATRE CREEK
GLITTER LAKE
LITTLE PIC RIVER
THE SHALLOWS
DREAMERS BAY
CADILLAC

TURKEY JOE'S, ST. JOHN'S, NL: A lively bar on George Street, established in 1995. It has an upstairs deck and live bands, and on Sundays Ladies Night draws the biggest crowd on the block (the "15 cents per ounce" beer deal on Wednesdays also brings in a lot of people). Patrons of Turkey Joe's tend to be a young, relaxed crowd, including many students from Memorial University. The owner of the place, according a bartender named Chris, is named Stefan—the only Joe in the place is the dapper, vest-wearing turkey featured on paintings around the bar.

JOE LE ROI DU SOUS MARIN, TERREBONNE, QC: The name translates to "Joe, the King of Submarines," which can then be reduced to "Joe Sub King." This Joe's is a family-owned sit-down pizza-and-sandwich restaurant, open since the late 1980s. Most of Joe's clientele have been regulars for many years. Anna, daughter of the owners, says there never was a Joe; her extended family owns other Sub King shops around Montreal with similar fictional names: Bob le Roi du Sous Marin, George le Roi du Sous Marin, and Ray le Roi du Sous Marin.

JOE'S MACHINE SHOP, WINNIPEG, MB: No one in this family-owned business is named Joe, either. Emile founded the business in 1957; his son Paul now runs it with his son Richard and a business partner named Gil. Joe's does engine rebuilds on cars, trucks and "anything that has an engine." When Joe's opened, it was well outside of Winnipeg—the building itself was once a tractor repair shed used by the farmer who owned the property. Over the years the city has grown around them, and the shop is now surrounded by Windsor Park, a residential suburb.

CRAZY JOE'S DRAPERY WAREHOUSE, NORTH YORK, ON: Joe Itskowitz, owner and manager, founded his first store in the mid-1970s, and later opened two more in the Greater Toronto Area (the others are on "discount rows" in Scarborough and Mississauga). Crazy Joe's sells cloth, window treatments, and hardware, mainly to bargain-seekers buying in bulk, though they do have a high-end home design service. According to a sales clerk at Crazy Joe's, yes, Joe is a little bit crazy, but in "a low-low-prices kind of way."

A FEW MORE CANADIAN JOES

Joe Clark, former prime minister; Joe Shuster, creator of Superman; Joe Krol, football player; Joseph Lannin, baseball team owner; Joe Malone, Joe Thornton, Joe Sakic, Joe Nieuwendyk, NHL players; Sami Jo Small, female hockey player; Joe Fortes, lifeguard; Joey Smallwood, former premier of Newfoundland; "Joe," fictional Molson Canadian beer spokesman; Joseph Boyden, writer; Joe Horton, chess player; Joey "Shithead" Keithley, punk rocker; Joe Crow, character on TV's *This Hour Has 22 Minutes*; Joey Jeremiah, character on TV's *Degrassi Junior High*; Joey Mayle, character in the film *Goin' Down the Road*; Joe Average, artist; Joe Fafard, artist; Mendelson Joe, artist and musician; Joseph Thayendanegea Brant, Mohawk missionary; Joe Cheng, auto racer; Joseph-Armand Bombardier, snowmobile inventor; Billyjojimbob, champion gelding racehorse; Canada Joe, lumberjack.

Map: Billeh Nickerson and Melissa Edwards

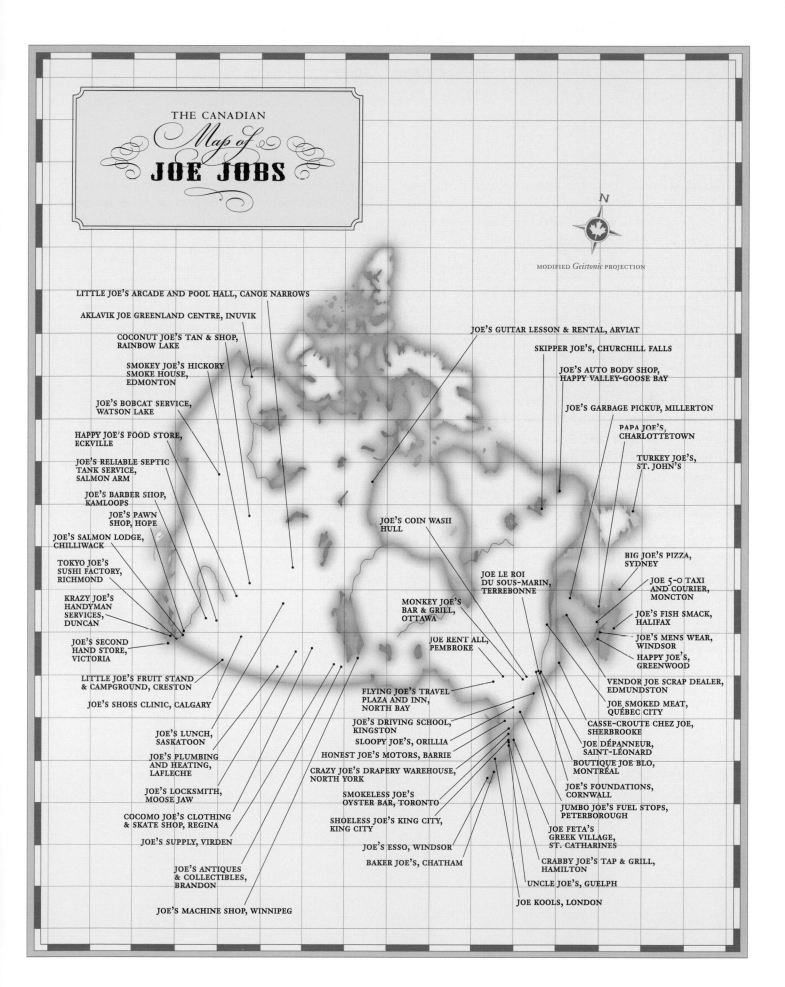

THE CANADIAN
Map of
JOE JOBS

N

MODIFIED *Geistonic* PROJECTION

LITTLE JOE'S ARCADE AND POOL HALL, CANOE NARROWS

AKLAVIK JOE GREENLAND CENTRE, INUVIK

COCONUT JOE'S TAN & SHOP, RAINBOW LAKE

SMOKEY JOE'S HICKORY SMOKE HOUSE, EDMONTON

JOE'S BOBCAT SERVICE, WATSON LAKE

HAPPY JOE'S FOOD STORE, ECKVILLE

JOE'S RELIABLE SEPTIC TANK SERVICE, SALMON ARM

JOE'S BARBER SHOP, KAMLOOPS

JOE'S PAWN SHOP, HOPE

JOE'S SALMON LODGE, CHILLIWACK

TOKYO JOE'S SUSHI FACTORY, RICHMOND

KRAZY JOE'S HANDYMAN SERVICES, DUNCAN

JOE'S SECOND HAND STORE, VICTORIA

LITTLE JOE'S FRUIT STAND & CAMPGROUND, CRESTON

JOE'S SHOES CLINIC, CALGARY

JOE'S LUNCH, SASKATOON

JOE'S PLUMBING AND HEATING, LAFLECHE

JOE'S LOCKSMITH, MOOSE JAW

COCOMO JOE'S CLOTHING & SKATE SHOP, REGINA

JOE'S SUPPLY, VIRDEN

JOE'S ANTIQUES & COLLECTIBLES, BRANDON

JOE'S MACHINE SHOP, WINNIPEG

JOE'S GUITAR LESSON & RENTAL, ARVIAT

SKIPPER JOE'S, CHURCHILL FALLS

JOE'S AUTO BODY SHOP, HAPPY VALLEY-GOOSE BAY

JOE'S GARBAGE PICKUP, MILLERTON

PAPA JOE'S, CHARLOTTETOWN

TURKEY JOE'S, ST. JOHN'S

JOE'S COIN WASH HULL

JOE LE ROI DU SOUS-MARIN, TERREBONNE

MONKEY JOE'S BAR & GRILL, OTTAWA

JOE RENT ALL, PEMBROKE

BIG JOE'S PIZZA, SYDNEY

JOE 5-O TAXI AND COURIER, MONCTON

JOE'S FISH SMACK, HALIFAX

JOE'S MENS WEAR, WINDSOR

HAPPY JOE'S, GREENWOOD

VENDOR JOE SCRAP DEALER, EDMUNDSTON

JOE SMOKED MEAT, QUÉBEC CITY

FLYING JOE'S TRAVEL PLAZA AND INN, NORTH BAY

JOE'S DRIVING SCHOOL, KINGSTON

SLOOPY JOE'S, ORILLIA

HONEST JOE'S MOTORS, BARRIE

CRAZY JOE'S DRAPERY WAREHOUSE, NORTH YORK

SMOKELESS JOE'S OYSTER BAR, TORONTO

SHOELESS JOE'S KING CITY, KING CITY

JOE'S ESSO, WINDSOR

BAKER JOE'S, CHATHAM

CASSE-CROUTE CHEZ JOE, SHERBROOKE

JOE DÉPANNEUR, SAINT-LÉONARD

BOUTIQUE JOE BLO, MONTRÉAL

JOE'S FOUNDATIONS, CORNWALL

JUMBO JOE'S FUEL STOPS, PETERBOROUGH

JOE FETA'S GREEK VILLAGE, ST. CATHARINES

CRABBY JOE'S TAP & GRILL, HAMILTON

UNCLE JOE'S, GUELPH

JOE KOOLS, LONDON

ISLE MADAME, NS: The name developed from Insula Sancte Mariae to Isle Notre Dame to Porte Ste. Marie and finally to Isle Madame. The island has been a bustling spot for commercial fishers since the mid-1700s.

LAKE SUPERIOR, ON: Samuel de Champlain called it Grand Lac in 1632, then the Jesuits renamed it Lac de Tracy ou Supérieur in 1670 after the Marquis de Tracy (a commander of French troops in North America). Because the word "superior" aptly summed up both the relative size and elevation of the lake, that part of the name became official. Originally, the Ojibwa called the lake Kitchigami ("great water")—a name Henry Wadsworth Longfellow translated into Gitche Gumee for his epic poem "The Song of Hiawatha" (1855). In the poem, which riffs off genuine Ojibwa stories of a legendary leader, a Native hero joyfully accepts the Christian message brought to him by "the Priest of Prayer, the Paleface," implores his people to do the same, then canoes off into the sunset.

LEADER, SK: The original name, Prussia, became a victim of wartime public relations (see notes on Kitchener, Map of Kitchen Implements, p. 30). The town was renamed during World War I.

PRESIDENTS SEAT, NU: Charles Francis Hall named this peak in 1861 to honour Abraham Lincoln, declaring it a "most conspicuous mountain on the coast of Frobisher Bay."

THE RAJAH, AB: At 3,018 metres (9,902 feet), this mountain is the highest in the Snake Indian River Valley of Jasper National Park. The king is kept company by its neighbour and queen, The Ranee (2,939 metres/9,642 feet). Both were named by Richard W. Cautley in 1921, during a colonial era of fascination with all things Indian—especially royal. Empress, AB, for example, was named a few years earlier to honour Queen Victoria, who had been declared Empress of India.

MANITOU, QC: Many, many places in Quebec carry the name Manitou, the Algonquian word for the Great Spirit and an early Quebecois slang word for an important person. This Manitou is an unincorporated area on the Rivière Manitou, not far from the ferry to l'Île d'Anticosti (see notes on Brick, Retail Map, p. 88). Manitoulin Island in Lake Huron is Canada's largest freshwater island. "Manitou" is also the root word of "Manitoba," a variant that means "the god that speaks."

THE CANADIAN PRESS BARON

When Sir Conrad Moffat Black, Baron Black of Crossharbour, a financier, newspaper magnate, and one of Canada's best-known authority figures, accepted a place in the British House of Lords in 2001, he contravened the Nickle Resolution, a Canadian law stating that a citizen of Canada may not hold a foreign title. In response, the Baron renounced his Canadian citizenship, stating that it was "an impediment to [his] progress in another, more amenable, jurisdiction."

The
AUTHORITY
MAP *of* CANADA

N

MODIFIED *Geistonic* PROJECTION

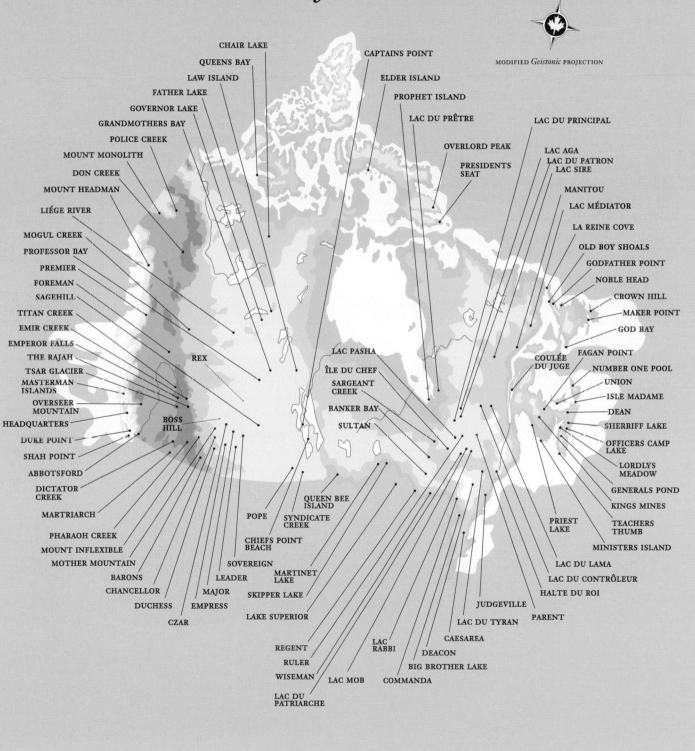

CHAIR LAKE
QUEENS BAY
LAW ISLAND
FATHER LAKE
GOVERNOR LAKE
GRANDMOTHERS BAY
POLICE CREEK
MOUNT MONOLITH
DON CREEK
MOUNT HEADMAN
LIÉGE RIVER
MOGUL CREEK
PROFESSOR BAY
PREMIER
FOREMAN
SAGEHILL
TITAN CREEK
EMIR CREEK
EMPEROR FALLS
THE RAJAH
TSAR GLACIER
MASTERMAN
ISLANDS
OVERSEER
MOUNTAIN
HEADQUARTERS
DUKE POINT
SHAH POINT
ABBOTSFORD
DICTATOR
CREEK
MARTRIARCH
PHARAOH CREEK
MOUNT INFLEXIBLE
MOTHER MOUNTAIN
BARONS
CHANCELLOR
DUCHESS
CZAR
EMPRESS
MAJOR
LEADER
SOVEREIGN
MARTINET
LAKE
SKIPPER LAKE
LAKE SUPERIOR
REGENT
RULER
WISEMAN
LAC DU
PATRIARCHE
LAC MOB
REX
BOSS
HILL
POPE
CHIEFS POINT
BEACH
SYNDICATE
CREEK
QUEEN BEE
ISLAND

CAPTAINS POINT
ELDER ISLAND
PROPHET ISLAND
LAC DU PRÊTRE
OVERLORD PEAK
PRESIDENTS
SEAT
LAC PASHA
ÎLE DU CHEF
SARGEANT
CREEK
BANKER BAY
SULTAN
LAC
RABBI
DEACON
BIG BROTHER LAKE
COMMANDA
CAESAREA
LAC DU TYRAN
JUDGEVILLE
LAC DU PRINCIPAL
LAC AGA
LAC DU PATRON
LAC SIRE
MANITOU
LAC MÉDIATOR
LA REINE COVE
OLD BOY SHOALS
GODFATHER POINT
NOBLE HEAD
CROWN HILL
MAKER POINT
GOD BAY
FAGAN POINT
NUMBER ONE POOL
UNION
ISLE MADAME
DEAN
SHERRIFF LAKE
OFFICERS CAMP
LAKE
LORDLYS
MEADOW
GENERALS POND
KINGS MINES
TEACHERS
THUMB
MINISTERS ISLAND
PRIEST
LAKE
LAC DU LAMA
LAC DU CONTRÔLEUR
HALTE DU ROI
PARENT
COULÉE
DU JUGE

LONDON, ON: It came very close to being named Georgina on the Thames, but the community and its river (originally Tranche, now Thames) were named in honour of the centre of the British Empire. In 1792 London was a front-runner for capital of Upper Canada (now Ontario), though it had yet to be settled—and wouldn't be for another thirty years. Even if it didn't become the capital of Ontario, London had a great impact on Canadian culture: the Labatt Brewery was founded here in 1847.

REYKJAVIK, MB: A man named Gunnlaugur "Góði" Úlfsson was convicted of murder in Iceland in the late 1800s, but he escaped and fled to Canada with a friend. Eventually he moved to Manitoba, took up farming, and became a model citizen. Úlfsson founded Reykjavik in 1883, naming it for the capital of his former homeland. The town never quite took off, and it is still very small today.

NORWAY, PE: No Scandinavian roots here: "Norway" is a shortened evolution of "North Way," so named because the village is on the way to North Cape.

STONEHENGE, SK: Home of the Moose Mountain Medicine Wheel, an over-2,000-year-old stone-laid pattern of mysterious origin whose survival is under serious threat from souvenir-takers. The town was named by the Craddock family, who came from—yes, Stonehenge, England.

TANGIER, NS: This place and Damascus stand out among the many Nova Scotia places named for English and Scottish villages. Tangier was named for the schooner *Tangier*, which sank off the coast of Nova Scotia in 1830. In 1858 a British Army officer and his Mi'kmaq guide found traces of gold in the Tangier River and the area became the centre of a mini-gold rush. Today Tangier survives on adrenaline—the region is big with sea kayakers and other outdoor adventurers.

ATHENS, ON: Named in the 1800s to honour the ancient Greeks' advancements in learning and respect for knowledge. The civic mandate of this Athens still includes an explicit mention of quality education for its children. The village is decorated with about a dozen murals depicting ancient times.

PARIS, YT: It developed as a resource centre for the mining of gypsum and was named for plaster of Paris, not the City of Light. Dawson City, YT, on the other hand, was called "the Paris of the North" during the Klondike Gold Rush—a reference to the French capital. At its peak in 1898, Dawson City had a population of 16,000 and an outlying population of a further 15,000, which together put away 545,000 litres of alcohol over the course of that year. One year later, gold was found in Nome, Alaska, and Dawson City's population crashed almost instantly. Dawson City still thrives (seasonally, at least) on tourism and a more discreet form of gold mining, but Paris, YT, is a ghost town.

WELCOME WAGON

235,824 people became new permanent residents of Canada in 2004. More than half of them settled in Ontario, 10,743 chose a non-urban area, and 8 made their home in Nunavut.

Map: Kevin Barefoot

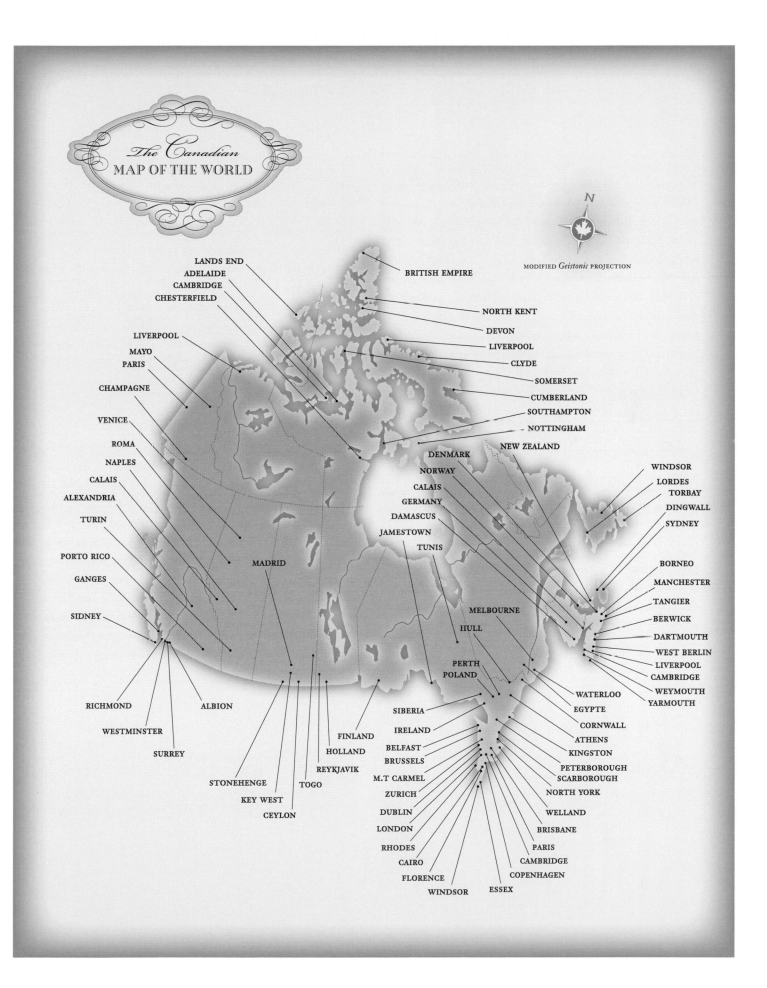

The *Canadian*
MAP OF THE WORLD

N

MODIFIED *Geistonic* PROJECTION

LANDS END
ADELAIDE
CAMBRIDGE
CHESTERFIELD

BRITISH EMPIRE

NORTH KENT

DEVON

LIVERPOOL

CLYDE

SOMERSET

CUMBERLAND

SOUTHAMPTON

NOTTINGHAM

NEW ZEALAND

LIVERPOOL

MAYO

PARIS

CHAMPAGNE

VENICE

ROMA

NAPLES

CALAIS

ALEXANDRIA

TURIN

PORTO RICO

GANGES

SIDNEY

DENMARK

NORWAY

CALAIS

GERMANY

DAMASCUS

JAMESTOWN

TUNIS

MADRID

WINDSOR
LORDES
TORBAY
DINGWALL
SYDNEY

BORNEO

MANCHESTER

TANGIER

BERWICK

DARTMOUTH

WEST BERLIN

LIVERPOOL

CAMBRIDGE

WEYMOUTH

YARMOUTH

MELBOURNE

HULL

PERTH
POLAND

WATERLOO

EGYPTE

CORNWALL

ATHENS

KINGSTON

PETERBOROUGH
SCARBOROUGH

NORTH YORK

SIBERIA

IRELAND

BELFAST

BRUSSELS

M.T CARMEL

ZURICH

DUBLIN

LONDON

RHODES

CAIRO

FLORENCE

WINDSOR

ESSEX

COPENHAGEN

CAMBRIDGE

PARIS

BRISBANE

WELLAND

RICHMOND

WESTMINSTER

SURREY

ALBION

STONEHENGE

KEY WEST

CEYLON

TOGO

REYKJAVIK

HOLLAND

FINLAND

— 59 —

VANCOUVER, WA: After the Anglo-American Convention of 1818, Oregon County was under joint British and American rule. Many believed the border between their territories would be set along the Columbia River, so the Americans established a fort on the south bank (now Astoria, Oregon) and the Hudson's Bay Company built Fort Vancouver on the north side and named it after Captain George Vancouver of the British Royal Navy, the namesake of Vancouver, BC. Fort Vancouver grew into a busy hub for fur trading in the Pacific Northwest; the predominant languages spoken there were French and Chinook Jargon (a trading language that blended English, French, and several Aboriginal languages). The fort became American in 1846, when the border was set at the 49th parallel. Today Vancouver, Washington, is part of the Portland, Oregon, metropolitan area and has a population of about 143,500.

JASPER, TX: The seat of Jasper County, named for William Jasper, a Civil War soldier. Jasper became a hero for raising the American flag in the face of British bombardment at Fort Moultrie in 1776; he was killed three years later during the Siege of Savannah. (Jasper, AB, was named for Jasper Hawes, a North West Company trading post manager.) Jasper County has made bad-news headlines three times in recent years: for the brutal, racially motivated murder of James Byrd, Jr. in 1998, the recovery of wreckage from the Space Shuttle *Columbia* disaster in 2003, and widespread damage and civil unrest after Hurricane Rita in 2005. Jasper, Texas, has a population of about 8,200.

TORONTO, OH: The Ohio town was called Newburg's Landing, then Sloan Station, but during a boom in the late 1800s, a civic leader named Thomas M. Daniels thought they ought to take the name of a big city and emulate its development. (For the naming history of the Canadian Toronto, see the Original Map, p. 64.) During the next century the town did enjoy some success as an industrial centre, but in the 1990s a manufacturing slump sent it into an economic downturn. Today, Toronto, Ohio, has a population of about 5,650.

YUKON, OK: A suburb of Oklahoma City, which lies in Canadian County, which was named for the North Canadian River. Yukon was founded in the late 1800s when the word "Yukon" evoked grandeur and success. (For the Yukon Territory's naming history, see the Original Map, p. 64.) Yukon, Oklahoma, became nationally famous in the late 1940s when a six-year-old Hereford cow named Grady got stuck in a metal storage silo. After three days, much study, and many articles in *Life*, *Time*, and other magazines, handlers released Grady using a ramp, some rope, some axle grease, and a handful of tranquilizers (for the cow). Yukon, Oklahoma, is also the hometown of the country singer Garth Brooks. It has a population of about 24,000.

GOING SOUTH

About 2.6 percent of US residents are Canadian (that's 820,771 people, not including the snowbirds who flock to Florida in winter).

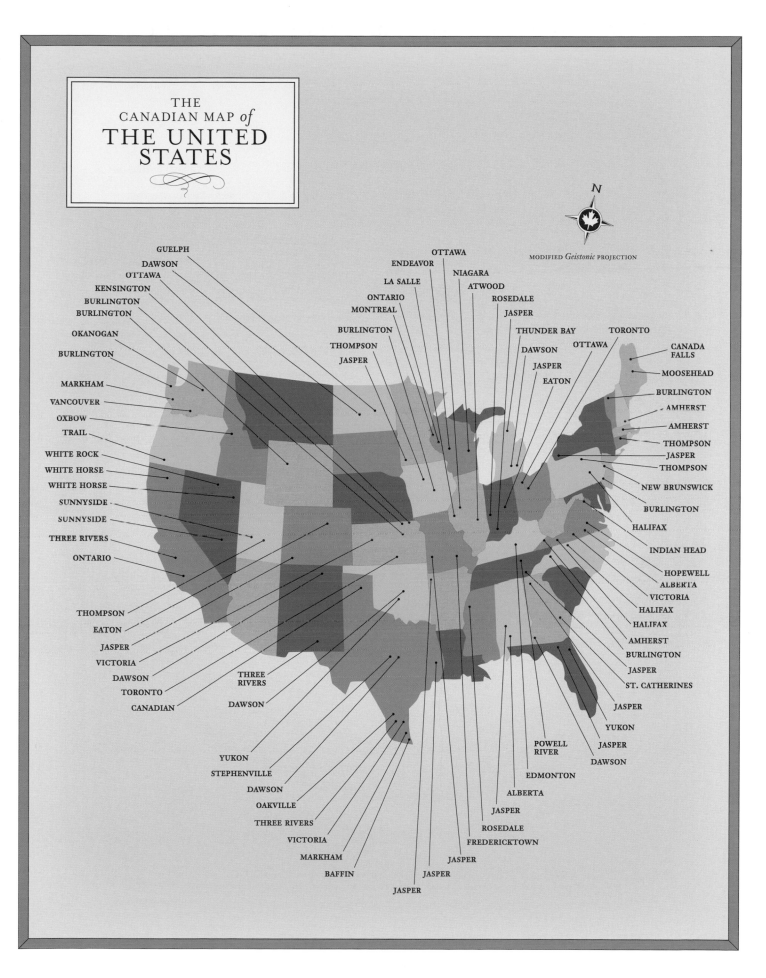

THE
CANADIAN MAP *of*
THE UNITED
STATES

MODIFIED *Geistonic* PROJECTION

GUELPH
DAWSON
OTTAWA
KENSINGTON
BURLINGTON
BURLINGTON
OKANOGAN
BURLINGTON
MARKHAM
VANCOUVER
OXBOW
TRAIL
WHITE ROCK
WHITE HORSE
WHITE HORSE
SUNNYSIDE
SUNNYSIDE
THREE RIVERS
ONTARIO
THOMPSON
EATON
JASPER
VICTORIA
DAWSON
TORONTO
CANADIAN

THREE
RIVERS
DAWSON

YUKON
STEPHENVILLE
DAWSON
OAKVILLE
THREE RIVERS
VICTORIA
MARKHAM
BAFFIN
JASPER

OTTAWA
ENDEAVOR
LA SALLE
ONTARIO
MONTREAL
BURLINGTON
THOMPSON
JASPER

NIAGARA
ATWOOD
ROSEDALE
JASPER

THUNDER BAY
DAWSON
JASPER
EATON

OTTAWA

TORONTO
CANADA
FALLS
MOOSEHEAD
BURLINGTON
AMHERST
AMHERST
THOMPSON
JASPER
THOMPSON
NEW BRUNSWICK
BURLINGTON
HALIFAX
INDIAN HEAD
HOPEWELL
ALBERTA
VICTORIA
HALIFAX
HALIFAX
AMHERST
BURLINGTON
JASPER
ST. CATHERINES
JASPER
YUKON
JASPER
DAWSON

POWELL
RIVER
EDMONTON
ALBERTA
JASPER
ROSEDALE
FREDERICKTOWN
JASPER
JASPER
JASPER

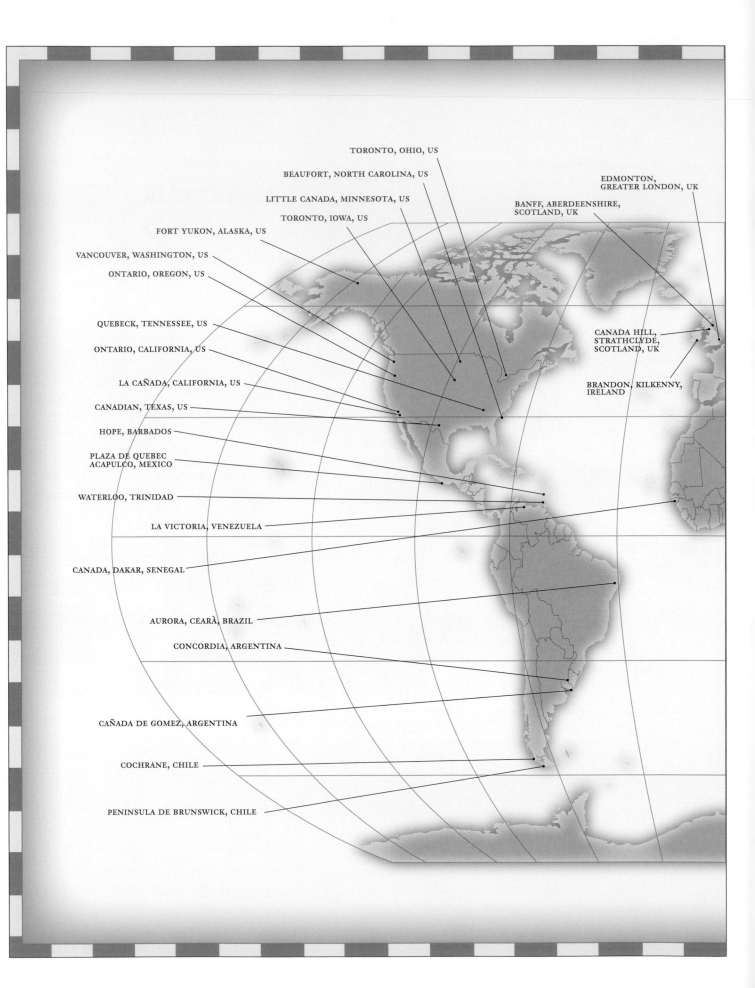

TORONTO, OHIO, US

BEAUFORT, NORTH CAROLINA, US

LITTLE CANADA, MINNESOTA, US

TORONTO, IOWA, US

FORT YUKON, ALASKA, US

VANCOUVER, WASHINGTON, US

ONTARIO, OREGON, US

QUEBECK, TENNESSEE, US

ONTARIO, CALIFORNIA, US

LA CAÑADA, CALIFORNIA, US

CANADIAN, TEXAS, US

HOPE, BARBADOS

PLAZA DE QUEBEC
ACAPULCO, MEXICO

WATERLOO, TRINIDAD

LA VICTORIA, VENEZUELA

CANADA, DAKAR, SENEGAL

AURORA, CEARÀ, BRAZIL

CONCORDIA, ARGENTINA

CAÑADA DE GOMEZ, ARGENTINA

COCHRANE, CHILE

PENINSULA DE BRUNSWICK, CHILE

EDMONTON,
GREATER LONDON, UK

BANFF, ABERDEENSHIRE,
SCOTLAND, UK

CANADA HILL,
STRATHCLYDE,
SCOTLAND, UK

BRANDON, KILKENNY,
IRELAND

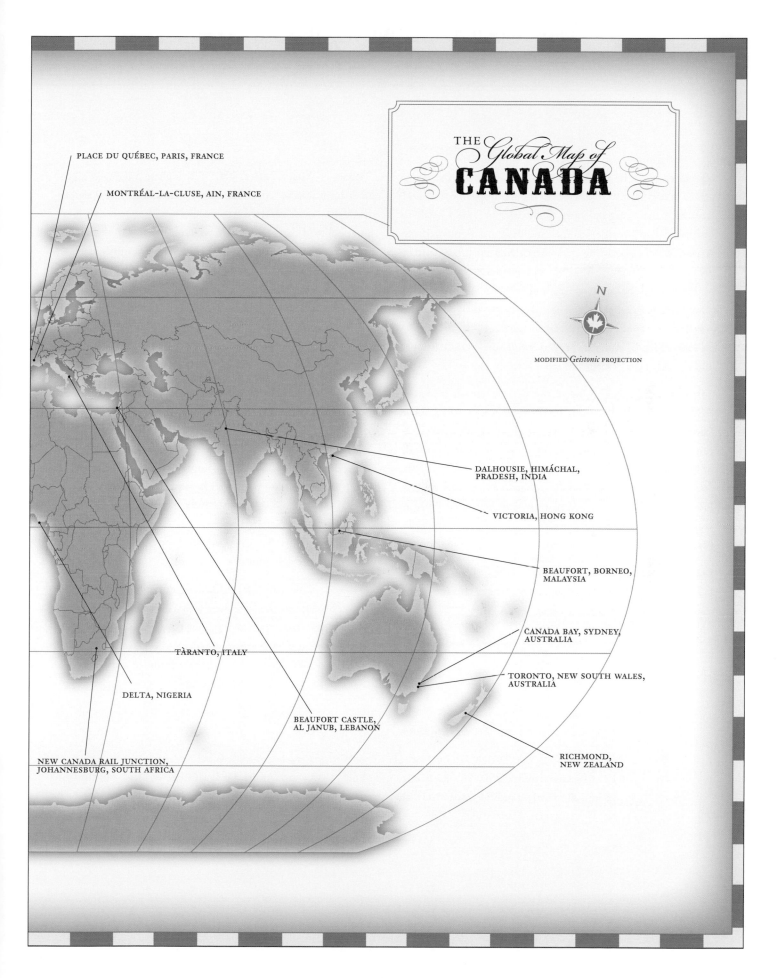

PLACE DU QUÉBEC, PARIS, FRANCE

MONTRÉAL-LA-CLUSE, AIN, FRANCE

THE *Global Map of* **CANADA**

N

MODIFIED *Geistonic* PROJECTION

DALHOUSIE, HIMÁCHAL,
PRADESH, INDIA

VICTORIA, HONG KONG

BEAUFORT, BORNEO,
MALAYSIA

CANADA BAY, SYDNEY,
AUSTRALIA

TÀRANTO, ITALY

TORONTO, NEW SOUTH WALES,
AUSTRALIA

DELTA, NIGERIA

BEAUFORT CASTLE,
AL JANUB, LEBANON

RICHMOND,
NEW ZEALAND

NEW CANADA RAIL JUNCTION,
JOHANNESBURG, SOUTH AFRICA

Our Home on Native Land

IQALUIT, NU: In the late 1980s and early 1990s, many places in northern Canada cast off their European names and reclaimed their original ones. Snowdrift became Lutselk'e, Frobisher Bay became Iqaluit, and Eskimo Point became Arviat (which, according to some calculations, is Canada's geographical centre). A 1995 plebiscite determined that Iqaluit would become the capital of Nunavut, Canada's newest territory. The region is sparsely populated, but the vote for the capital got a 79 percent turnout—some 10,000 ballots were cast. Roughly 60 percent of voters chose Iqaluit, and the other 40 percent preferred Rankin Inlet.

TUKTOYAKTUK, NT: One of the first Northern towns to reclaim its original name—English speakers had called it Port Brabant until 1950. "Tuk" is the farthest north you can drive in Canada (and even then only in winter—north of Inuvik, the route is an ice road). The name—in English, "resembling a caribou"—refers to an area of reefs that at low tide look like caribou. One Inuvialuit legend says that as some caribou waded in the water, a woman gazed upon the herd and turned them into stone.

OTTAWA, ON: The band that lived on the Ottawa River was called "the traders" by the Algonquins, as they controlled the main commerce route.

TORNGAT MOUNTAINS, NL: The highest mountain range in eastern Canada (Mt. Caubvick, 1,652 metres/5,420 feet, is the highest peak), and their rocks are the oldest on Earth. The Innu believed that the spirit world and the world of mortals overlap in these mountains. The cold, strange, mostly treeless landscape is inhabited by a few caribou and black bears, but no people, except occasional adventurers. The closest community is Kangiqsualujjuaq, which is 150 kilometres (ninety miles) away.

QU'APPELLE, SK: Founded as Troy in 1882 and once a front-runner for the administrative seat of southern Saskatchewan. Regina was chosen instead, and Qu'Appelle struggled economically until it was redeveloped as a bedroom community to Regina. The name is a French sound-alike from Cree legends about a spirit who travels along the Qu'Appelle River and cries in a human voice. Voyageurs expanded this into a story about a Native man who heard his bride-to-be calling his name as he canoed down the river. The man replied, "Who calls?" and was answered by mocking spirits. On his return, he discovered that his intended had died and had called his name with her dying breath.

CANADA: The story of Huron-Iroquois villagers directing Jacques Cartier to *kanata* is very well known by now: Cartier believed the word was the name of the land, and eventually it became so. The Natives were actually directing him to Stadacona. Ville de Québec was later founded on that site.

FIRST NATIONS BY THE NUMBERS

Approximately 900,000 Aboriginal people live in Canada. About 600,000 belong to one of fifty-two First Nations, about 290,000 are Metis, and about 45,000 are Inuit. The members of these cultural groups are represented by, respectively, the Assembly of First Nations, the Metis National Council, and the Inuit Tapiriit Kanatami.

THE
ORIGINAL
MAP *of* CANADA

N

MODIFIED *Geistonic* PROJECTION

NUNAVUT
INUKTITUT: "OUR LAND"

TUKTOYAKTUK
INUVIALUIT:
"RESEMBLING A CARIBOU"

MANITOBA
(*MANIOT-WAPOW*) CREE:
"STRAIT OF THE SPIRIT"

ARVIAT
INUKTITUT: "PLACE OF
THE BOWHEAD WHALE"

LUTSELK'E
DENE: "PLACE OF SMALL FISH"

IQALUIT
INUKTITUT:
"PLACE OF FISH"

QUÉBEC
(*KEBEK*) ALGONQUIN:
"NARROW PASSAGE"

YUKON
(*LOYU-KUN-AH*) LOUCHEUX:
"GREAT RIVER"

TORNGAT MOUNTAINS
(*TURNGAIT*) INUKTITUT:
"SPIRITS"

GASPÉ
(*GESPEG*) MI'KMAQ:
"WHERE IT ENDS"

KLONDIKE RIVER
(*TR'ONDËK*) HAN:
"A STONE HAMMER"

WABUSH
NASCOPI INNU:
"RABBIT GROUND"

AGUATHUNA
(*AQUATHOONT*)
BEOTHUK:
"GRINDSTONE"

KLUANE NATIONAL PARK
(*KLÙ'AN*) TUTCHONE:
"BIG FISH"

KOUCHIBOUGUAC
MI'KMAQ: "RIVER OF
THE LONG TIDEWAY"

FORT CHIPEWYAN
CREE: "POINTED SKINS"

CANADA
(*KANATA*) HURON-IROQUOIS;
"COLLECTION OF HOUSES"

MISCOUCHE
(*MENISGOTJG*)
MI'KMAQ:
"LITTLE MARSHY
PLACE"

ATHABASCA
(*ATHAPASKE*) CREE:
"WHERE THERE ARE REEDS"

ABEGWEIT PASSAGE
(*EPEGWITG*)
MI'KMAQ: "PARALLEL
WITH THE LAND"

HAIDA GWAII
HAIDA: "OUR LAND"

TORONTO
(*TKARONTO*) MOHAWK:
"WHERE THERE ARE
TREES STANDING IN WATER"

BADDECK
(*PETEKOOK*) MI'KMAQ:
"PLACE ON THE
BACKWARD TURN"

KAMLOOPS
(*TK'EMLUPS*) SHUSWAP:
"MEETING OF THE RIVERS"

ANTIGONISH
(*NALEGITKOONECHK*)
MI'KMAQ: "WHERE
BRANCHES ARE TORN OFF"

NANAIMO
(*SNU-NY-MUXW*)
HUL'QUMI'NUM:
"PEOPLE OF MANY NAMES"

SHUBENACADIE
(*S'P'GNE'GATIG*)
MI'KMAQ: "WHERE THE
POTATOES GROW"

CHILLIWACK
(*CH-IHL-KWAY-UHK*)
STÓ:LŌ HUL'QUMI'NUM:
"GOING BACK UP"

WINNIPEG
(*WIN-NIPI*) CREE:
"MURKY WATER"

OROMOCTO
(*WELAMOOKTOOK*) MALISEET:
"GOOD RIVER"

SPUZZUM
(*SPATSUM*) CHINOOK JARGON:
"TYPE OF REED"

ASSINIBOINE RIVER
(*ASSIN-BWAN*) OJIBWA:
"STONE PEOPLE"

MEMPHRÉMAGOG
(*MEMROBAGAK*) ABENAKI:
"GREAT EXPANSE OF WATER"

WETASKIWIN
(*WI-TA-SKI-OO CHA-KA-TIN-OW*)
CREE: "HILL OF PEACE"

QU'APPELLE
(*KÂ-TÊPWÊT*)
CREE: "RIVER THAT CALLS"

TAMAGAMI
ASHINAABE:
"DEEP WATERS"

CHICOUTIMI
(*SHKOUTIMEAU*) MONTAGNAIS:
"END OF THE DEEP WATER"

SASKATOON
(*MISAŚKWATŌMIN*) CREE:
"SASKATOON BERRY"

KAPUSKASING
ANISHINAABE:
"BEND IN THE RIVER"

OTTAWA
(*ADAWE*) ALGONQUIN:
"TO TRADE"

SASKATCHEWAN
(*KISISKATCHEWANI SIPI*)
CREE: "SWIFT FLOWING RIVER"

ONTARIO
(*ONTARIIO*) HURON:
"BEAUTIFUL LAKE"

NIAGARA FALLS
(*ONGUIAAHRA*) IROQUOIS:
"THE STRAIT"

GZOWSKI, ON: It bears the surname of Peter, the late host of *Morningside* on CBC Radio, but was named for his great-grand-father, Sir Kazimierz (Casimir) Stanislaw Gzowski, an engineer who served as acting Lieutenant-Governor of Ontario for one year in 1896. Gzowski had fled with his family to Canada during the Polish revolt against Russia in the early 1800s. He learned English, studied law and engineering, and eventually become influential in politics (he was a personal friend of John A. Macdonald). His career as an engineer included work on the Welland Canal, Yonge Street, and the Grand Trunk Railway. He was knighted in 1890 by Queen Victoria. A Toronto park and a few other natural features in Ontario are named for him.

MYSTERY LAKE, AB: F.W. Harris, an early settler, spotted the lake while exploring the region. Later, when he took some friends back there to hunt muskrat, he couldn't find it again. It was a mystery. . . .

ROGERS PASS, BC: In the original version of this map published in *Geist* magazine, Rogers Coulee, AB, was chosen to stand for Shelagh Rogers, the CBC Radio One host. (The Rogers Pass area on the map was already crowded and the coulee was conveniently located in an empty spot.) But some letters to the editor insisted that Rogers Pass was a better selection, so both are included here. Rogers Pass National Historic Site is the Trans-Canada Highway's route through the Selkirk Mountains. Major A.B. Rogers, a CPR engineer described by a historian as a "short, sharp, snappy little chap," chose it in 1882 as the best way through when he scaled Avalanche Mountain and envisioned the route from there. The Pass proved to be fatally dangerous: between 1885 and 1916, 250 railway workers died in snow avalanches. The CPR went underground and built the eight-kilometre (five-mile) long Connaught Tunnel (later replaced by the fourteen-kilometre/eight-and-a-half-mile Mt. Macdonald Tunnel). By the 1950s, when the Trans-Canada was being upgraded, better avalanche-control systems were in place and the Pass was once again put to use for car traffic.

GREEN GABLES, PE: A district within the village of Cavendish. The site was given official status in 1953 to mark the celebrity of Lucy Maud Montgomery's 1908 novel *Anne of Green Gables*, which was set in this pastoral region of Queens in central Prince Edward Island. The book's reputation got another boost in the 1980s from of a hugely successful CBC mini-series, which has spawned a number of spin-offs and at least one spoof. Approximately 700 people visit the Green Gables House and other nearby Anne-themed sites each day during high season.

"AS CANADIAN AS . . ."

In 1972 Peter Gzowski asked listeners of the CBC Radio program *This Country in the Morning* to come up with the best conclusion to the phrase "As Canadian as . . ." in an attempt to find a Canadian equivalent to "As American as apple pie." The winning response came from an Ontarian teenager named Heather Scott. It went: "As Canadian as possible, under the circumstances."

THE CBC
MAP *of* CANADA

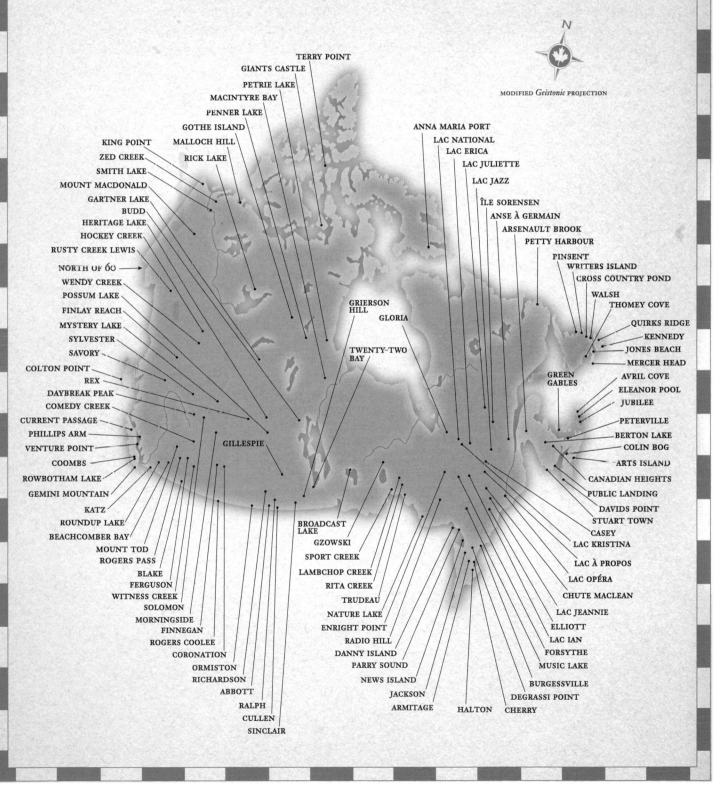

N

MODIFIED *Geistonic* PROJECTION

TERRY POINT
GIANTS CASTLE
PETRIE LAKE
MACINTYRE BAY
PENNER LAKE
GOTHE ISLAND
MALLOCH HILL
KING POINT
ZED CREEK
RICK LAKE
SMITH LAKE
MOUNT MACDONALD
GARTNER LAKE
BUDD
HERITAGE LAKE
HOCKEY CREEK
RUSTY CREEK LEWIS
NORTH OF 60
WENDY CREEK
POSSUM LAKE
FINLAY REACH
MYSTERY LAKE
SYLVESTER
SAVORY
COLTON POINT
REX
DAYBREAK PEAK
COMEDY CREEK
CURRENT PASSAGE
PHILLIPS ARM
VENTURE POINT
COOMBS
ROWBOTHAM LAKE
GEMINI MOUNTAIN
KATZ
ROUNDUP LAKE
BEACHCOMBER BAY
MOUNT TOD
ROGERS PASS
BLAKE
FERGUSON
WITNESS CREEK
SOLOMON
MORNINGSIDE
FINNEGAN
ROGERS COOLEE
CORONATION
ORMISTON
RICHARDSON
ABBOTT
RALPH
CULLEN
SINCLAIR

GILLESPIE

GRIERSON HILL
GLORIA

TWENTY-TWO BAY

BROADCAST LAKE
GZOWSKI
SPORT CREEK
LAMBCHOP CREEK
RITA CREEK
TRUDEAU
NATURE LAKE
ENRIGHT POINT
RADIO HILL
DANNY ISLAND
PARRY SOUND
NEWS ISLAND
JACKSON
ARMITAGE
HALTON
CHERRY

ANNA MARIA PORT
LAC NATIONAL
LAC ERICA
LAC JULIETTE
LAC JAZZ
ÎLE SORENSEN
ANSE À GERMAIN
ARSENAULT BROOK
PETTY HARBOUR
PINSENT
WRITERS ISLAND
CROSS COUNTRY POND
WALSH
THOMEY COVE
QUIRKS RIDGE
KENNEDY
JONES BEACH
MERCER HEAD
AVRIL COVE
ELEANOR POOL
JUBILEE
PETERVILLE
BERTON LAKE
COLIN BOG
ARTS ISLAND
CANADIAN HEIGHTS
PUBLIC LANDING
DAVIDS POINT
STUART TOWN
CASEY
LAC KRISTINA
LAC À PROPOS
LAC OPÉRA
CHUTE MACLEAN
LAC JEANNIE
ELLIOTT
LAC IAN
FORSYTHE
MUSIC LAKE
BURGESSVILLE
DEGRASSI POINT

GREEN GABLES

THE MAP OF PEGGY'S CANADA

Margaret Atwood, Coast to Coast

ATWOOD CHEESE COMPANY, ATWOOD, ON: Along with a Campbell's soup factory, it is an economic mainstay for the town of Atwood, which was founded as Elma Centre in 1854 and renamed in 1883 by William Dunn, for the surrounding woodlands. The town has a population of about 500 and, other than cheese and soup, subsists mainly on agriculture. The Atwood Cheese Company produces Italian, Danish, Greek, Swiss, and, of course, Canadian cheeses.

ATWOOD ENTERPRISES, RAINY RIVER, ON: An electronics store whose signage says "The Source by Circuit City" (formerly known as Radio Shack), but its owner, Lance, founded it as Atwood, and that name still appears on his letterhead and business documents. Lance named the store after the district of Atwood, which itself was named for Thomas Attwood, an English currency reformer. The area includes Rainy River, whose name evolved from the original French Lac de la Pluie, which likely referred to spray from nearby waterfalls (the Ojibwa called the area *tekamamaouen*, "it rains all the time"). Rainy River is the terminus of Yonge Street, the world's longest street which begins in Toronto.

BOMBAY PEGGY'S, DAWSON CITY, YT: The building that houses this inn and restaurant was constructed in 1900 and has served as a home, a mining company hostel, an art gallery, and a brothel. Its current name comes from the brothel era (the mid-1950s). "Bombay Peggy" was the nickname of Margaret Vera Dorval, the brothel's madam and a part-time bootlegger. The current owners, Wendy and Kim, bought the house in 1998, when it was falling apart and sinking slowly into a swamp. They had it lifted out of its mire, moved to its current location at the corner of 2nd and Princess streets, rebuilt and restored, blessed by a priest, then opened as a hotel (a classy one, despite still being referred to as "the whorehouse"). For more information on the naming of Dawson City, see the notes on the Geographer's Map, p. 82.

TOAD SCHOOL, SIDNEY, BC: A preschool daycare, named for the founders' new baby daughter Andrea, affectionately called "Toad." (Toad School and Toad Hall, a Winnipeg toy store, appear on this map as allusions to O.W. Toad, Margaret Atwood's anagrammatically named literary company.)

ATWOOD OBSCURA

Killam (Atwood's maternal line); Graeme and Gibson (Atwood's partner); Ruby Red Shoes (*The Red Shoes* is the title of a biography of Atwood); Thru a Woman's Eyes (the Atwoodian perspective). All other place names refer to titles of Atwood's works.

Map: Kris Rothstein and Melissa Edwards

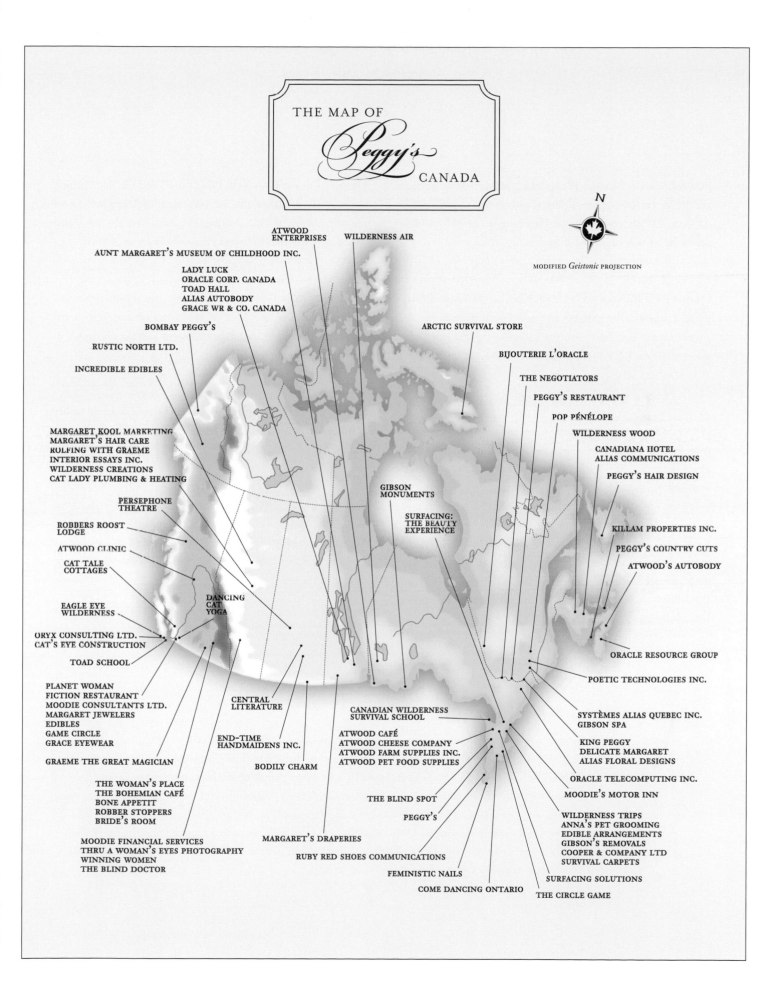

THE MAP OF
Peggy's
CANADA

N

MODIFIED *Geistonic* PROJECTION

ATWOOD ENTERPRISES
WILDERNESS AIR
AUNT MARGARET'S MUSEUM OF CHILDHOOD INC.
LADY LUCK
ORACLE CORP. CANADA
TOAD HALL
ALIAS AUTOBODY
GRACE WR & CO. CANADA
BOMBAY PEGGY'S
RUSTIC NORTH LTD.
INCREDIBLE EDIBLES
ARCTIC SURVIVAL STORE
BIJOUTERIE L'ORACLE
THE NEGOTIATORS
PEGGY'S RESTAURANT
POP PÉNÉLOPE
WILDERNESS WOOD
CANADIANA HOTEL
ALIAS COMMUNICATIONS
PEGGY'S HAIR DESIGN

MARGARET KOOL MARKETING
MARGARET'S HAIR CARE
ROLFING WITH GRAEME
INTERIOR ESSAYS INC.
WILDERNESS CREATIONS
CAT LADY PLUMBING & HEATING

PERSEPHONE THEATRE
ROBBERS ROOST LODGE
ATWOOD CLINIC
CAT TALE COTTAGES

EAGLE EYE WILDERNESS
ORYX CONSULTING LTD.
CAT'S EYE CONSTRUCTION
TOAD SCHOOL

DANCING CAT YOGA

GIBSON MONUMENTS

SURFACING: THE BEAUTY EXPERIENCE

KILLAM PROPERTIES INC.
PEGGY'S COUNTRY CUTS
ATWOOD'S AUTOBODY

ORACLE RESOURCE GROUP
POETIC TECHNOLOGIES INC.

PLANET WOMAN
FICTION RESTAURANT
MOODIE CONSULTANTS LTD.
MARGARET JEWELERS
EDIBLES
GAME CIRCLE
GRACE EYEWEAR

GRAEME THE GREAT MAGICIAN

CENTRAL LITERATURE

END-TIME HANDMAIDENS INC.

CANADIAN WILDERNESS SURVIVAL SCHOOL

ATWOOD CAFÉ
ATWOOD CHEESE COMPANY
ATWOOD FARM SUPPLIES INC.
ATWOOD PET FOOD SUPPLIES

SYSTÈMES ALIAS QUEBEC INC.
GIBSON SPA

KING PEGGY
DELICATE MARGARET
ALIAS FLORAL DESIGNS

ORACLE TELECOMPUTING INC.
MOODIE'S MOTOR INN

THE WOMAN'S PLACE
THE BOHEMIAN CAFÉ
BONE APPETIT
ROBBER STOPPERS
BRIDE'S ROOM

BODILY CHARM

THE BLIND SPOT

PEGGY'S

WILDERNESS TRIPS
ANNA'S PET GROOMING
EDIBLE ARRANGEMENTS
GIBSON'S REMOVALS
COOPER & COMPANY LTD
SURVIVAL CARPETS

MOODIE FINANCIAL SERVICES
THRU A WOMAN'S EYES PHOTOGRAPHY
WINNING WOMEN
THE BLIND DOCTOR

MARGARET'S DRAPERIES

RUBY RED SHOES COMMUNICATIONS

FEMINISTIC NAILS

COME DANCING ONTARIO

SURFACING SOLUTIONS

THE CIRCLE GAME

THE STAN ROGERS MAP OF CANADA

Uncommon Folk

PORTAGE AND MAIN, WINNIPEG, MB: "It's at Portage and Main you'll see them again/On their way to the hills of Alberta./With lop-side grins, they waggle their chins/And they brag of the wage they'll be earning."

"Free in the Harbour," Northwest Passage

FISHERMAN'S WHARF, HALIFAX, NS: "... I looked from the Citadel down to the narrows and asked what it's coming to./I saw Upper Canadian concrete and glass right down to the water line/And I heard an old song down on Fisherman's Wharf/Can I sing it just one time."

"Fisherman's Wharf," Fogarty's Cove

NEWFOUNDLAND: "He spied a pretty, fair young maid and took her by the hand./'Oh will you go to Newfoundland along with me?' he cried./But the answer that she gave to him was 'Oh no, not I.'"

"Oh No, Not I," Turnaround

LAKE ST. CLAIR, ON: "I am Alexander MacIntosh, a nephew to the Laird/And I do distain men who are vain, the men with powdered hair./I command the Nancy Schooner from the Moy on Lake St. Claire./On the third day of October, boys, I did set sail from there."

"The Nancy," From Fresh Water

GRAND TRUNK RAILWAY, ON: "Who fled the first Famine wearing all that they owned,/Were called 'Navigators,' all ragged and torn,/And built the Grand Trunk here, and found a new home/Wherever their children were born."

"The House of Orange," From Fresh Water

GLEICHEN, AB: "Now when I climbed up on him, he so naturally took to the air,/That every time we went aloft, he tried to leave me there,/Until at last we went so high, the lights in Gleichen shone ..."

"Two-Bit Cayuse," For the Family

TORONTO, ON: "Ontario, y'know I've seen a place I'd rather be/Your scummy lakes and the City of Toronto don't do a damn thing for me/I'd rather live by the sea."

"Watching the Apples Grow," Fogarty's Cove

FRASER RIVER, BC: "And through the night, behind the wheel, the mileage clicking west/I think upon Mackenzie, David Thompson and the rest/Who cracked the mountain ramparts and did show a path for me/To race the roaring Fraser to the sea."

"Northwest Passage," Northwest Passage

ABOUT STAN ROGERS

Stan Rogers was a major force in the development of modern Canadian folk music. His simple, powerful songs conveyed a profound connection with labourers, fishers, sailors, and explorers. His lyrics are original but have such an air of historic authenticity that many people think his songs are traditional folk tunes. Rogers was also thought by many to be from the Atlantic region: he did spend many summers in Nova Scotia when he was a child, but he was born in Hannon, Ontario, and lived in Hamilton. Rogers' talent as a musician and his stature as a folk music lyricist were only beginning to grow when he was killed in an airplane fire in Cincinnati, Ohio on June 2, 1983, when he was only thirty-three years old. (*Lyrics reprinted with the permission of Fogarty's Cove Music.*)

Map: Gwen Foss, Chris Conway, and Melissa Edwards

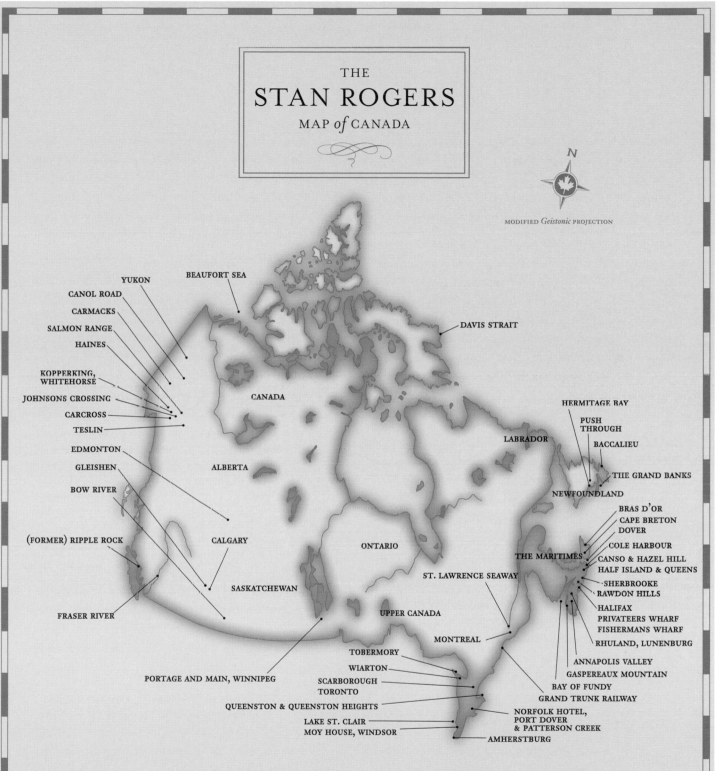

THE
STAN ROGERS
MAP *of* CANADA

MODIFIED *Geistonic* PROJECTION

BEAUFORT SEA
YUKON
CANOL ROAD
CARMACKS
SALMON RANGE
HAINES
DAVIS STRAIT
KOPPERKING, WHITEHORSE
JOHNSONS CROSSING
CARCROSS
TESLIN
CANADA
HERMITAGE BAY
PUSH THROUGH
BACCALIEU
LABRADOR
EDMONTON
GLEISHEN
BOW RIVER
ALBERTA
THE GRAND BANKS
NEWFOUNDLAND
BRAS D'OR
CAPE BRETON
DOVER
(FORMER) RIPPLE ROCK
CALGARY
ONTARIO
COLE HARBOUR
THE MARITIMES
CANSO & HAZEL HILL
HALF ISLAND & QUEENS
SASKATCHEWAN
ST. LAWRENCE SEAWAY
SHERBROOKE
RAWDON HILLS
HALIFAX
PRIVATEERS WHARF
FISHERMANS WHARF
FRASER RIVER
RHULAND, LUNENBURG
UPPER CANADA
MONTREAL
ANNAPOLIS VALLEY
GASPEREAUX MOUNTAIN
TOBERMORY
WIARTON
PORTAGE AND MAIN, WINNIPEG
SCARBOROUGH
TORONTO
BAY OF FUNDY
GRAND TRUNK RAILWAY
QUEENSTON & QUEENSTON HEIGHTS
NORFOLK HOTEL,
PORT DOVER
& PATTERSON CREEK
LAKE ST. CLAIR
MOY HOUSE, WINDSOR
AMHERSTBURG

The place names on this map are named in the following songs by the late great Stan Rogers:

Barrett's Privateers, Bluenose, Canol Road, Cliffs of Baccalieu, Field Behind the Plow, Fisherman's Wharf, Fogarty's Cove, Free in the Harbour, Giant, House of Orange, Last Watch, Lazy Head, Lock-Keeper, Macdonnell on the Heights, Make or Break Harbour, Man with a Blue Dolphin, Northwest Passage, Oh No, Not I, Rawdon Hills, Ripple Rock, Scarborough Settler's Lament, So Blue, Strings and Dory Plug, The Jeannie C, The Nancy, Tiny Fish for Japan, Two-Bit Cayuse, Watching the Apples Grow, White Squall, Wild Rose

DUNGEON PROVINCIAL PARK, NL: The park has a sea cave that resembles a medieval dungeon, and twin tunnels that run through it to a collapsed open area. Brave people go spelunking in the cave, others picnic on the grassy field above it. (The park also appears on the Map of Board Games, p. 28.)

CAPE RESCUE, NU: Named for the US vessel *Rescue*, one of several victims of failed attempts to find the Franklin Expedition (see also notes on Satellite Bay, Celestial Map, p. 22). A passage from *Life with the Esquimaux* (1864) by Captain Charles Francis Hall reads, "The *Rescue*'s quondam consort, after having given forth freely of its planks and timbers for the preservation and warmth of Dr. Kane and his party, was finally given up to the ices of the North which unrelentingly grasped it."

MIRROR, AB: Originally a stop on the Edmonton–Calgary line of the Grand Trunk Pacific Railway and named in 1911 for the *Daily Mirror*, a newspaper in London, England. The Grand Trunk company had bought advertising in the paper and the *Mirror* published an article that promoted Mirror as a "rising township" and Alberta itself as a land of opportunity.

GOLDEN, BC: This mountain town was originally called The Cache, until residents changed the name to Golden City to one-up nearby Silver City, which was founded by a couple of gold-rush crooks who cashed in and abandoned the town. Silver City petered out soon after that, and Golden dropped the "City" from its name (which may have saved it—see notes on Star City, Celestial Map, p. 22). In February 2006 Golden passed a resolution to temporarily change its name to Hockey in an effort to win a CBC-sponsored contest that had Canadian towns compete to show the most enthusiasm for the game. For the next three months, the town's highway signs, banners, and civic stationery used the new name, but to no avail: the town of Salmon River, NS won the title.

CASTLEGAR, BC: A centre for the Doukhobor sect and home to the Doukhobor Heritage Village, among other things. The *Doukhobortsi* were a Russian sect declared dissidents and heretics by the Russian Orthodox Church in the late 1700s. The name, which means "spirit wrestlers," was meant to be derogatory, but the group adopted it as their own. The Doukhobors were (and continue to be) pacifists and vegetarians. They refused both conscription and allegiance to a political state, and over the next hundred years its members were arrested, tortured, and persecuted. Finally, in 1899, several thousand Doukhobors were allowed to emigrate to Canada. The community eventually established itself peacefully in BC's Kootenay region though they still protest when government bodies or other Doukhobor splinter groups appear to threaten their religious freedom.

TINY, ON: Named in 1822 in honour of one of Lady Sarah Maitland's pets (her other two dogs were named Flos and Tay). Maitland (1792–1873) was the wife of Sir Peregrine Maitland, a Lieutenant-Governor of Upper Canada. Tiny's population is small, but not tiny: 9,035. A town in Saskatchewan of the same name (see Entomological Map, p. 16) may have been named by Ontarian settlers after this Tiny town.

A CANADIAN LEGEND

A beautiful woman named Nokomis was pushed off the moon. She fell all the way to Earth and landed in a lake, where she was greeted by a group of villagers. They welcomed her into their community, built her a wigwam, and learned to seek out her advice. Nokomis had a daughter named Winona, and Winona had a son named Nanabozho. Nanabozho controlled the seasons, formed mountains, and taught the Ojibwa people how to hunt, grow food, tap maple trees, and use healing herbs.

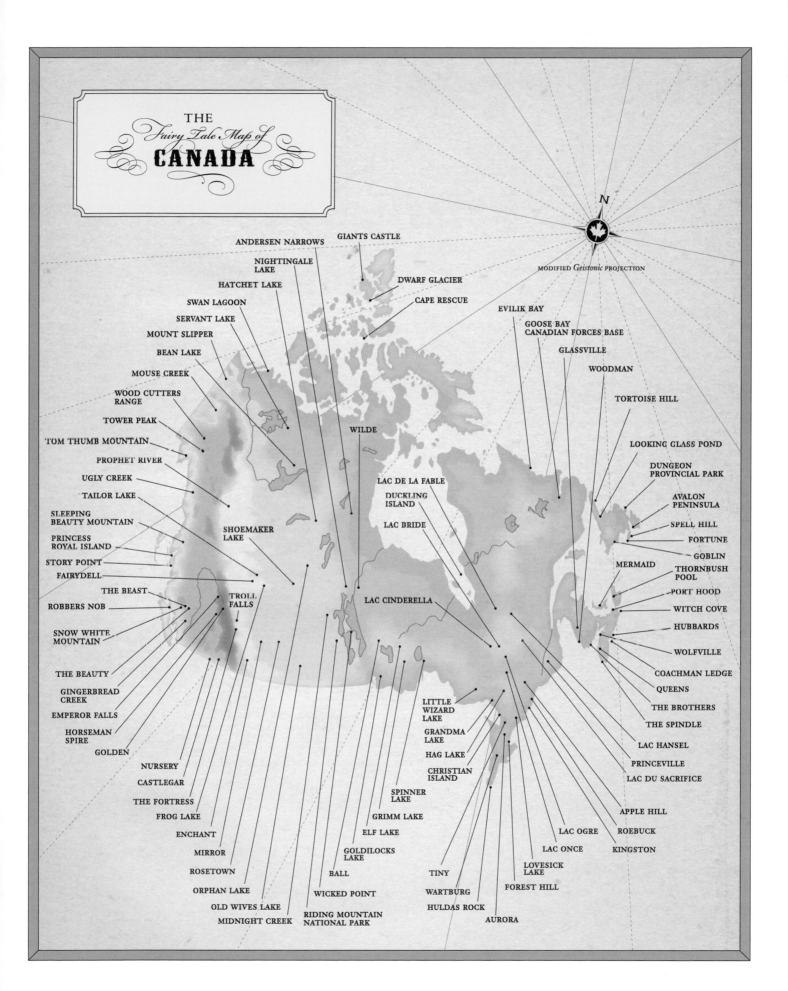

THE
Fairy Tale Map of
CANADA

N

MODIFIED *Geistonic* PROJECTION

ANDERSEN NARROWS

GIANTS CASTLE

NIGHTINGALE LAKE

DWARF GLACIER

HATCHET LAKE

CAPE RESCUE

SWAN LAGOON

SERVANT LAKE

MOUNT SLIPPER

BEAN LAKE

MOUSE CREEK

WOOD CUTTERS RANGE

TOWER PEAK

TOM THUMB MOUNTAIN

PROPHET RIVER

UGLY CREEK

TAILOR LAKE

SLEEPING BEAUTY MOUNTAIN

PRINCESS ROYAL ISLAND

STORY POINT

FAIRYDELL

THE BEAST

ROBBERS NOB

SNOW WHITE MOUNTAIN

THE BEAUTY

GINGERBREAD CREEK

EMPEROR FALLS

HORSEMAN SPIRE

GOLDEN

NURSERY

CASTLEGAR

THE FORTRESS

FROG LAKE

ENCHANT

MIRROR

ROSETOWN

ORPHAN LAKE

OLD WIVES LAKE

MIDNIGHT CREEK

WILDE

SHOEMAKER LAKE

TROLL FALLS

LAC DE LA FABLE

DUCKLING ISLAND

LAC BRIDE

LAC CINDERELLA

LITTLE WIZARD LAKE

GRANDMA LAKE

HAG LAKE

CHRISTIAN ISLAND

SPINNER LAKE

GRIMM LAKE

ELF LAKE

GOLDILOCKS LAKE

BALL

WICKED POINT

RIDING MOUNTAIN NATIONAL PARK

TINY

WARTBURG

HULDAS ROCK

AURORA

LOVESICK LAKE

FOREST HILL

LAC ONCE

LAC OGRE

KINGSTON

ROEBUCK

APPLE HILL

LAC DU SACRIFICE

PRINCEVILLE

LAC HANSEL

THE SPINDLE

THE BROTHERS

QUEENS

COACHMAN LEDGE

WOLFVILLE

HUBBARDS

WITCH COVE

PORT HOOD

THORNBUSH POOL

MERMAID

GOBLIN

FORTUNE

SPELL HILL

AVALON PENINSULA

DUNGEON PROVINCIAL PARK

LOOKING GLASS POND

TORTOISE HILL

WOODMAN

GLASSVILLE

GOOSE BAY CANADIAN FORCES BASE

EVILIK BAY

EVILIK BAY

— 73 —

POWERVIEW, MB: A village named for its view of a large hydro-electric power plant, constructed in 1951, that blocks the Winnipeg River. Powerview is just east of Pine Falls, home of the annual Canadian Walleye Fishing Championships.

UTOPIA, NB: An unincorporated region on the banks of Lake Utopia, whose name is a facetious reference to an unusual land grant given in 1784 to Captain Peter Clinch, the founder of nearby St. George. The lake is a source of mystery, partly because it has its own sea serpent, which is said to bust its head through the ice occasionally to snap at people, but mostly because it is the site where a stonemason looking for a hearthstone found a strange rock medallion of unknown origins in 1863. The smooth, round disk, about five centimetres (two inches) thick and forty-five centimetres (eighteen inches) wide, bore a carving of a man's face. Some say ancient indigenous people carved it; some say it is a portrait of Ouagimou, a Passamoquoddy chief, carved by artisans who travelled with the explorer Samuel de Champlain in 1605; some say it proves the Egyptians visited North America; others say it is a hoax. The medallion is now kept in Saint John at the New Brunswick Museum.

MYSTIC, QC: The first settlers in this region were an Anglophone family named Clapper, and Mystic's original name was Clapperton. The Clappers were known as a superstitious family who believed in ghosts and witches who incorporated mystical rites and ceremonies into their day-to-day tasks. The name "Mystic," given in 1864, could therefore be in honour of the Clappers, but it may be a translation of an earlier Aboriginal name.

ROCOCO POINT, NU: R.M. Eaton, a researcher on the Polar Continental Shelf Project, named this point in 1964 for the ornate, extravagant appearance of the pillars of eroded rock that bordered the point.

RAT ART

In Vancouver in 1990, a performance artist named Rick Gibson issued a press release announcing the forthcoming public execution of a rat named Sniffy by crushing it with a twenty-five-kilogram (fifty-five-pound) concrete block. Sniffy had been purchased from a snake-food bin at a pet store. He would be smashed onto a canvas; the result would be Gibson's artistic creation. The event was to take place downtown in front of the Vancouver Public Library, but a national public outcry (which may have been part of Gibson's intention) brought the event to a halt, and Sniffy was spared. Since then, Sniffy has been memorialized in Sniffy-the-Rat-for-Mayor campaigns and Sniffy the Rat Bus Tours.

THE ART-MAKING MAP *of* CANADA

N

MODIFIED *Geistonic* PROJECTION

MUSEUM RANGE
REFERENCE ISLAND
LOGICAL POINT
ARTISTS BAY
SINGING LANE
SCHOOL DRAW
STRUCTURAL RIVER
SHADE CREEK
ROCOCO POINT
OTHERSIDE BAY
THE GALLERY
FOLK LAKE
ERA ISLAND
ILLUSION CREEK
EPHEMERAL COVE
DESTRUCTION BAY
ACCESS PASSAGE
OPERA GLASS CAPE
FANTASQUE LAKE
TRAGEDY POINT
CARVER LAKE
APPROACH POINT
POPULAR POINT
LAC DE L'IMAGINAIRE
MUSIC LAKE
POSTVILLE
FABLE LAKE
LAC SCULPTÉ
VITAL RANGE
LAC JUXTAGLACIAIRE
TUTU BAY
LAC ÉPIC
LAC DÉCOUPÉ
CULTIVATION POINT
LAC TABLEAU
KILN BAY
NOISE CREEK
FORM POND
CINEMA
THE GAZE
POSER
THE PAINTER
POET PEAK
IRONY CREEK
LAC DU
LAC DE L'IDIOME
BÉRET
ACTRESS PASSAGE
NATURALISTS
MOUNTAINS
EXPERIMENT
BIGHT
DANCERS POINT
LIBERATED
FANTASYLAND
GROUP
BOURGEOIS
DEVIATION PEAK
UTOPIA
STORY
MOSAIC GLACIER
LAC SUBLIME
HEAD
LAC DU MASQUE
BALLET BAY
LAC CAMÉRA
INSPIRATION
COVE
MYSTIC
MONT CLICHE
TONES CREEK
CANON
ICONOCLAST
COMEDY
PARC DES APPRENTIS
MOUNTAIN
CREEK
PARC DE LA RENAISSANCE
EXPRESS
PURITY PASS
POINT
LAC DU VISIONNAIRE
PIANO
TABOO CREEK
RUISSEAU MODERNE
THE GOTHICS
LAKE
ORTHODOX
MASTER
OPAQUE LAKE
MOUNTAIN
EGO MOUNTAIN
SAGA
LAKE
REBUS
PSYCHE SHOAL
MACABRE TOWER
ISLAND
TROUPE
LAKE
THE OUTLET
BEAUTY CREEK
SKETCH
SIGN ISLAND
MYTH LAKE
CREEK
WRITING CREEK
CHANTLER
POP LAKE
GRANT
CREATION LAKE
THEATRE
CREEK
HISTORY LAKE

PHOTO
LAKE

PARADOX
CREEK
LAC
COMPOSITE
FIGURE
LAKE
ÎLE
RÉAL

ANIMUS
LAKE

GIFT
LAKE

MURAL
GLACIER

LAC
DADA

WORK

POWERVIEW

IDEAL

IMAGE CREEK

KITSCH LAKE

FRAME LAKE

UNIVERSITY

EYE LAKE

UNITY

ARTY HILL

CRAFT
CREEK

— 75 —

LOCKE POINT, NS: Locke Point, Locke Island, and the town of Lockeport are all named for Jonathan Locke, an American from Rhode Island who settled here in 1767. During the 1770s, privateers on the fringes of the US Civil War conducted frequent raids along the southern shores of Nova Scotia, which turned many US ex-pats in the region against the revolutionaries. Locke helped organize a campaign to petition the Massachusetts Council for relief from the attacks. In return, his name became attached to what had been known as the Ragged Islands.

AUGUSTINE LAKE, NT: Unlike many other places in the North named by Europeans, this one was named by residents to honour a local trapper after his death.

PLATO, SK: The CNR accepted the name in 1915 after it was suggested by Richard Burst, one of the town's first settlers, who came from Plato, Minnesota.

POPE, QC: Named in 1899 for politician John Henry Pope (1824–1889), a principal minister in Sir John A. Macdonald's cabinet who served in the House of Commons for twenty-two years. Some business interests owned by Pope were influential in the development of Quebec's railway system.

SENECA, ON: A town believed to have been named for the Seneca First Nation, one of the founding Iroquois bands of the Six Nations Confederacy (also known as Haudenosaunee, or the League of Peace and Power). The Six Nations was a trade confederacy among independent Iroquois bands, formed sometime between 1100 and 1600 CE. The confederacy had a form of "international" currency and a complete constitution, called *Gayanashagowa* or the "Great Law of Peace."

OFF THE MAP

The BC town of Likely was named for "Plato John" Likely, a gold prospector from New Brunswick who ran an unofficial philosophy school for his fellow miners near Quesnel, BC, in the late 1800s. He held classes in his "Philosophy Grove," a stand of giant cedars near Quesnel Lake, and he kept a retreat on an island in the lake, to which he took his most apt pupils. Most of Likely's lectures focussed on the teachings of his two favourite philosophers, Socrates and Plato. Prospectors who came to hear him often rewarded him with closely guarded tips on lucrative mining sites. The town of Likely grew into a real hot spot during the Cariboo Gold Rush. Its Bullion Pit, a three-kilometre (two-mile) long man-made mining trench, was the biggest hydraulic mine in the world in the early 1900s; water from the surrounding lakes was pumped through the trench to flush out $1.25 million worth of gold. The pit is still a popular tourist attraction.

EPISTEMOLOGY HIGH

Ontario has the most developed high-school philosophy programs in Canada. To acquire an Ontario academic credit in philosophy, a student must demonstrate knowledge of the major philosophers, philosophical concepts, and techniques used in formal and informal logic. The student must also show the ability to "explore the current limits to knowledge and understanding," and should be able to "articulate an understanding of connections between reason and feeling."

Map: Neil MacDonald

The **PHILOSOPHER'S** *Map of Canada*

N

MODIFIED *Geistonic* PROJECTION

CAPE BERKELEY

BENTHAM FIORD

MARCUS CHANNEL

SPENCER CAPE

HUME ISLAND

GRANT LAKE

CAPE SEARLE

PYTHAGORAS LAKE

BERKELEY PASSAGE

SHAFTESBURY INLET

DUNS LAKE

MOUNT GRANT

RIVIÈRE FOUCAULT

MOUNT PLATO

SINGER POINT

MOUNT SOCRATES

ROUSSEAU

MOUNT ARISTOTLE

LAC ROUSSEAU

SHAFTESBURY
SETTLEMENT

CAMUS SHOAL

ROUSSEAU CREEK

POINTE AUGUSTINE

POPE CREEK

BACON COVE

MARCUS PASSAGE

MILL COVE

LOCKE ISLAND

KINGWELL

AUGUSTINE LAKE

MARCEL HILLS

HUME ROCKS

LAC WHITEHEAD

AUGUSTINE ISLANDS

AUGUSTINE MOUND

MOUNT BERKELEY

EMERSON

MILL CREEK

COLLINGWOOD
POINT

AUGUSTINE COVE

CHURCHLAND

ERASMUS ISLAND

MARCEL LAKE

ENGELS ROCK

FOUCAULT BLUFF

LOCKE ISLAND

CICERO CREEK

LOCKE POINT

ANSELM CREEK

LAC LOCKE

HUME PASS

LOCKE BAY

LAC SIMONE

EMERSON

SCHELLING

LAC AUGUSTINE

RUSSELL PEAK

WHITEHEAD

ROUSSEAU
ISLAND

LAC NAGEL

BACON CREEK

RUSSELL

MOUNT ERASMUS

POPE

GOETHE LAKE

BACON
ISLAND

BACON BROOK

GRANT

FOUCAULT

LAC SENECA

PLATO

BACON BONE ROCK

MILL BEACH

PLATO CREEK

RUSSELL LAKE

CAPE SEARLE

LAC ZENO

BERKELEY

SENECA

COLLINGWOOD

SENECA CREEK

TOLSTOI, MB: Russian immigrants who once lived on the estate of Count Leo Tolstoy settled here near the turn of the last century, and in 1911 the CNR made the name official. The new name replaced the original Oleskiw, which honoured Josef Oleskiw, a Ukranian doctor who encouraged thousands of his countrymen to emigrate to Canada.

BALZAC, AB: Named by W.C. Van Horne, president of the CPR, who was instrumental in the creation of Banff National Park and was an admirer of the works of Honoré de Balzac. Poe, AB was also named for the actual writer, but it is not known by whom. Huxley, AB was named, not for the author of *Brave New World*, but for Thomas Huxley (1825–1895), a scientist and avid defender of Darwinism. Other literary-sounding Alberta towns not named for writers are Fitzgerald, Waugh, Conrad, and Kinsella (though the author W.P. Kinsella was born not far from Kinsella).

KIPLING, SK: Rudyard Kipling was an avid supporter of the British Empire, and he spent a lot of time touring the colonies, including the Canadian Prairies. He was even influential in preserving the name of Medicine Hat, AB (see notes on Medicine Hat, Sartorial Map, p. 48).

DICKENS POINT, NU: Sir Francis Leopold McClintock named this point for Charles Dickens. Many other places in the Arctic with European monikers were named by and for Sir John Franklin and all of the people who went looking for him (see notes on Belcher Islands, Beer Map, p. 14; Satellite Bay, Celestial Map, p. 22; and Cape Rescue, Fairy Tale Map, p. 72).

CONRAD, YT: In 1905 Colonel John Howard Conrad, an American mining promoter, acquired control of the silver and lead rights in the region and opened a series of mines, including Montana, Aurora, The Big Thing, and The Venus. He had a good business going for a while, but the seams in the area proved to be erratic and by 1914 all of Conrad's mines were closed.

DUNCAN, BC: In 1886, when a train bearing Sir John A. Macdonald and industrialist Robert Dunsmuir made its inaugural trip up the new Esquimalt & Nanaimo Railway, it was stopped by a crowd of 2,000 people at a spot near Alderlea Farm, owned by William Chalmers Duncan. The locals sang messages of welcome to the men and petitioned them for a stop on the line. Dunsmuir responded by yelling, "You will have a station here, boys!" He was true to his word—the train stop was called Duncan's Station, a site that eventually became the city of Duncan.

LE PREMIER LIVRE

The first French-Canadian novel was *L'Influence d'un Livre* (1837) by Philippe-Joseph Aubert de Gaspé, a journalist and occasional rabble-rouser. He wrote the novel while in hiding at his father's house (he was wanted for throwing a stink bomb into the National Assembly of Quebec). The book, a satire of Quebec's spiritual culture that involved folk stories gleaned from Aubert de Gaspé's father's memories, was not well received in its time, and the author died from hard living only a few years after it was published.

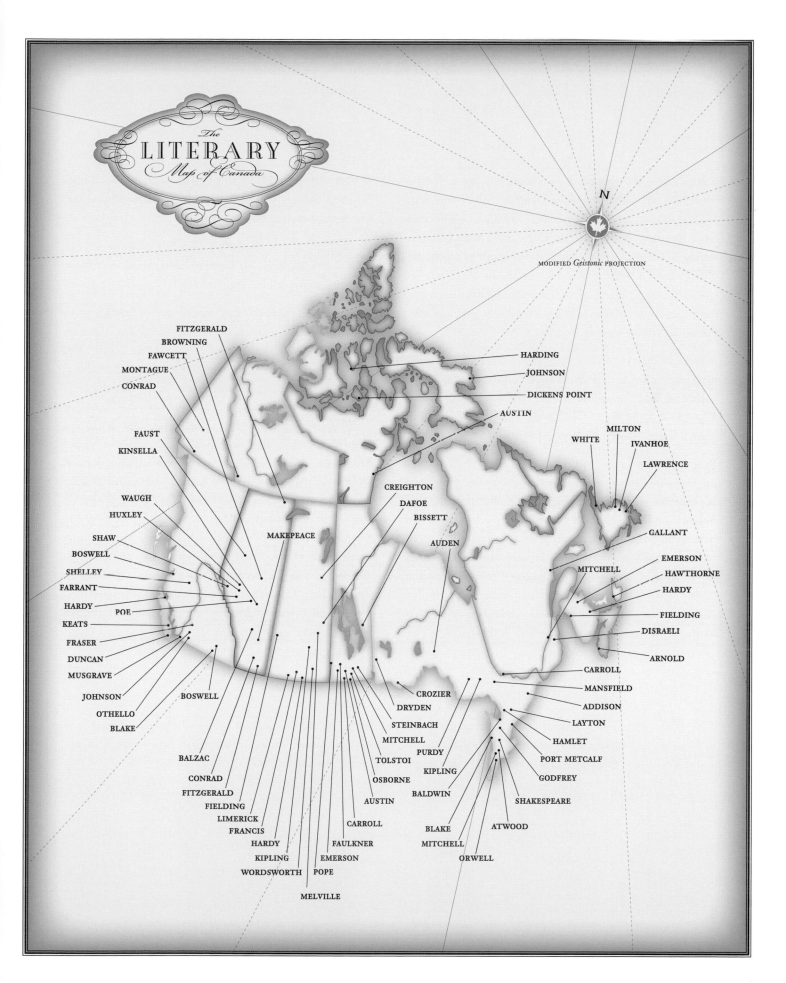

The LITERARY Map of Canada

N

MODIFIED *Geistonic* PROJECTION

FITZGERALD
BROWNING
FAWCETT
MONTAGUE
CONRAD

FAUST
KINSELLA

WAUGH
HUXLEY

SHAW
BOSWELL
SHELLEY
FARRANT
HARDY
POE
KEATS
FRASER
DUNCAN
MUSGRAVE
JOHNSON
OTHELLO
BLAKE

BOSWELL

MAKEPEACE

BALZAC
CONRAD
FITZGERALD
FIELDING
LIMERICK
FRANCIS
HARDY
KIPLING
WORDSWORTH

MELVILLE

POPE

EMERSON
FAULKNER

CARROLL

AUSTIN

OSBORNE
TOLSTOI
MITCHELL
STEINBACH
DRYDEN
CROZIER

CREIGHTON
DAFOE
BISSETT
AUDEN

HARDING
JOHNSON

DICKENS POINT

AUSTIN

WHITE
MILTON
IVANHOE
LAWRENCE

GALLANT

MITCHELL

EMERSON
HAWTHORNE
HARDY
FIELDING
DISRAELI
ARNOLD

CARROLL
MANSFIELD
ADDISON
LAYTON
HAMLET
PORT METCALF
GODFREY

PURDY
KIPLING
BALDWIN

BLAKE
MITCHELL
ORWELL

SHAKESPEARE

ATWOOD

ESPANOLA, ON: Founded as a company town for the Spanish River Pulp and Paper Company (the name is an anglicization of the Spanish word for "Spanish"). The entire town was shut down during the Depression, but was revived during World War II, when it was used briefly as a prisoner-of-war camp. The camp closed in the middle of the war and the Kalamazoo Vegetable Parchment Paper Company, a pulp mill, reopened the town. Today the town's economy relies mainly on cottage-country tourism.

VOWEL MOUNTAIN, BC: May have been named (though misspelled) for Arthur W. Vowell, a politician who was appointed gold commissioner of the Kootenay Mining District of BC in the late 1800s. Also in the Kootenays are Vowell Creek, Vowell Glacier, and Vowell peak.

PARC DE L'ESPÉRANTO, QC: A park established in 1988 in Trois-Rivières to commemorate *l'importante communauté* of Esperantophones who reside in Quebec, though their numbers and areas of residence are not calculated. About 1 million people around the world can understand Esperanto; of those, 1,000 speak it as a first language and 10,000 speak it fluently. Dr. Ludwik Lejzer Zamenhof invented, not tied to any country or ethnic group, the language in the late 1800s. A few sample words: *amikeco* (friendship); *ruĝiĝi* (to blush); *fihomo* (a wicked person); *aminda* (lovable).

MAORI POINT, NT: Named to honour Bishop George Augustus Selwyn (1809–1878), a missionary who worked among the Maori in New Zealand.

GREEK RIVER, PE: Possibly an English evolution of "*kuhtowedek*" or "*giotôgoeteg*," Mi'kmaq words meaning "reverberating echo" and "surrounding," respectively.

VULCAN, AB: Named for the Roman god of fire and metalworking, but its name has been reinterpreted to represent the stoic, logical race from the TV series *Star Trek*. In 1995 the town erected a 9.5-metre (thirty-one-foot) model of the *Enterprise* (its design based on the ships from the original series, not the subsequent *The Next Generation*), and gave it the identification number FX6-1995-A (the "FX6" is a Federation code identifying the ship as part of a Vulcan fleet, the middle number is the year in which it was made, and the "A" identifies it as the first of its kind in Canada). Gary McKinnon, the owner of a welding shop in the region, built the starship based on designs by an engineer named D. Day; McKinnon neglected his own business for months in his dedication to the project. The replica has turned Vulcan, AB, into a Trekkie Mecca: the town hosts two annual *Star Trek* festivals, Galaxyfest and Spock Days. A message of welcome is inscribed on the starship's base in English, Vulcan, and Klingon.

THE MOTHER TONGUE

Approximately 100 languages are spoken in Canada. Twenty-two percent of Canadians speak French at home, 67.5 percent speak English, and 10.5 percent speak something else. The largest Aboriginal language groups in Canada are Cree, Inuktitut, and Ojibwa.

THE LINGUISTIC
MAP *of* CANADA

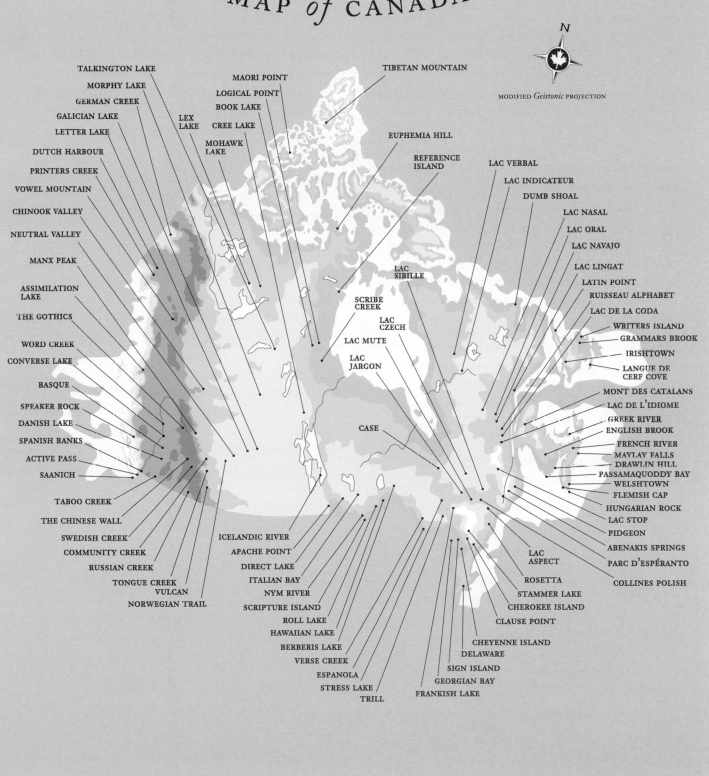

N

MODIFIED *Geistonic* PROJECTION

TALKINGTON LAKE
MORPHY LAKE
GERMAN CREEK
GALICIAN LAKE
LETTER LAKE
DUTCH HARBOUR
PRINTERS CREEK
VOWEL MOUNTAIN
CHINOOK VALLEY
NEUTRAL VALLEY
MANX PEAK
ASSIMILATION LAKE
THE GOTHICS
WORD CREEK
CONVERSE LAKE
BASQUE
SPEAKER ROCK
DANISH LAKE
SPANISH BANKS
ACTIVE PASS
SAANICH
TABOO CREEK
THE CHINESE WALL
SWEDISH CREEK
COMMUNITY CREEK
RUSSIAN CREEK
TONGUE CREEK
VULCAN
NORWEGIAN TRAIL

LEX LAKE
MOHAWK LAKE

MAORI POINT
LOGICAL POINT
BOOK LAKE
CREE LAKE

TIBETAN MOUNTAIN

EUPHEMIA HILL

REFERENCE ISLAND

LAC SIBILLE

SCRIBE CREEK
LAC CZECH
LAC MUTE
LAC JARGON

CASE

ICELANDIC RIVER
APACHE POINT
DIRECT LAKE
ITALIAN BAY
NYM RIVER
SCRIPTURE ISLAND
ROLL LAKE
HAWAIIAN LAKE
BERBERIS LAKE
VERSE CREEK
ESPANOLA
STRESS LAKE
TRILL

LAC VERBAL
LAC INDICATEUR
DUMB SHOAL
LAC NASAL
LAC ORAL
LAC NAVAJO
LAC LINGAT
LATIN POINT
RUISSEAU ALPHABET
LAC DE LA CODA
WRITERS ISLAND
GRAMMARS BROOK
IRISHTOWN
LANGUE DE CERF COVE
MONT DES CATALANS
LAC DE L'IDIOME
GREEK RIVER
ENGLISH BROOK
FRENCH RIVER
MAYLAY FALLS
DRAWLIN HILL
PASSAMAQUODDY BAY
WELSHTOWN
FLEMISH CAP
HUNGARIAN ROCK
LAC STOP
PIDGEON
ABENAKIS SPRINGS
PARC D'ESPÉRANTO
COLLINES POLISH

LAC ASPECT
ROSETTA
STAMMER LAKE
CHEROKEE ISLAND
CLAUSE POINT

CHEYENNE ISLAND
DELAWARE
SIGN ISLAND
GEORGIAN BAY
FRANKISH LAKE

MT. LOGAN, YT: The second-highest peak in North America (5,959 metres/19,551 feet), named for Sir William Edmond Logan (1798–1875), who founded the Geological Survey of Canada. For his achievements in geography and geology, which include determining the origins of Quebec's Laurentides (Laurentian Mountains), Logan received twenty-two medals—including one from Emperor Napoleon III—and a knighthood. In 2000, when Pierre Trudeau died, it was suggested that Mt. Logan be renamed for Trudeau, supposedly because then Prime Minister Jean Chrétien had once climbed the mountain with Trudeau, but a huge outcry from the earth-sciences community ended the discussion. Trudeau got an unnamed mountain near Valemont, BC, that was unofficially known as Ski Hill Mountain, though it has no ski hill. Mt. Trudeau is in the Premier Range, which was put aside in the 1920s to honour great prime ministers.

A LAKE, NB: It is tied with Lac Y in Quebec, for shortest place name in Canada. The longest place name is "Dysart, Dudley, Harcourt, Guilford, Harburn, Bruton, Havelock, Eyre, and Clyde" in Ontario. The longest single-word place name is Pekwachnamaykoskwaskwaypinwanik in Nunavut. The longest place name in the world is Taumatawhakatang ihangakoauauotamateaturipukakapikimaungahoronukupok aiwhenuakitanatahu, a hill in New Zealand.

BIG MUDDY, SK: An unincorporated region that takes its name from nearby Big Muddy Lake, which is just that—one of a chain of shallow, silty lakes that lead down to the Missouri watershed. The surrounding region is known as the Big Muddy Badlands, a wide, flat area dotted with striking land formations that were created by thousands of years of glacial traffic. A fifty-five-kilometre (thirty-three-mile) trench cuts through the middle of the Badlands, and Butch Cassidy is said to have hidden from the law in its caves.

MAGNETIC HILL, NB: The secret of this spot near Moncton, where cars seem to coast upwards, is that the stretch of road only *appears* to go uphill. It's listed as one of Canada's top tourist attractions.

DAWSON CITY, YT: George Mercer "Little Doctor" Dawson, born in Pictou, NS, in 1849, was (among other things) a botanist, linguist, geographer, geologist, and surveyor. A childhood illness left him with weak lungs and other physical disabilities, but he was known for his drive and passion for exploration and sociological study. Dawson City's best-known accomplishment was to undertake a 2,200-kilometre (1,350-mile) overland journey of the Yukon and northern BC, during which he made detailed maps of the area and became one of the first to pinpoint the Klondike as a potential goldmine. Eventually he was appointed Director of the Geological Survey of Canada, a position he held until his death in 1901. Aside from Dawson City, twenty-five other Canadian places—and one breed of caribou—have been named for him.

HAPPY BIRTHDAY

The year 2006 marks the 100th Anniversary of the first edition of *The Atlas of Canada*. Very few countries had a national atlas in 1906. Finland claims to be the first to have produced one, in 1899, though there are records of an American national atlas published in 1874. *The Atlas of Canada* has now been published in six editions—the latest, released in 1998, is entirely digital and available online.

Map: Gary T. Whiteford, PhD and Melissa Edwards

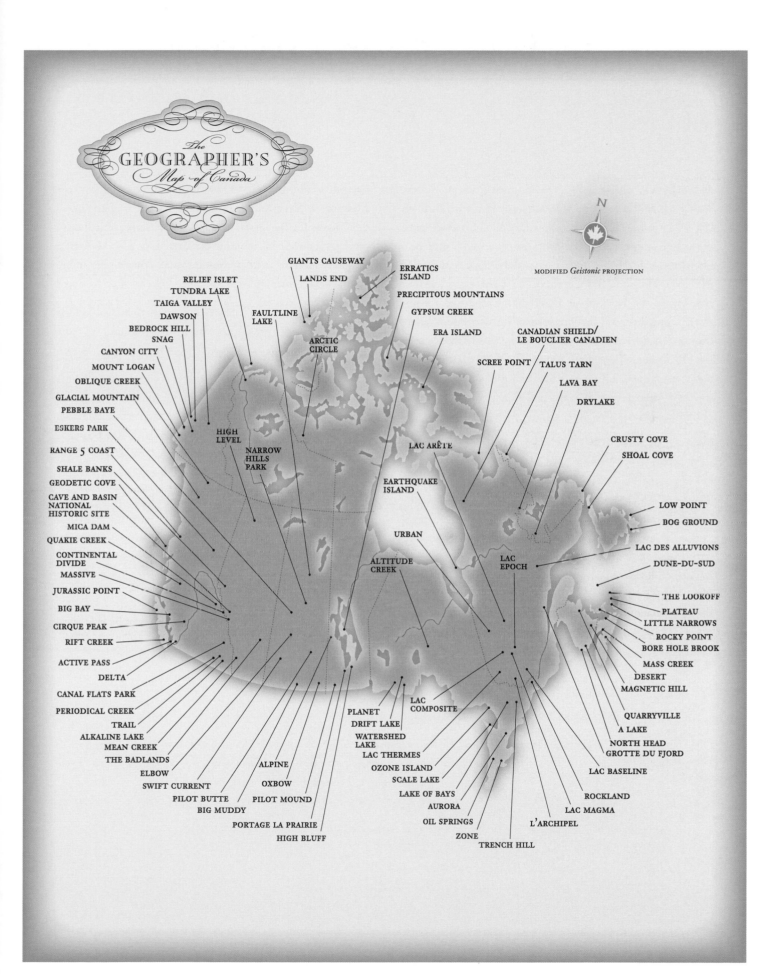

Tête Jaune Cache, BC: "Tête jaune" means "yellow head," and like the Yellowhead Highway that runs through Jasper National Park, it was named for blond-haired Pierre Hatsinaton, a.k.a. Pierre Bostonais (see notes on Boston Bar, Doughnut Map, p. 20), an Iroquois-Metis trapper and guide who led a Hudson's Bay Company party through their first crossing of the Rockies in 1820. The Cache was a point at the confluence of the Fraser and Robson rivers where Hatsinaton stored his furs before taking them to trade with the HBC. The village was a thriving hub during the building of the Grand Trunk Railway, and today is just a small service centre for tourist traffic. "Tête Jaune" is frequently pronounced "tee-John."

Chaffeys Locks, ON: The locks are in the Rideau Canal, a 202-kilometre (125-mile) waterway that links Kingston to Ottawa and then links to Montreal via the Ottawa River. The canal, which opened in 1832, was built to enable supply boats to reach Montreal without travelling the St. Lawrence Seaway, where they were vulnerable to attack and piracy by Americans. The scenic waterway is now a popular tourist attraction for Americans. The locks are near the town of Chaffeys Mills, which was named for Samuel Chaffey, a sawmill owner who helped develop the area after the War of 1812. He died of swamp fever before construction of the canal began.

Clarke's Head, NL: The possessive apostrophe is not always used in Canadian place names; thus we have Lions Bay, Giants Castle, Devils Thumb, and Chaffeys Locks (see previous entry). Newfoundland and Labrador, however, thumbed its nose at this trend and puts apostrophes wherever it pleases, starting with the capital, St. John's.

The Helmet, BC: J.H. Scattergood gave this hard-headed name in 1900 to a peak northeast of Mt. Robson.

Hair Lake, NT: The name was translated from the original Tli Cho (formerly known as Dogrib) language, in which the words for "hair" and "grass" are interchangeable. The Tli Cho Nation was involved in a pivotal 2003 land-claims case, in which the Canadian government ceded a 39,000-square-kilometre (15,600-square-mile) stretch of land between Great Slave Lake and Great Bear Lake to Tli Cho governance.

Hairy Hill, AB: In spring, buffalo rolled around on the nearby hill to shed their winter coats, covering the grass and shrubs with a thick layer of fur. The first settlers didn't know what to make of the matted clumps they saw all around them, until the buffalo herds appeared the following spring.

Business in the Front, Party in the Back

Though not native to Canada, the Mullet haircut has become another identifying feature of the Canadian hoser—if not of the classic Bob-and-Doug hoser, certainly the modern hoser, as seen in the Canadian film *Fubar* (2002). With a short top and sides and a long back, the style is also referred to as Hockey Hair, the Beaver Paddle, the Yep-Nope, Shorty Long-back, the Commonwealth Crewcut, and the Canadian Passport.

Map: A collaboration by the Geist mapping team

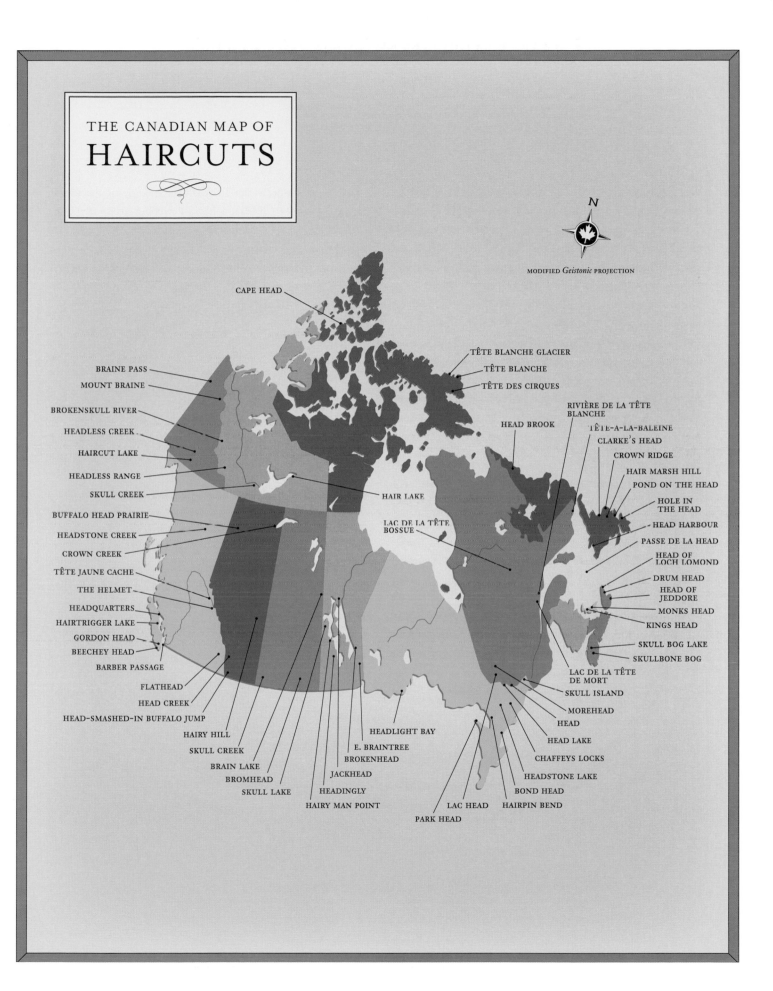

THE CANADIAN MAP OF
HAIRCUTS

N

MODIFIED *Geistonic* PROJECTION

CAPE HEAD

TÊTE BLANCHE GLACIER
TÊTE BLANCHE
TÊTE DES CIRQUES

BRAINE PASS
MOUNT BRAINE

RIVIÈRE DE LA TÊTE BLANCHE
HEAD BROOK
TÊTE-A-LA-BALEINE
CLARKE'S HEAD
CROWN RIDGE
HAIR MARSH HILL
POND ON THE HEAD
HOLE IN THE HEAD
HEAD HARBOUR
PASSE DE LA HEAD
HEAD OF LOCH LOMOND
DRUM HEAD
HEAD OF JEDDORE
MONKS HEAD
KINGS HEAD

BROKENSKULL RIVER
HEADLESS CREEK
HAIRCUT LAKE
HEADLESS RANGE
SKULL CREEK
HAIR LAKE

BUFFALO HEAD PRAIRIE
HEADSTONE CREEK
CROWN CREEK
LAC DE LA TÊTE BOSSUE

TÊTE JAUNE CACHE
THE HELMET
HEADQUARTERS
HAIRTRIGGER LAKE
GORDON HEAD
BEECHEY HEAD
BARBER PASSAGE

SKULL BOG LAKE
SKULLBONE BOG

LAC DE LA TÊTE DE MORT
SKULL ISLAND
MOREHEAD
HEAD

FLATHEAD
HEAD CREEK
HEAD-SMASHED-IN BUFFALO JUMP
HAIRY HILL
SKULL CREEK
BRAIN LAKE
BROMHEAD
SKULL LAKE

HEADLIGHT BAY
E. BRAINTREE
BROKENHEAD
JACKHEAD
HEADINGLY
HAIRY MAN POINT

HEAD LAKE
CHAFFEYS LOCKS
HEADSTONE LAKE
BOND HEAD
HAIRPIN BEND

LAC HEAD
PARK HEAD

WEST EDMONTON MALL, EDMONTON, AB: The largest mall in the world when it was built in 1981. Though it has kept growing, it lost the "world's largest" crown in 1992 to the Mall of America, near the Twin Cities in Minnesota, which in turn was outdone by a mega-mall in Beijing, which in turn was trumped by a monster mall in Dubai. The Edmonton complex is still an impressive construction, covering almost 500,000 square metres (600,000 square yards) and containing 800 shops and services including 110 restaurants, twenty-one theatre screens, six department stores, ten aviaries, seven amusement parks, an ice rink, an indoor car lot, a 12.3 million-litre (2.7 million-gallon) wave pool with constant tropical temperatures (even in the dead of an Edmonton winter), and a replica of Christopher Columbus's ship *Santa Maria*.

PATH, TORONTO, ON: *The Guinness Book of World Records* lists PATH as the word's largest underground shopping complex. A twenty-seven-kilometre (sixteen-mile) network of subterranean walkways snakes between Union Station and Dundas Street, connecting fifty office towers, twenty indoor parking lots, six hotels, a railway terminal, and five subway stations, and it is entirely lined with retail outlets. The only comparable Canadian system is the plus-15/plus-30 networks in Calgary, which also connect malls, parking lots, and office towers (and one four-storey bar), but with fifty-eight enclosed bridges that crisscross over downtown streets—4.5 metres (at fifteen feet) and nine metres (thirty feet) above, respectively. The Calgary system was the setting of *Waydowntown* (2000), a film in which a group of young office workers wager not to step outdoors, for weeks on end. Another enclosing project with the same intent—shelter from the weather—is Fermont, QC. The entire town—shops, apartments, schools—is composed of one giant building, called *le mur*, or "the wall."

ORCHARD PARK MALL, KELOWNA, BC: Its name is indicative of the subsuming tendencies of urban sprawl. The large mall and its larger parking lot lie along Highway 97 in the Okanagan Valley, on what was once an orchard.

HORWOOD'S MALL, WHITEHORSE, YT: Situated at First Avenue and Main Street, Horwood's Mall occupies what used to be known as the Taylor and Drury Building, a wood-frame depot thrown up in 1905 after a fire destroyed the original building. Many renovations and additions have been added since, most notably a second-floor expansion in the 1950s. Isaac Taylor and William Drury were businessmen from England who came to the region in 1900 with $200 between them and ended up making good money trading used prospecting gear near Atlin, BC. They developed their business into a merchandising firm with locations throughout the Klondike, including this building in Whitehorse. The mall takes its name from its main shop, Horwood's Office Supplies, and also houses an art gallery, gift store, self-storage centre, café, and recreation centre.

CROSS-CANADA CONSUMERISM

There are 2,261 official shopping centres in Canada. Prince Edward Island has twelve, and the Yukon and Northwest Territories each have one.

Map: Billeh Nickerson

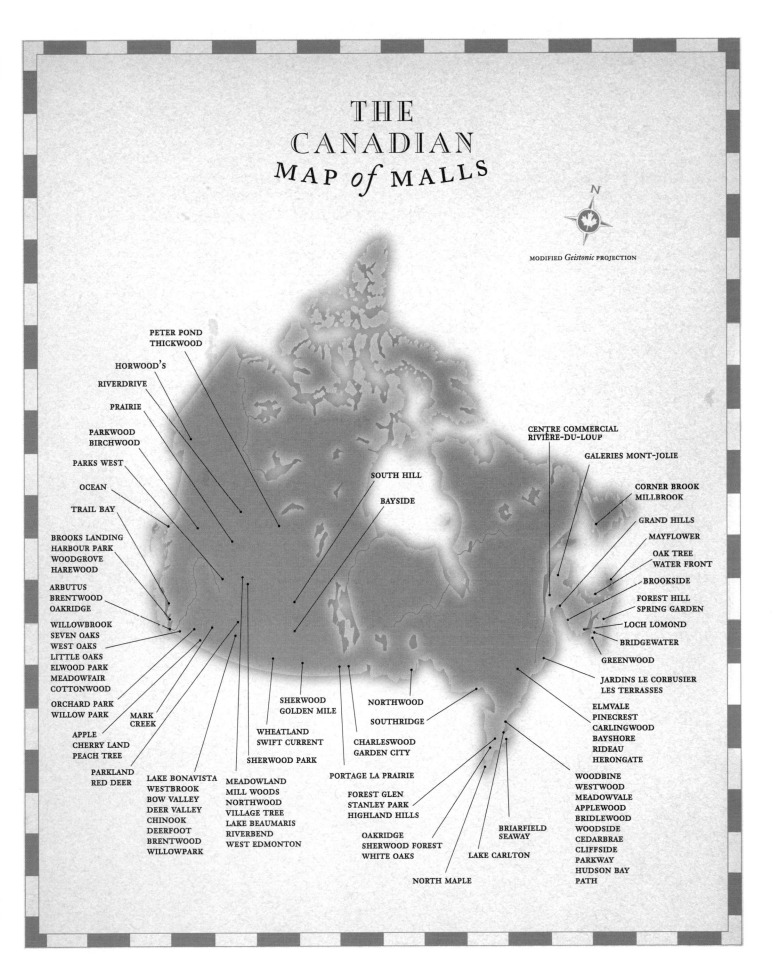

THE CANADIAN MAP *of* MALLS

MODIFIED *Geistonic* PROJECTION

PETER POND
THICKWOOD

HORWOOD'S

RIVERDRIVE

PRAIRIE

PARKWOOD
BIRCHWOOD

PARKS WEST

OCEAN

TRAIL BAY

BROOKS LANDING
HARBOUR PARK
WOODGROVE
HAREWOOD

ARBUTUS
BRENTWOOD
OAKRIDGE

WILLOWBROOK
SEVEN OAKS
WEST OAKS
LITTLE OAKS
ELWOOD PARK
MEADOWFAIR
COTTONWOOD

ORCHARD PARK
WILLOW PARK

MARK
CREEK

APPLE
CHERRY LAND
PEACH TREE

PARKLAND
RED DEER

LAKE BONAVISTA
WESTBROOK
BOW VALLEY
DEER VALLEY
CHINOOK
DEERFOOT
BRENTWOOD
WILLOWPARK

MEADOWLAND
MILL WOODS
NORTHWOOD
VILLAGE TREE
LAKE BEAUMARIS
RIVERBEND
WEST EDMONTON

SHERWOOD
GOLDEN MILE

WHEATLAND
SWIFT CURRENT

SHERWOOD PARK

SOUTH HILL

BAYSIDE

NORTHWOOD

SOUTHRIDGE

CHARLESWOOD
GARDEN CITY

PORTAGE LA PRAIRIE

FOREST GLEN
STANLEY PARK
HIGHLAND HILLS

OAKRIDGE
SHERWOOD FOREST
WHITE OAKS

NORTH MAPLE

BRIARFIELD
SEAWAY

LAKE CARLTON

CENTRE COMMERCIAL
RIVIÈRE-DU-LOUP

GALERIES MONT-JOLIE

CORNER BROOK
MILLBROOK

GRAND HILLS

MAYFLOWER

OAK TREE
WATER FRONT

BROOKSIDE

FOREST HILL
SPRING GARDEN

LOCH LOMOND

BRIDGEWATER

GREENWOOD

JARDINS LE CORBUSIER
LES TERRASSES

ELMVALE
PINECREST
CARLINGWOOD
BAYSHORE
RIDEAU
HERONGATE

WOODBINE
WESTWOOD
MEADOWVALE
APPLEWOOD
BRIDLEWOOD
WOODSIDE
CEDARBRAE
CLIFFSIDE
PARKWAY
HUDSON BAY
PATH

All-Consuming

HUDSON BAY, QC/ON/MB/NU: Perhaps Canada's most recognizable feature: a 1.23-million-square-kilometre (475,000-square-mile) scoop of ice water in the middle of the Canadian Shield. It is named for Henry Hudson, an explorer who charted parts of its coastline on the Discovery in 1610. The ship became trapped in ice in James Bay, and after a hard winter there, Hudson's crew mutinied and abandoned him (and his teenage son) on the ice. There were several attempts to rescue Hudson (see notes on Button, Sartorial Map, p. 48 and Belcher Islands, Beer Map, p. 14), but his body was never found. Many years later, his surname was put to use again in the name of the Hudson's Bay Company (which, after more than 300 years in Canada, was sold to an American financier in 2006).

FAIRWEATHER MOUNTAIN, BC: The highest peak in British Columbia (4,663 metres/15,400 feet), if you ignore the half of it that lies in Alaska. Otherwise, Mt. Waddington (4,019 metres/13,200 feet) near Bella Coola gets the crown (or crowns—it has twin peaks). Fairweather was named in 1778 by Captain James Cook (see notes on Mt. Cook, Map of Kitchen Implements, p. 30) in celebration of some good weather. In fact, the mountain is close to the open ocean and surrounded by a low-pressure system most of the time, so it is subject to year-round storms and very heavy snowfall. Fairweather Mountain can also be found on the Happy Map (p. 104).

BRICK, QC: A chalet on the banks of the Rivière du Brick (Brig) on l'Île d'Anticosti. Anticosti Island is the twentieth-largest island in Canada and the nintieth-largest in the world, but it has a very small population (250). Its name suggests that it has no safe harbour—it is ringed by a dangerous limestone reef. Jacques Cartier claimed Anticosti for the French in 1534; in 1763 it was ceded to Newfoundland, which kept it briefly until Canada took it for Quebec in 1774. The island was overfished and overhunted to near barrenness, but in 1896 a French chocolatier named Henri Menier bought it for $125,000 and converted it to a game preserve. He founded a tiny, fairly utopian farming community there but only visited it six times. Over the next twenty years, the deer he had imported stripped the island of edible material and then died off in droves. The evolutionary result of this today is a smaller and smarter breed of Anticosti deer.

EATONIA, SK: Named for Timothy Eaton, founder of the Eaton's department store chain, which closed for good in 2002. Eatonia was established after World War I, making it one of the last places in Saskatchewan to be founded by settlers. The original name was Eaton, and the "ia" was added later to avoid confusion with nearby Eston. For small prairie towns at the time, Eaton's mail-order catalogues were a lifeline, for clothing and household supplies, as literacy tools for farm kids and, finally, as paper for the outhouse. Eaton's stopped distributing its catalogue in 1976. Writer W.O. Mitchell read a eulogy for it on CBC Radio, saying the publication was one of his strongest memories of a prairie childhood.

SPENDING PATTERNS

Canadian consumers spent $6.1 billion on men's clothing and accessories and $11.5 billion on women's clothing and accessories in 2002. Overall, $307 billion ended up in retailer cash boxes, 15 percent of which was spent on women's underwear and hosiery.

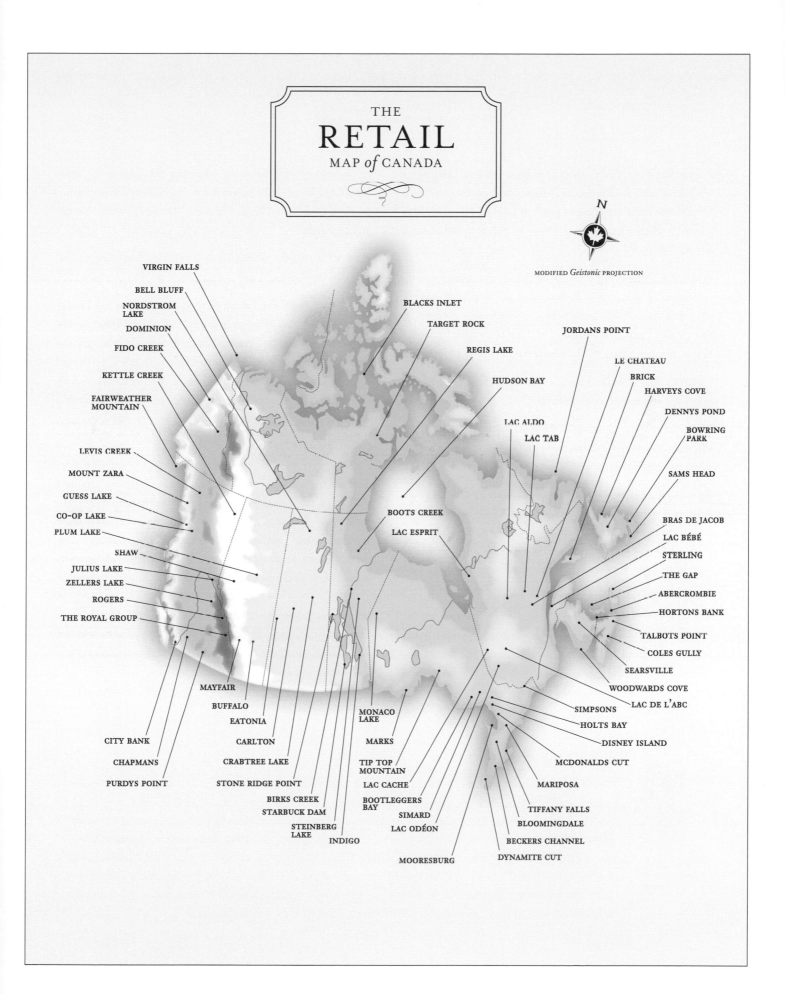

THE

RETAIL

MAP *of* CANADA

N

MODIFIED *Geistonic* PROJECTION

VIRGIN FALLS

BELL BLUFF

NORDSTROM LAKE

DOMINION

FIDO CREEK

KETTLE CREEK

FAIRWEATHER MOUNTAIN

LEVIS CREEK

MOUNT ZARA

GUESS LAKE

CO-OP LAKE

PLUM LAKE

SHAW

JULIUS LAKE

ZELLERS LAKE

ROGERS

THE ROYAL GROUP

MAYFAIR

BUFFALO

EATONIA

CITY BANK

CHAPMANS

CARLTON

PURDYS POINT

CRABTREE LAKE

STONE RIDGE POINT

BIRKS CREEK

STARBUCK DAM

STEINBERG LAKE

INDIGO

BLACKS INLET

TARGET ROCK

REGIS LAKE

HUDSON BAY

LAC ALDO

LAC TAB

BOOTS CREEK

LAC ESPRIT

MONACO LAKE

MARKS

TIP TOP MOUNTAIN

LAC CACHE

BOOTLEGGERS BAY

SIMARD

LAC ODÉON

MOORESBURG

DYNAMITE CUT

BECKERS CHANNEL

BLOOMINGDALE

TIFFANY FALLS

MARIPOSA

MCDONALDS CUT

DISNEY ISLAND

HOLTS BAY

SIMPSONS

LAC DE L'ABC

WOODWARDS COVE

SEARSVILLE

COLES GULLY

TALBOTS POINT

HORTONS BANK

ABERCROMBIE

THE GAP

STERLING

LAC BÉBÉ

BRAS DE JACOB

SAMS HEAD

BOWRING PARK

DENNYS POND

HARVEYS COVE

BRICK

LE CHATEAU

JORDANS POINT

ECONOMY, NS: The name is an anglicization of *"kenomee,"* a Mi'kmaq word for "land spit." Acadians transliterated it to *Vil Conomie*; after they were expelled, English resettlers kept a version of the name (a rare act—the policy being to erase Acadian history).

FORTUNE, NL: From *"fortuna,"* a Portuguese word meaning "richness." The village is honoured in a Newfoundland folk song that goes, "Sally got a bouncin' new baby,/ Father said that he didn't care;/ Because he liked the feller from Fortune/ What was down here fishin' last year."

CRYSTAL CITY, MB: Thomas Greenway chose the name to salute the water in a local stream.

ARGENTIA, NL: Originally a fishing outport called Little Placentia, it was renamed to celebrate the opening of a nearby silver mine in the early 1900s (*argentum* is Latin for "silver").

RESOURCE, SK: Cobena Smith's farm lay in the thirteen-kilometre (eight-mile) stretch between railway sidings at Silver Park and Clemens, and he wanted a stop closer to home. The railway authority refused, but Smith lobbied so vigorously that they finally relented. They named the new station Resource because Smith had used "every resource he could think of" to change their minds.

BRAS D'OR, NS: The name (pronounced "bra-door") may refer to the sun's reflection off this pretty lake resembling "arms of gold," or it may have come from an early mapping error. A few sixteenth-century maps placed "the Sea of Labrador" too far south, showing the lake as an inlet into Cape Breton. A chairman of the National Geographic Society once called Bras d'Or his "favourite landscape on planet Earth."

LAC VALUE, QC: Surpassed by Lac de la Plus-Value, in the Côte-Nord region.

DOLLARTON, BC: A company town founded by the Dollar Lumber Company, owned by Captain Robert Dollar. It has two literary claims to fame: Captain Dollar was the inspiration for Cappy Ricks, a character in stories by Peter Kyne; and Dollarton plays a role in many of the stories and novels of Malcolm Lowry, who in the 1940s and 1950s lived in a squatter's shack on the beach (which has been preserved).

OFF THE MAP

During the Klondike Gold Rush, Yukon Territory acquired too many place names related to gold and wealth to fit into this map (Too Much Gold Creek, for example, was named by a weary prospector who found no gold there at all). The most intense Klondike frenzy was sparked in 1897, when the *Excelsior* docked in San Francisco and unloaded crates of gold found by a few early-bird prospectors. The next ship to arrive was greeted by thousands of onlookers, and gold fever spread fast. Passage on ships returning to the North sold out immediately and the *New York Herald* reported, "Seattle has gone stark, staring mad on gold."

GOLD STANDARDS

Canada got its own currency in 1858. Before that, the trading medium in the Dominion was Spanish dollars, a currency developed by Spain for its colonies. (There had been an attempt to use British pounds, but the coins were hard to come by.) Canada, under French rule at the time, used a colonial currency called the New France livre, while Newfoundland, Nova Scotia, and New Brunswick maintained their own currencies. In 1841 the Province of Canada created the dollar and pinned it to the US dollar at 5 shillings. In 1858 the new currency incorporated the decimal system and quickly became standard. In 1871, the Uniform Currency Act brought all the provinces together under the same dollar (Newfoundland maintained its own currency until 1949, when it joined the Confederation).

THE
MONEY
MAP *of* CANADA

N

MODIFIED *Geistonic* PROJECTION

PENNY BAY
LOON STRAITS
YEN LAKE
BENJAMIN MOUNTAIN
TREASURE ISLAND
PROSPEROUS LAKE
PROSPECTOR
CHARITY GULCH
ENTERPRISE
NICKEL CREEK
EARN HILLS
COIN CREEK
THE PYRAMID
WORTH
BONANZA
PROGRESS
LEGAL
VENTURE BANKS
KRONE ISLAND
PAY BAY
BUCK LAKE
POUNDMAKER
BOND SOUND
CACHE CREEK
TENDER MOUNTAIN
JACKPOT CREEK
MARK BAY
MONEYMAKER REEF
DOLLARTON
DIVIDEND MOUNTAIN
TRADERS COVE
GOLDEN
TRUST CREEK
COMMERCE CREEK

RESOURCE
SCRIP
BAHT LAKE

EQUITY
EBENEEZER
BOUNTY
SUCCESS
REWARD

CRYSTAL CITY
GAINSBOROUGH

RICHER
DIME LAKE
PATRON LAKE
WEALTHY LAKES
RAND
STOCK
SHILLINGTON
DYMOND
SCRATCH ISLAND
SIMOLEA LAKE
FORKS OF THE CREDIT

SILVER DOLLAR
LAC VALUE
LAC SPENDET
LAC FRANC

DRACHME POINT
SELLER LAKE
BUYERS POINT
DEPOSIT COVE
GROSS ISLAND
LAC FLIP
LAC BILLET
ARGENTENAY
CUT THROAT HARBOUR
LAC AUX CLAMS
THE BANK
ÎLE MONGER
PRICE
CHANGE ISLANDS
BUSINESS POND
ARGENTIA
FORTUNE
PROFITTS POINT
BRAS D'OR
STERLING
GRANTVILLE
BEANS LAKE
BREADALBANE
DOLLAR LAKE
CENTRAL ECONOMY
SPECULATOR POND
GREENVILLE
MONEY POINT
GRAND RIVER

PARC DE L'AFFLUENT
LAC PESO
LAC RICHE
LAC MERCHANT
THE QUARTERS
MONEYSUNK ISLAND
VALLÉE-DE-L'OR
CASHTOWN CORNERS
NEW CREDIT

— 91 —

CRAPAUD, PE: From *Rivière aux Crapauds*, the early name for a river near the townsite (the river was later renamed Brocklesby, then Westmoreland). "Crapauds" means "toads," but the river's name may have referred to an Acadian term for an eel: *le crapaud de mer* ("sea toad"). Variations of the town's name showed up in records as early as 1818, but "Crapaud" wasn't official until 1850. Crapaud is in the county of Queens, a short drive from the Confederation Bridge.

ASBESTOS, QC: Site of the world's largest asbestos mine, founded by the mining company MRC d' Asbestos. When "asbestos" became synonymous with "poison," residents began to debate—and continue to debate—a name change. Possibilities include Trois Lacs and Phoenix—the latter possibly a nod to the town's economic survival after asbestos was made illegal. In 1949 a massive miners strike here changed the course of Quebec labour history. It lasted four months and involved 5,000 miners, and is considered one of the seeds of Quebec's Quiet Revolution.

LA FRAGILITÉ DES CHOSES, QC: Named for a story by François Charron. In 1997 the Government of Quebec commemorated the twentieth anniversary of the French Language Charter (Bill 101) by naming 101 islands in the Caniapiscau Reservoir after post-war Quebecois literary works (see also La Vingt-Septieme Lettre, Number 1 Map, p. 24).

SNAFU CREEK, YT: Snafu is a military acronym for "situation normal: all fouled up" (in less polite use, substitute that other F-word). Canada's other place names made of syllabic abbreviations include Kenora, ON (an amalgamation of the post office names Keewatin, Norman, and Rat Portage), Lake Koocanusa, BC (Kootenai River, Canada, and USA), Transcona, MB (Transcontinental Railway and Strathcona), and Carcross, YT (Caribou Crossing).

TIN TOWN, MB: An "unpopulated locality" in the middle of Delta Marsh west of Flee Island and a gathering place for sport hunters, who erect tin shacks and hunting lodges during high season. Tin Town was also the original name for Powerview (see notes on Art-Making Map, p. 74).

BROKEN GROUP ISLANDS, BC: A cluster of about 100 small islands covering 106 square kilometres (forty-one square miles) in Pacific Rim National Park on the west coast of Vancouver Island. It is a beautiful region and quite accessible; as a result it booms with so many whale watchers, scuba divers, kayakers, and other tourists that the crowds, and their litter and poorly buried human waste, are creating some conflict between the old-time nature lovers and the new-time tourism entrepreneurs.

DISCOUNT DOLLARS

The Great Canadian Dollar Store has 121 outlets across Canada (New Brunswick has the largest concentration of stores). Other notable Canadian discount stores, many of which pay homage to our uniquely Canadian dollar coin: A Buck or Two, Amy's Loonie-Toonie Town, Happy Loonie, Loonie Bin, Loonie King, Loonie Lane, Loonie Plus, Dollar Barn, Dollarama, Dollar Bazaar, Dollar Giant, Dollar Land, Everything 99 Cents, 99 Cents or Less, Tout a $1, Dollar Chanceux, Dollartheque, Le Meilleur Prix un Dollars Plus, La Boutique du Dollar, and Loonie on the Lake Dollar Plus.

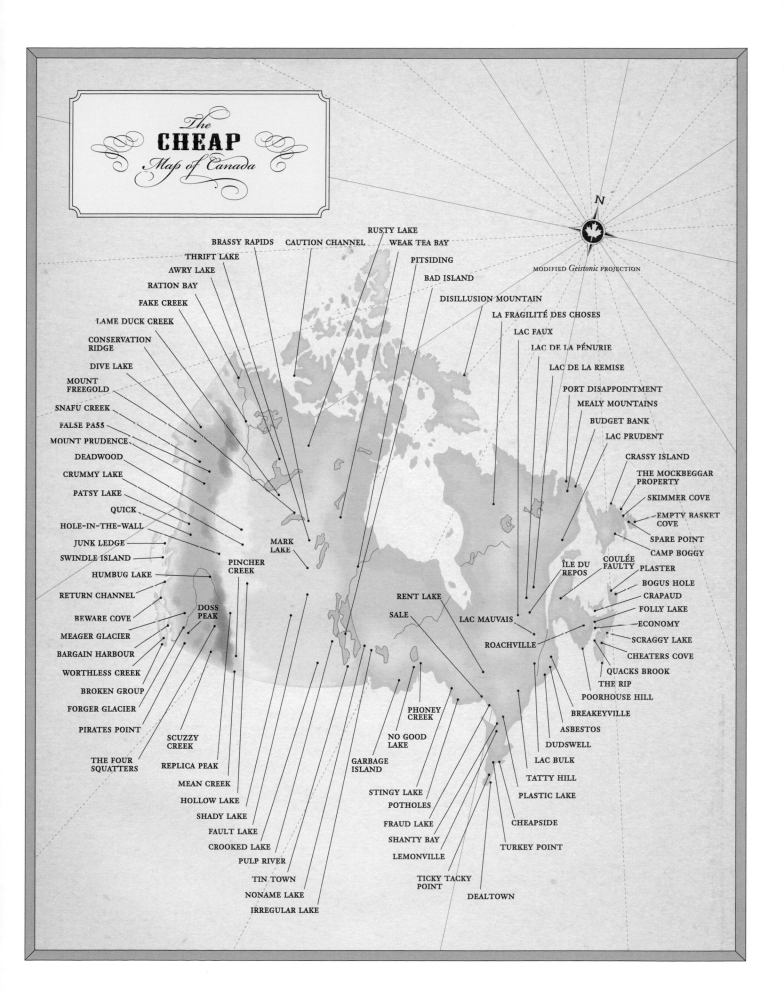

The CHEAP Map of Canada

MODIFIED *Geistonic* PROJECTION

N

BRASSY RAPIDS
CAUTION CHANNEL
RUSTY LAKE
WEAK TEA BAY
THRIFT LAKE
PITSIDING
AWRY LAKE
BAD ISLAND
RATION BAY
FAKE CREEK
DISILLUSION MOUNTAIN
LAME DUCK CREEK
LA FRAGILITÉ DES CHOSES
CONSERVATION RIDGE
LAC FAUX
DIVE LAKE
LAC DE LA PÉNURIE
MOUNT FREEGOLD
LAC DE LA REMISE
SNAFU CREEK
PORT DISAPPOINTMENT
FALSE PA55
MEALY MOUNTAINS
MOUNT PRUDENCE
BUDGET BANK
DEADWOOD
LAC PRUDENT
CRUMMY LAKE
CRASSY ISLAND
PATSY LAKE
THE MOCKBEGGAR PROPERTY
QUICK
SKIMMER COVE
HOLE-IN-THE-WALL
EMPTY BASKET COVE
JUNK LEDGE
SWINDLE ISLAND
MARK LAKE
SPARE POINT
HUMBUG LAKE
PINCHER CREEK
CAMP BOGGY
COULÉE FAULTY
PLASTER
RETURN CHANNEL
ÎLE DU REPOS
BOGUS HOLE
BEWARE COVE
DOSS PEAK
CRAPAUD
MEAGER GLACIER
RENT LAKE
FOLLY LAKE
BARGAIN HARBOUR
SALE
ECONOMY
WORTHLESS CREEK
LAC MAUVAIS
SCRAGGY LAKE
BROKEN GROUP
ROACHVILLE
CHEATERS COVE
FORGER GLACIER
QUACKS BROOK
PIRATES POINT
THE RIP
POORHOUSE HILL
SCUZZY CREEK
PHONEY CREEK
BREAKEYVILLE
THE FOUR SQUATTERS
REPLICA PEAK
NO GOOD LAKE
ASBESTOS
MEAN CREEK
DUDSWELL
GARBAGE ISLAND
LAC BULK
HOLLOW LAKE
TATTY HILL
SHADY LAKE
STINGY LAKE
PLASTIC LAKE
FAULT LAKE
POTHOLES
CROOKED LAKE
FRAUD LAKE
CHEAPSIDE
PULP RIVER
SHANTY BAY
TURKEY POINT
TIN TOWN
LEMONVILLE
NONAME LAKE
TICKY TACKY POINT
IRREGULAR LAKE
DEALTOWN

FREEDOM, AB: One of many Canadian places settled by Germans and renamed during World Wars I and II (see notes on Kitchener, Map of Kitchen Implements, p. 30). The town was renamed from Dusseldorf to Freedom during World War I.

BAIE DE GIRLS, QC: Two unnamed female friends "adopted" the bay and established a very successful fishing venture together. In 1999 they were immortalized in the name.

STONEWALL, MB: Named by a local mill operator for the nineteenth-century American General Andrew "Stonewall" Jackson.

PINK MOUNTAIN, BC: Fireweed flowers turn this mountain pink when they bloom, and during blossom season, the mountain appears to glow at sunrise. The fireweed also attracts a rare species of Arctic butterfly to the area (for more on Arctic butterflies, see notes on Butterfly Bay, Entomological Map, p. 16).

BENTS, SK: Founded as Piche, but the residents didn't like the name, and when the railway line came through in 1928, James Elder, town secretary, wrote to the railway proposing some alternative names. In a postscript, he mentioned that his family was from Bents in Scotland. Be careful what you ask for: officials wrote back to say that all of Elder's requested names had been taken, so they had gone ahead and called it Bents. The town is now known for an annual giant beef-barbecue held by the Longworth family, who run a purebred cattle business.

BAY BULLS, NL: The first place in Newfoundland to be given an English name—it appears in a manuscript from 1592. Before that, almost all recorded European names there had been Portuguese or French. The "bulls" may be dovekies, or little auks (sometimes called bull birds or ice birds). Or the name may be a corruption of "Baie de Bois," French for "wooded bay." The harbour has been the site of several military conflicts and the bottom of the bay is littered with shipwrecks, some still visible from shore. The best-known wreck is that of HMS *Sapphire*, which was scuttled and burned to prevent an approaching French ship from taking her. The French crew boarded the wreck to salvage it just as the fire reached the ammunition stores, and the entire boarding party died in the explosion.

TRANSITION BAY, NU: A bay on Transition Lake, which sits in an area of layered intrusions, or geologic transition. The rocks to the southeast of the lake are peridotites; those to the northwest are gabbros.

ALTERITY

Homosexuality was decriminalized in Canada under Prime Minister Pierre Trudeau in 1969, two years after then Justice Minister Trudeau introduced a controversial act called the Omnibus Bill, which removed many sexual acts from the Criminal Code. When the media questioned Trudeau about the bill, he responded with one of his more famous statements: "There is no place for the state in the bedrooms of the nation."

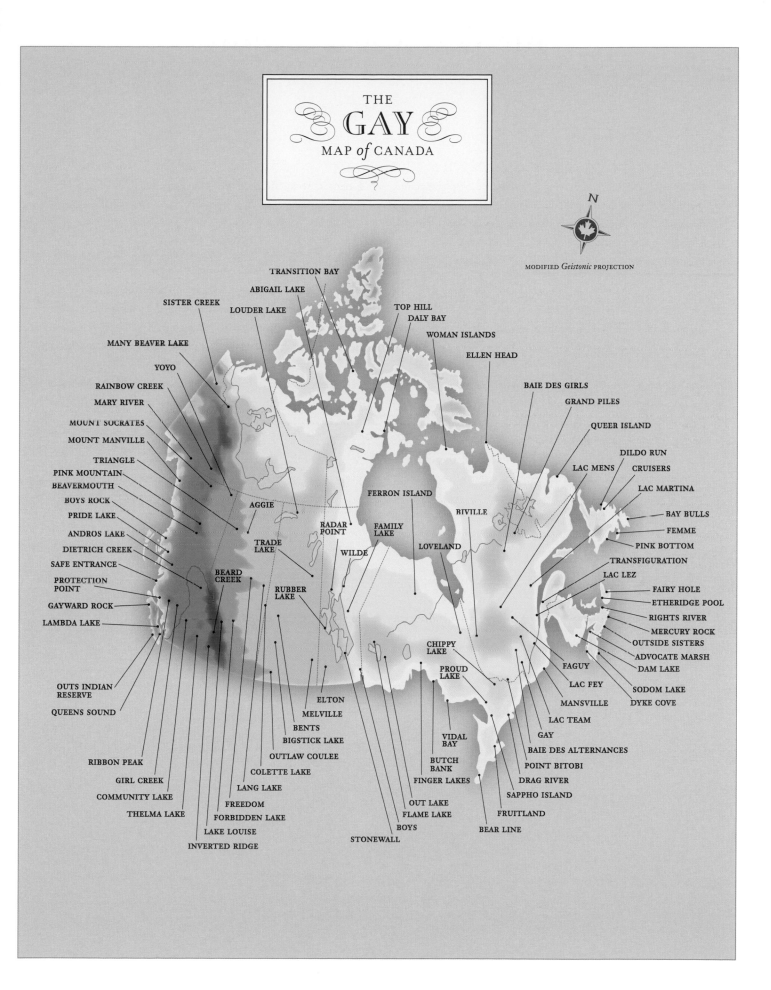

THE GAY MAP of CANADA

MODIFIED *Geistonic* PROJECTION

TRANSITION BAY
ABIGAIL LAKE
SISTER CREEK
LOUDER LAKE
MANY BEAVER LAKE
YOYO
RAINBOW CREEK
MARY RIVER
MOUNT SOCRATES
MOUNT MANVILLE
TRIANGLE
PINK MOUNTAIN
BEAVERMOUTH
BOYS ROCK
PRIDE LAKE
ANDROS LAKE
DIETRICH CREEK
SAFE ENTRANCE
PROTECTION POINT
GAYWARD ROCK
LAMBDA LAKE

TOP HILL
DALY BAY
WOMAN ISLANDS
ELLEN HEAD
BAIE DES GIRLS
GRAND PILES
QUEER ISLAND
DILDO RUN
LAC MENS
CRUISERS
LAC MARTINA
BAY BULLS
FEMME
PINK BOTTOM
TRANSFIGURATION
LAC LEZ
FAIRY HOLE
ETHERIDGE POOL
RIGHTS RIVER
MERCURY ROCK
OUTSIDE SISTERS
ADVOCATE MARSH
DAM LAKE
SODOM LAKE
DYKE COVE

FERRON ISLAND
RIVILLE
AGGIE
RADAR POINT
TRADE LAKE
FAMILY LAKE
WILDE
LOVELAND
BEARD CREEK
RUBBER LAKE

FAGUY
LAC FEY
MANSVILLE
LAC TEAM
GAY
BAIE DES ALTERNANCES
POINT BITOBI
DRAG RIVER
SAPPHO ISLAND
FRUITLAND
BEAR LINE

CHIPPY LAKE
PROUD LAKE

OUTS INDIAN RESERVE
QUEENS SOUND
ELTON
MELVILLE
BENTS
BIGSTICK LAKE
OUTLAW COULEE
RIBBON PEAK
COLETTE LAKE
GIRL CREEK
LANG LAKE
COMMUNITY LAKE
FREEDOM
THELMA LAKE
FORBIDDEN LAKE
LAKE LOUISE
INVERTED RIDGE

VIDAL BAY
BUTCH BANK
FINGER LAKES
OUT LAKE
FLAME LAKE
BOYS
STONEWALL

— 95 —

BACON, QC: Quebec's provincial database of place names describes this region as *inhabité et marécageux* ("uninhabited and marshy"). It was named in 1938 for Louis Bacon (1689–1767), a provincial land surveyor. Edward Bacon, a commissioner of trade in the mid-1700s, got Bacon Cove, PE (Map of Condiments, p. 32), while Bacon Creek, AB (Philosopher's Map, p. 76) may have been named for the actual meat.

MEAT COVE, NS: The original version of this map, published in *Geist*, neglected to include Meat Cove, and readers responded with a flood of letters asserting the significance—and eeriness—of the place. All of the letters describe the beauty of Cape Breton; several refer to (but do not describe) dark moments in the history of Meat Cove, and the strange or terrifying experiences of visitors in earlier years. Meat Cove consists of a tiny collection of houses at the end of a narrow road skirting a cliff, a community shack, and a campground managed by a man whose family has lived in Meat Cove for several hundred years. He tells visitors that the panoramic ocean view covers the graves of 300 fishermen, and that anyone who dared visit the island across from the cove would be "walking on bones." Meat Cove may have got its name from the abundance of game found here by explorers of the north coast; or from a cargo of meat that washed ashore after a shipwreck and became a feast for a group of early settlers.

CHOICELAND, SK: In 1927 a farmer named Pete Rotz suggested the name because this place was "a choice land and lots to choose from."

HEAD-SMASHED-IN-BUFFALO-JUMP, AB: The best known of several Alberta "buffalo jumps"—high cliffs that Blackfoot hunters once used to kill large numbers of buffalo by driving them through V-shaped fences over the cliff; more hunters waited at the bottom to finish them off. The "head-smashed-in" part comes from the story of a young hunter who waited too close to the bottom of the cliff and was crushed to death. Deep layers of buffalo bones and ancient tools found here have made Head-Smashed-In-Buffalo-Jump a UNESCO World Heritage Site.

BEEF TRAIL CREEK, BC: Ranchers used this Dean River tributary as a route to drive their cattle from the Chilcotin region of BC to markets on the coast at Bella Coola. There is a similar older colloquial term for the Alexander Mackenzie Trail, a historic hiking route that follows nearly the same path: the "Grease Trail." It was used to carry oolichan oil, a valuable trade item for coastal First Nations, from the coast to the interior, and became part of Mackenzie's trail in 1793. The oolichan is a silvery smelt so rich with oil that it can burst into flame when held over an open fire.

HOG STATS

Maple Leaf, Canada's largest pork producer, processed more than 6 million hogs in 2002, and in 2003 Canada exported almost 1 million tons of pork meat. At current production rates, Canada will become the world's fifth-largest pork producer, processing just shy of 2 million tonnes (2.2 million tons) of pork each year.

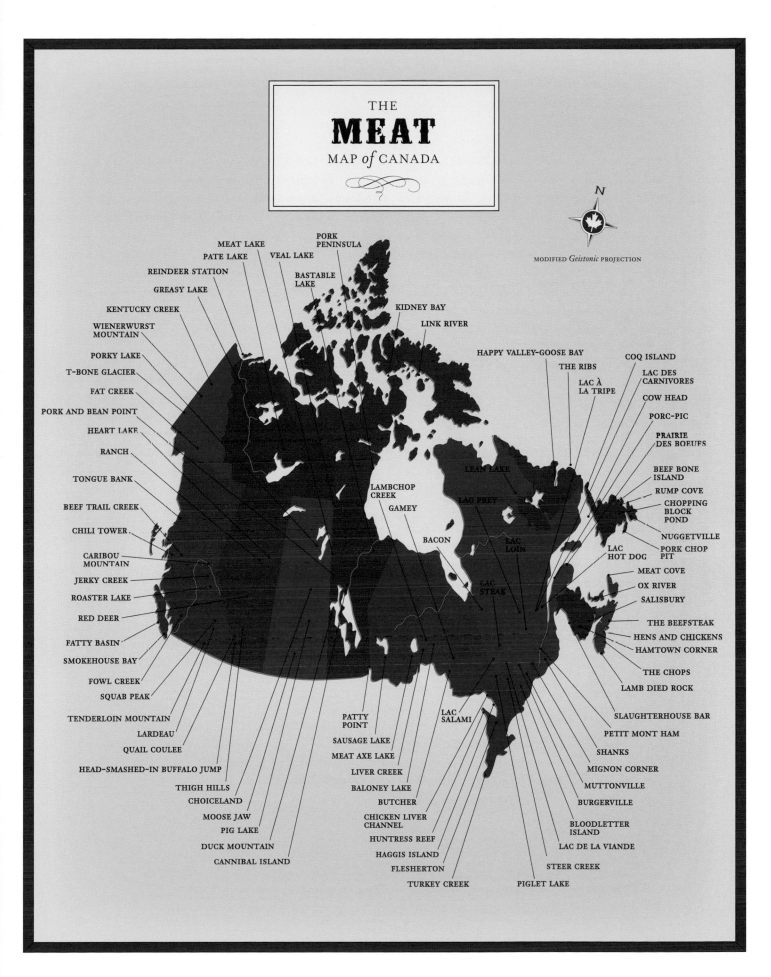

THE **MEAT** MAP *of* CANADA

N

MODIFIED *Geistonic* PROJECTION

MEAT LAKE
PATE LAKE
VEAL LAKE
REINDEER STATION
GREASY LAKE
KENTUCKY CREEK
WIENERWURST MOUNTAIN
PORKY LAKE
T-BONE GLACIER
FAT CREEK
PORK AND BEAN POINT
HEART LAKE
RANCH
TONGUE BANK
BEEF TRAIL CREEK
CHILI TOWER
CARIBOU MOUNTAIN
JERKY CREEK
ROASTER LAKE
RED DEER
FATTY BASIN
SMOKEHOUSE BAY
FOWL CREEK
SQUAB PEAK
TENDERLOIN MOUNTAIN
LARDEAU
QUAIL COULEE
HEAD-SMASHED-IN BUFFALO JUMP
THIGH HILLS
CHOICELAND
MOOSE JAW
PIG LAKE
DUCK MOUNTAIN
CANNIBAL ISLAND

PORK PENINSULA
BASTABLE LAKE
KIDNEY BAY
LINK RIVER

HAPPY VALLEY-GOOSE BAY
THE RIBS
LAC À LA TRIPE

COQ ISLAND
LAC DES CARNIVORES
COW HEAD
PORC-PIC
PRAIRIE DES BOEUFS
BEEF BONE ISLAND
RUMP COVE
CHOPPING BLOCK POND
NUGGETVILLE
PORK CHOP PIT
MEAT COVE
OX RIVER
SALISBURY
THE BEEFSTEAK
HENS AND CHICKENS
HAMTOWN CORNER
THE CHOPS
LAMB DIED ROCK
SLAUGHTERHOUSE BAR
PETIT MONT HAM
SHANKS
MIGNON CORNER
MUTTONVILLE
BURGERVILLE
BLOODLETTER ISLAND
LAC DE LA VIANDE
STEER CREEK
PIGLET LAKE

LAC HOT DOG

LEAN LAKE
LAG PREY
LAMBCHOP CREEK
GAMEY
BACON
LAC LOIN
LAC STEAK

LAC SALAMI
PATTY POINT
SAUSAGE LAKE
MEAT AXE LAKE
LIVER CREEK
BALONEY LAKE
BUTCHER
CHICKEN LIVER CHANNEL
HUNTRESS REEF
HAGGIS ISLAND
FLESHERTON
TURKEY CREEK

DILDO, NL: The name dates back to at least 1711 (as Dildoe), and its origins are much debated. It may be an old slang word for having the blues, a meaningless word used in a song refrain (a sort of old-fashioned "ob-la-di, ob-la-da"), a local word for an oarlock peg, an antiquated word for rippling water—or exactly what it means today: a phallus. Dildo, along with Dildo Arm, Dildo Cove, Dildo Run, Dildo Island, and South Dildo, is one of many curious Canadian town names that have survived repeated attempts to change them (see notes on Malignant Cove, Angst Map, p. 18, and Swastika, ON, Map of Kitchen Implements, p. 30, and many places noted on the Impolite Map, p. 42). *Harrowsmith* magazine named Dildo one of the ten prettiest small towns in Canada in 2001. The mascot of a school in Dildo is a teddy bear named "Woody."

CLIMAX, SK: Ranchers from the US settled the region at the end of the nineteenth century. Its first big ranch was called Turkey Track, and the owners had to sell it after the bitterly cold winter of 1906–1907 killed off much of their herd. The name was registered when the railway reached the village in the 1920s. It was selected by two Scandinavian settlers, Fred and Christer Fuglestad, who may have chosen it to reflect some pinnacle of economic success. Today, Climax is a favourite spot for road-trippers who like to have their picture taken in front of the large, well-kept Climax grain elevator.

BEAVER CREEK, YT: Canada's national mascot lends its name to hundreds of towns, rivers, and lakes across the country. Beaver Creek, YT, is among the more notable of these because it is the westernmost town in Canada. It was founded in 1955 as a service station for vehicles on the Alaska Highway, and marks the spot where the bulldozers working on the southern and northern legs of the highway met, blade to blade, in 1942. At that time the highway—now considered one of the world's most scenic drives—was a narrow dirt track marked by 133 log bridges and frequently mired by muskeg.

BAIE HOPES ADVANCE, QC: The bay and cape of Hopes Advance and its sister cape of Hopes Checked reflect the ups and downs of Captain Thomas Button, who searched for the Northwest Passage and Henry Hudson (see notes on Button, Sartorial Map, p. 48) in the early 1600s. Hudson had already recorded the spot on his charts as Cape Prince Henri, following the notes of Samuel de Champlain. The Inuktitut name for the cape is Nuvuk ("the cape").

FLESHERTON, ON: A Grey County village founded in 1853 by William Kingston Flesher, a sawmill developer. The town was originally called Artemesia, but the post office stood on a site called Flesher's Corners and the town was better known by that name, so a compromise was eventually made official. Flesherton, which gets a lot of tourist traffic, is now known as the "Gateway to Beaver Valley."

SEXY STATS

A 2002 survey in *Maclean's* magazine found that Quebec had the greatest percentage of people who consider themselves sexually active (75 percent), followed by Newfoundland (66 percent). Residents of BC, Manitoba, and Saskatchewan were tied for having the fewest sexually active people (58 percent).

The
EROTIC
Map of Canada

N

MODIFIED *Geistonic* PROJECTION

HUMP ISLAND   KNOB HILL
LOVE LAKE
BRAS D'OR LAKE   STRIP LAKE
GREASY LAKE   CAPE COME AGAIN
WET GULCH   THE BUTTOCKS
BEAVER CREEK   BURSTING BROOK
STEAMBATH LAKE   BAIE HOPES ADVANCE
SCREW CREEK   GOOSE BAY
TIGHTFIT LAKE   LAC DU PÉNIS   THE TITS
SPANKIE LAKE   DU CARIBOU   BED HEAD
SIN LAKE   LEADING TICKLES
MOAN CREEK   LOVE BAY   NAKED MAN
THE NIPPLES   LUST LAKE   LOVE MAN BANK
                               SWALLOW LAKE   SPREAD EAGLE
SHAG ROCK   CUDDLE LAKE   COCK AND   DICK BURNS
INSIDE PASSAGE   HEN HOLE   ROCK
LEATHER PEAK   UNITY   STRIP RAPIDS   PINCHGUT
LUST SUBDIVISION   COUPLE LAKE   GASPÉ   TICKLE
THE BLOWHOLE   DILDO
TICKLETOETEASER   BALL LAKE   SOUTH DILDO
   TOWER   MOUNT   BARE BUM POND
EASY INLET   SEXSMITH   BARE   DOMINANT   TOUCH AND TICKLE SHOAL
GOLDEN HINDE   BUTT   LAC ÉROS   ÉTANG
MATE ISLANDS   BAY   SLIPPERY STICK
NYMPH POINT   THE TONGUE
CUMSACK MOUNTAIN   KISSING BROOK
TABOO CREEK   BOOBEY BROOK
PEEKABOO FALLS   LOVERS COVE
MOUNT LOVEWAY   HARDWICK LAKE
BEAVER DELL   LUCKY   LAC LOVELACE SODOM LAKE
LICK PEAK   LAKE   LAC DE
SUCK CREEK   CLIMAX   LA CARESSE
                                             LAC LATEX
                    BIGSTICK   SWELL   CUMMING DRAIN
                    LAKE   BAY   RIVIÈRE ASSUP
                    CONSORT   LIP CREEK   PEELER
                    MOUND   CUMAWAY CREEK   LAKE
              FORBIDDEN LAKE   TEASE LAKE   BATH
          BREASTWORK HILL   PUSSY LAKE   BOTTOM LANDS
                              CRUISE LAKE   LAC BRASSIÈRE
            NUT MOUNTAIN   CREAM LAKE   FLESHERTON
            RUBBER LAKE   GRAB LAKE   OIL SPRINGS
         HAIRY MAN POINT   MIDDLESEX
            LONG POINT
         HARDMANS LAKE

PORT MOODY, BC: A suburb of Vancouver named by George Richards, captain of HMS *Plumper*, for Colonel Richard Clement Moody, a former Commissioner of Lands and Works for BC. Vancouver was once a subordinate town to Port Moody, which was the original western terminus of the Canadian Pacific Railway—but power, like moods, shifts quickly. The station at Port Moody welcomed the first transcontinental passenger train in 1886.

PLACENTIA, NL: Named by the French in 1662 as Plaisance, though similar-sounding names were used before then by Basque fishers (who may have named it for a Spanish town called Plasencia). Placentia was a fortified base for French attacks on the British until it was handed over in defeat in 1713.

BELLY RIVER, AB: The Oldman, the river that runs through Lethbridge, used to be the Belly River, but "belly" was considered a rude word in the 1890s. In *Naming Canada*, Alan Rayburn quotes from a letter from the Lethbridge Board of Trade: "We are certainly much disgusted with the present name, and wish to make a change of some kind." It took the belly-haters until 1915 to distance the town from the name: the final fix was to extend the Oldman officially until it met the Bow River, making the remains of Belly River a tributary far from Lethbridge city limits. The name comes from the Blackfoot word "*mokowanis*" ("big bellies"), a pejorative name for the Atsina First Nation, who lived on the river and whom the Blackfoot supposedly considered to be spongers.

LAC TAMPON, QC: Not such a strange name, considering that "*tampon*" is French for "plug."

RED RIVER, MB: Until about 1740, Rivière Rouge, translated from the original Cree name, Miscousipi ("red water river"). In the eighteenth and nineteenth centuries, the Red River was a critical trading route for the Hudson's Bay Company. Lord Selkirk, then governor of the HBC, founded the Red River Colony in 1812, but after years of regular flooding, conflict with the North West Company and skirmishes with the Metis, the HBC handed the land over to Canada. The Metis resisted this new domination by the anglophone confederation and began the Red River Rebellion, which eventually led to the establishment of the province of Manitoba. Communities along the river still face annual flooding—a problem exacerbated by retreating mountain glaciers farther south and, some say, by the floodway built to protect Winnipeg in 1968.

REGULATING THE DEVICE

Tampons are considered medical devices in Canada, and, as a result, are regulated by Health Canada. The rules say that all tampons sold in Canada must conform to a standardized system of quality measurement. This means that the absorbency of every tampon is exactly the same within the "light," "regular," and "ultra" specifications—no brand can legally be more absorbent than any other.

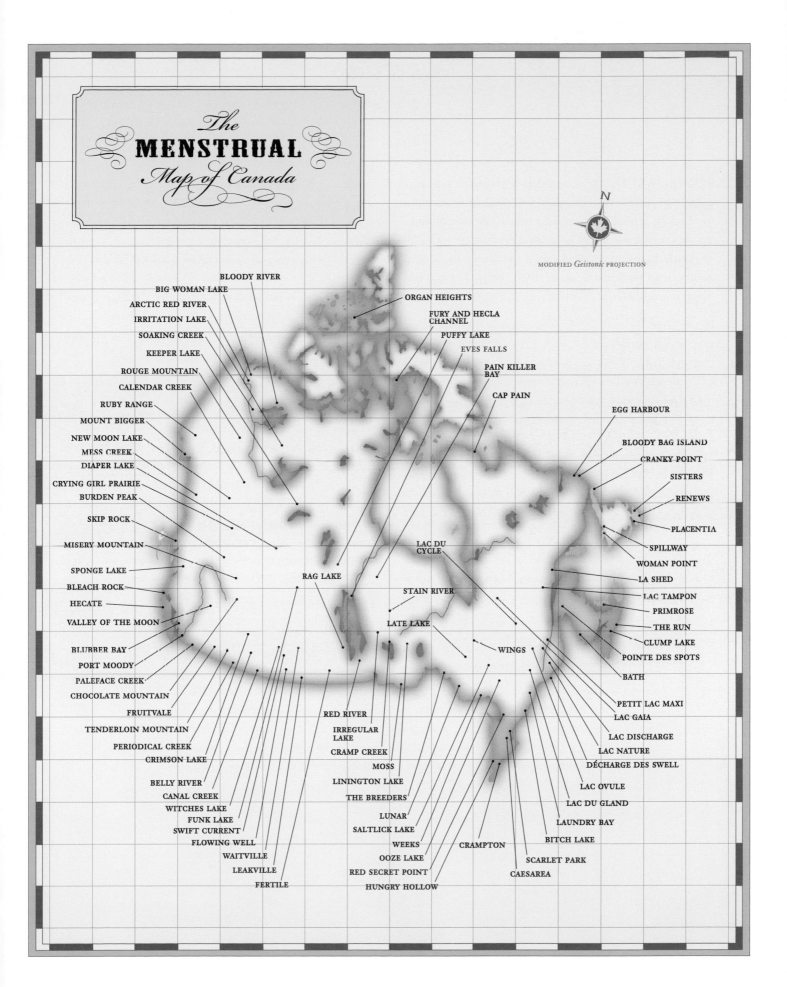

The
MENSTRUAL
Map of Canada

N

MODIFIED *Geistonic* PROJECTION

BLOODY RIVER
BIG WOMAN LAKE
ARCTIC RED RIVER
IRRITATION LAKE
SOAKING CREEK
KEEPER LAKE
ROUGE MOUNTAIN
CALENDAR CREEK
RUBY RANGE
MOUNT BIGGER
NEW MOON LAKE
MESS CREEK
DIAPER LAKE
CRYING GIRL PRAIRIE
BURDEN PEAK
SKIP ROCK
MISERY MOUNTAIN
SPONGE LAKE
BLEACH ROCK
HECATE
VALLEY OF THE MOON
BLUBBER BAY
PORT MOODY
PALEFACE CREEK
CHOCOLATE MOUNTAIN
FRUITVALE
TENDERLOIN MOUNTAIN
PERIODICAL CREEK
CRIMSON LAKE
BELLY RIVER
CANAL CREEK
WITCHES LAKE
FUNK LAKE
SWIFT CURRENT
FLOWING WELL
WAITVILLE
LEAKVILLE
FERTILE

ORGAN HEIGHTS
FURY AND HECLA CHANNEL
PUFFY LAKE
EVES FALLS
PAIN KILLER BAY
CAP PAIN

RAG LAKE

LAC DU CYCLE
STAIN RIVER
LATE LAKE
WINGS

RED RIVER
IRREGULAR LAKE
CRAMP CREEK
MOSS
LININGTON LAKE
THE BREEDERS
LUNAR
SALTLICK LAKE
WEEKS
OOZE LAKE
RED SECRET POINT
HUNGRY HOLLOW
CRAMPTON

EGG HARBOUR
BLOODY BAG ISLAND
CRANKY POINT
SISTERS
RENEWS
PLACENTIA
SPILLWAY
WOMAN POINT
LA SHED
LAC TAMPON
PRIMROSE
THE RUN
CLUMP LAKE
POINTE DES SPOTS
BATH
PETIT LAC MAXI
LAC GAIA
LAC DISCHARGE
LAC NATURE
DÉCHARGE DES SWELL
LAC OVULE
LAC DU GLAND
LAUNDRY BAY
BITCH LAKE
SCARLET PARK
CAESAREA

Manifold Destiny

BENTLEY, AB: The agrarian settlers in this town wanted to name it for Major Macpherson, a US civil war veteran who founded the general store and post office. The sawmill workers wanted to name it for George Bentley, a sawyer with a lot of friends. Each group used its own name, but the millworkers outnumbered the farmers, and by 1906 Bentley had won out. Today it is the home of Alberta's largest recumbent bike shop.

PLYMOUTH (PARK), NS: An unincorporated region near Stellarton in Pictou County, named for Plymouth in England. In May 1992 a huge explosion at the Westray Mine in Plymouth killed twenty-six miners, who were at work on the Foord coal seam, which is rich in methane gas. A nearby mine that had previously worked the Foord seam had suffered eight explosions between the 1920s and the 1950s. The explosion at Plymouth occurred a mile underground, yet it blew the top off the mine entrance and shook houses on the surface. More than 600 people have died in mining accidents in Pictou County since coal mining began there in the early 1800s.

TOW HILL, BC: A small mountain on the north coast of the Queen Charlotte Islands (Haida Gwaii) and the most visible feature on North Beach, which according to Haida legend is the birthplace of creation, where Raven released humanity from its clamshell. The hill is a well-known landmark to residents of Masset, the largest community on the Charlottes, and the path to its peak (you can see Alaska from there on a clear day) is popular with hikers. The name may have come from a Haida word relating to grease or food. In English it was originally pronounced to rhyme with "cow," but the mountain's slight resemblance to a toe changed the common pronunciation over time.

LAC DU MOTEUR GRUGÉ, QC: A lake named in 1996 to commemorate a boat engine that was dinged up by a porcupine.

KARS, ON: A town on the Rideau River originally called Wellington and renamed for General Sir William Fenwick Williams, a hero of the battle of Waterloo. Williams had led the Turks in a defence of the village of Kars against the Russians during the Crimean War. The town got on the *Geist* map because its name evokes KARR, the evil twin of KITT, the crime-fighting robot car that starred alongside David Hasselhoff in the 1980s TV show *Knight Rider*.

CANADAUTO

One of the better known of a very few Canadian automobiles is the Bricklin, an acrylic-bodied sports car with gull-wing doors, developed and manufactured in the 1970s in Saint John, NB. The Bricklin inspired a lot of excitement in New Brunswick but it sold poorly, and when the company folded in 1975 (after producing only 2,854 vehicles), it left the province with a debt of $23 million. A few collectible Bricklins are still on the road, and about 100 Bricklin drivers meet regularly in Saint John to share their enthusiasm. Another more successful Canadian car, ultramodern in its time, was the Studebaker, produced in Hamilton, ON, from 1948 until 1966.

THE AUTOMOTIVE
MAP *of* CANADA

N

MODIFIED *Geistonic* PROJECTION

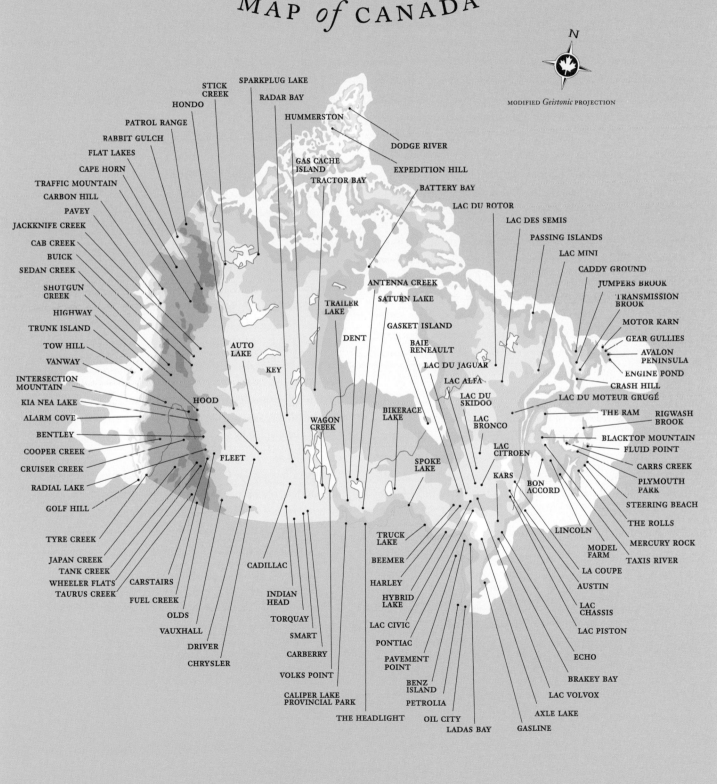

STICK CREEK
SPARKPLUG LAKE
HONDO
RADAR BAY
PATROL RANGE
HUMMERSTON
RABBIT GULCH
DODGE RIVER
FLAT LAKES
GAS CACHE ISLAND
EXPEDITION HILL
CAPE HORN
TRACTOR BAY
TRAFFIC MOUNTAIN
BATTERY BAY
CARBON HILL
LAC DU ROTOR
PAVEY
LAC DES SEMIS
JACKKNIFE CREEK
PASSING ISLANDS
CAB CREEK
LAC MINI
BUICK
CADDY GROUND
SEDAN CREEK
JUMPERS BROOK
ANTENNA CREEK
SHOTGUN CREEK
SATURN LAKE
TRANSMISSION BROOK
HIGHWAY
TRAILER LAKE
MOTOR KARN
TRUNK ISLAND
GASKET ISLAND
GEAR GULLIES
TOW HILL
DENT
AVALON PENINSULA
VANWAY
AUTO LAKE
BAIE RENEAULT
ENGINE POND
INTERSECTION MOUNTAIN
KEY
LAC DU JAGUAR
CRASH HILL
KIA NEA LAKE
LAC ALFA
LAC DU MOTEUR GRUGÉ
ALARM COVE
HOOD
LAC DU SKIDOO
THE RAM
RIGWASH BROOK
BENTLEY
BIKERACE LAKE
LAC BRONCO
BLACKTOP MOUNTAIN
COOPER CREEK
WAGON CREEK
FLUID POINT
CRUISER CREEK
FLEET
LAC CITROEN
CARRS CREEK
RADIAL LAKE
SPOKE LAKE
KARS
PLYMOUTH PARK
GOLF HILL
BON ACCORD
STEERING BEACH
TYRE CREEK
THE ROLLS
JAPAN CREEK
TRUCK LAKE
LINCOLN
MERCURY ROCK
TANK CREEK
CARSTAIRS
BEEMER
MODEL FARM
WHEELER FLATS
CADILLAC
HARLEY
TAXIS RIVER
TAURUS CREEK
FUEL CREEK
HYBRID LAKE
LA COUPE
OLDS
INDIAN HEAD
AUSTIN
VAUXHALL
TORQUAY
LAC CIVIC
LAC CHASSIS
DRIVER
SMART
PONTIAC
LAC PISTON
CHRYSLER
CARBERRY
PAVEMENT POINT
ECHO
VOLKS POINT
BENZ ISLAND
BRAKEY BAY
CALIPER LAKE PROVINCIAL PARK
PETROLIA
LAC VOLVOX
THE HEADLIGHT
OIL CITY
AXLE LAKE
LADAS BAY
GASLINE

HAPPY ADVENTURE, NL: Named by a sea captain who considered the discovery of a safe harbour in a gale a "happy adventure," or for a pirate ship belonging to Captain Peter Easton. Heart's Content, another cheery-sounding Newfoundland village, is also believed to be named for a ship. Heart's Content was the western terminus of the world's first functional underwater transatlantic telegraph cable (extending to Valentia Island, Ireland) and for a while was a thriving global communications hub. Heart's Delight and Heart's Desire, two nearby towns, were likely named for PR reasons.

HOPE, BC: Founded as a military fort during the Fraser River Gold Rush in the 1850s, on the site of an old Hudson's Bay Company trading post and named for the hope that the trail leading from the fort would be a secure route for British troops to travel to and from Fort Kamloops (it was). Today, Hope is considered the end of Vancouver's urban footprint: everyone southwest of the town is urban and everyone northeast is not. People on each side refer to those on the other side to be "beyond Hope."

MT. NIRVANA, NT: An unofficial name, given to this peak in the Ragged Range in the 1960s by mountaineer William Buckingham. It is the highest mountain in the Northwest Territories (2,773 metres/9,098 feet). Another happy hill, Tip Top Mountain, ON (appearing on the Retail Map, p. 88), was considered the highest mountain in Ontario (640 metres/2,100 feet) until 1966, when the Ishpatina Ridge (Ojibwa for "high hill," another happy name) was discovered to be fifty-three metres (175 feet) higher.

PLEASANT GROVE, PE: Named by its first postmaster, for a stand of beech trees.

GLADSTONE, MB: Originally Third Crossing, for the third crossing of the Saskatchewan Trail over the Whitemud River. In 1871 it was changed to Palestine to reflect the bounty of the Promised Land (as in the children's rhyme that goes "Jenny Hammel now divine/ Called the country Palestine"). In 1879 the name was changed again to Gladstone, perhaps to honour W.E. Gladstone, a British prime minister who served several terms during the 1800s. Or it may have been named for a local politician's uppity horse (which may, in turn, have been named for the prime minister). Today, Gladstone has a large monument of a smiling, top-hatted rock on the highway outside of town, which didn't make the World's Largest Map (p. 108) because it wasn't the world's largest rock, though it does resemble the smiling, top-hatted World's Largest Potato outside Maugerville, NB. Gladstone made it onto the Map of City Nicknames (p. 40), however, thanks to its moniker, "Happy Rock." The town is a leader in the promotion of bat habitat as a weapon against mosquitoes, a true enemy of Canadian happiness. Gladstone's website includes free plans for building bat houses on personal property.

HAPPINESS IS . . .

A survey in 2005 found that 93 percent of Canadians consider themselves to be happy. Slightly more than half of those described their feelings as "very" happy. Three-quarters of Canadians said they were happier than they were five years ago.

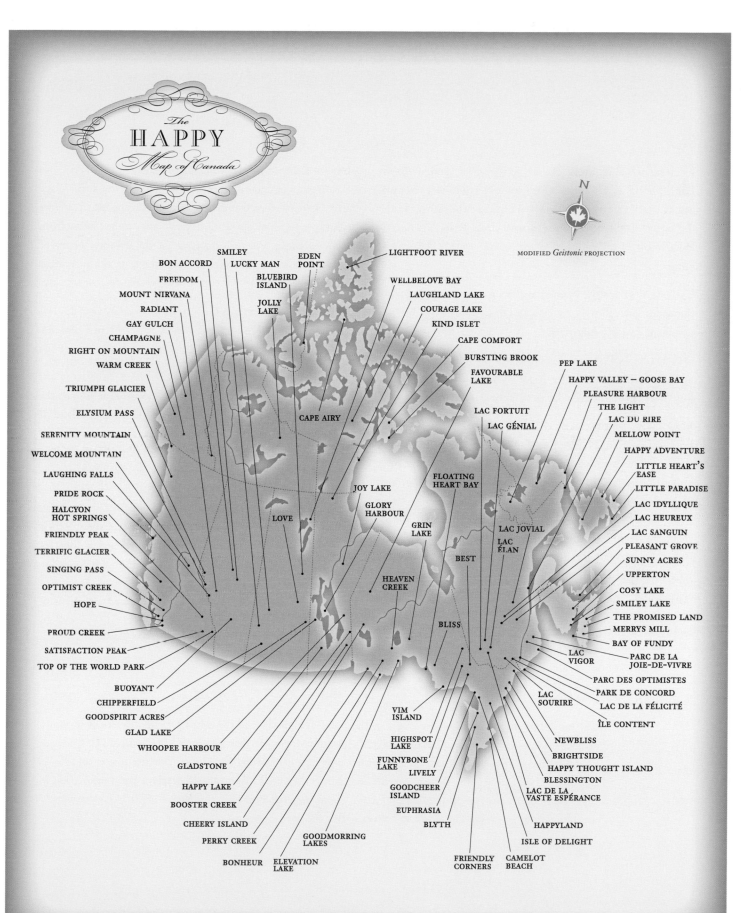

The HAPPY Map of Canada

N

MODIFIED *Geistonic* PROJECTION

SMILEY
BON ACCORD
LUCKY MAN
EDEN POINT
LIGHTFOOT RIVER
FREEDOM
BLUEBIRD ISLAND
WELLBELOVE BAY
MOUNT NIRVANA
JOLLY LAKE
LAUGHLAND LAKE
RADIANT
COURAGE LAKE
GAY GULCH
KIND ISLET
CHAMPAGNE
CAPE COMFORT
RIGHT ON MOUNTAIN
BURSTING BROOK
PEP LAKE
WARM CREEK
FAVOURABLE LAKE
HAPPY VALLEY – GOOSE BAY
TRIUMPH GLAICIER
PLEASURE HARBOUR
ELYSIUM PASS
CAPE AIRY
LAC FORTUIT
THE LIGHT
SERENITY MOUNTAIN
LAC GÉNIAL
LAC DU RIRE
WELCOME MOUNTAIN
MELLOW POINT
LAUGHING FALLS
HAPPY ADVENTURE
JOY LAKE
FLOATING HEART BAY
LITTLE HEART'S EASE
PRIDE ROCK
GLORY HARBOUR
LITTLE PARADISE
HALCYON HOT SPRINGS
LOVE
LAC IDYLLIQUE
FRIENDLY PEAK
GRIN LAKE
LAC HEUREUX
TERRIFIC GLACIER
LAC JOVIAL
LAC SANGUIN
SINGING PASS
LAC ÉLAN
PLEASANT GROVE
OPTIMIST CREEK
BEST
SUNNY ACRES
HOPE
UPPERTON
HEAVEN CREEK
COSY LAKE
PROUD CREEK
SMILEY LAKE
SATISFACTION PEAK
THE PROMISED LAND
BLISS
MERRYS MILL
TOP OF THE WORLD PARK
BAY OF FUNDY
LAC VIGOR
PARC DE LA JOIE-DE-VIVRE
BUOYANT
PARC DES OPTIMISTES
CHIPPERFIELD
LAC SOURIRE
PARK DE CONCORD
GOODSPIRIT ACRES
VIM ISLAND
LAC DE LA FÉLICITÉ
GLAD LAKE
ÎLE CONTENT
WHOOPEE HARBOUR
HIGHSPOT LAKE
NEWBLISS
GLADSTONE
FUNNYBONE LAKE
BRIGHTSIDE
LIVELY
HAPPY THOUGHT ISLAND
HAPPY LAKE
GOODCHEER ISLAND
BLESSINGTON
BOOSTER CREEK
LAC DE LA VASTE ESPÉRANCE
CHEERY ISLAND
EUPHRASIA
PERKY CREEK
GOODMORRING LAKES
BLYTH
HAPPYLAND
BONHEUR
ELEVATION LAKE
ISLE OF DELIGHT
FRIENDLY CORNERS
CAMELOT BEACH

FREEZEOUT BAY, MB: A bay at the south end of Reed Lake, once a winter camp where workers could rest the pull horses that dragged loads from the mines to the railway loading point. Today the lake is part of Grass River Provincial Park, home of the historic "Grass Route" canoe trails and a number of high-end fishing resorts.

LAC DU VIRUS, QC: Named in 1999 for an employee of the Outardes sawmill who got sick and passed out while he was operating forestry machinery.

OVERTON, NS: A small community on the western shore of Yarmouth's narrow inlet. It got its name because the town was "over the harbour" relative to Yarmouth.

MASSACRE BUTTE, AB: A landmark off the Crowsnest Highway near the confluence of the Crowsnest and Oldman rivers. At this site in 1867, a patrol group of Blood warriors under the leadership of Chief Medicine Calf killed a group of twelve settlers. The travellers had been heading from Minnesota to Oregon with Captain Fiske's wagon train, but they split from that group after hearing rumours of gold near Fort Edmonton. A popular version of the story glorifies the settlers' side of the battle, in which they circle their wagons against the oncoming warriors and fight valiantly for days, but in reality Chief Medicine Calf and his men lay in wait and launched an ambush after nightfall.

LANDS END, NT: Harald Ulrik Sverdrup (1888–1957), an oceanographer and explorer from Norway, named this place after drift ice forced him to camp off the north tip of the island, more than three kilometres (two miles) away from land. Sverdrup was the originator of the balance theory of ocean circulation, which relates wind forces to the movement of the upper ocean.

DOWN FALL ISLAND, NU: Named in 1968 by Dr. J.D. Ives of the Institute of Arctic and Alpine Research in Colorado, after a helicopter he was travelling in hit a 300-metre (984-foot) air pocket and nearly crashed on the island.

ALERT BAY, BC: A village on tiny Cormorant Island, the oldest community on the north coast of Vancouver Island. It has a population of about 1,500 people, approximately half of whom belong to the Kwakwaka'wakw First Nation. The economy of Alert Bay depends mainly on fishing, but tourism is a growing concern (Alert Bay has the world's tallest totem pole). In summer it is also a hotspot for sighting killer whales, which come to the region to float and scratch their hides in the gravel shallows. Alert Bay was named in 1860 for HMS *Alert*, a seventeen-gun British warship that belonged to the Pacific fleet.

VISIONS OF THE END

Eleven Canadian members of the Order of the Solar Temple died in the mid-1990s in a series of group suicides that occurred in Switzerland and at the group's Morin Heights compound in Quebec. The Order was founded in Geneva by Luc Jouret, a former motivational speaker for Hydro Quebec. Jouret told his followers that Quebec was the Promised Land, where they could wait out the warfare and famine that were destined to destroy civilization on Earth. There were rumours that insiders at Hydro Quebec were building dams to power the surviving colonies after the apocalypse.

THE
APOCALYPSE
MAP *of* CANADA

N

MODIFIED *Geistonic* PROJECTION

LANDS END

TERROR BAY

IMPACT LAKE

METHANE LAKE

END LAKE

FIRE LAKE

LAST CALL LAKE

DESTRUCTION BAY

RED STAR

DEATH RIVER

THE TERMINATOR

THE VOLCANO

DISASTER POINT

EXTINGUISHER
MOUNTAIN

RAGNAROK GLACIER

FINALITY MOUNTAIN

KALI PEAK

THE BEAST

KINGCOME

EXPERIMENT
BIGHT

ALERT BAY

DOOM MOUNTAIN

INCINERATOR ROCK

ADIEU
MOUNTAIN

EXPLOSIVES CREEK

FALL OF THE WAVES

HORSEMAN SPIRE

REVELATION LAKE

METEOR BASIN

GOG LAKE & MOUNT MAGOG

MOUNT ANDROMEDA

FLARE CREEK

MASSACRE BUTTE

CARBON

DINOSAUR

CLIMAX

WARTIME

BIOLOGY BAY

BLIGHT LAKE

CATASTROPHE
CREEK

POPULUS
LAKE

LIMITED LAKE

DIE LAKE

OZONE CREEK

NOVA

FLOOD

COMET

ATOMIC
LAKE

BURNS

BRIMSTONE

MORLOCK ISLAND

LOCUST HILL

ASHBALL LAKE

LAC ADVENT

LAC SYBILLIN

LAC DE L'ASTÉRÖIDE

LAC BABYLONE

LAC DE LA CODA

POISON LAKE

OVERTON

DEVASTATION
SHOAL

CHEMICAL CREEK

BLACK HOLE

THE BOOM

LAC ALIEN

CURTAINS COVE

WAR HEAD

CHANGE LOOKOUT

LAC DU FEU

LAC DU VIRUS

THE SINKER

LAC FAMINE

LAC ICEBOUND

ÎLE PROPHET

EARTHQUAKE ISLAND

DOWN FALL ISLAND

ZENITH POINT

RIOT ROCK

OMEGA LAKE

FREEZOUT
BAY

JUDGE LAKE

Where the Big Things Are

VEGREVILLE, AB: The Vegreville *pysanka* (traditional Ukrainian Easter egg) is nine metres (thirty-one feet) high and eight metres (twenty-six feet) long, and is decorated in an intricate pattern of squares and triangles, similar to the design of a quilt. The pole base on which it sits allows the big egg to swivel with the prairie winds. The monument was erected in 1974 to mark the centennial of the northern Alberta branch of the RCMP. The region has a large Ukrainian population: a large perogy has been installed in Glendon, AB, and in Mundare, AB, a large Ukrainian sausage. Though it is still predominantly a farming community, Vegreville's economy got a big boost in 1994 when it became a large federal immigration-processing centre. Most applications to immigrate to Canada are processed and judged by residents of Vegreville.

MAUGERVILLE, NB: O'Leary, PE, and this town claim to have the biggest potatoes on the east coast, though the O'Leary potato is a Russet Burbank and the Maugerville potato (that's pronounced "mayor-ville," not "mogger-ville") wears a hat. Both potatoes were included on this map to help balance the disproportionately higher concentration of "largest" things in the Prairie provinces.

COLEMAN, AB: Both this town and Williams Lake, BC, claimed to have the world's largest piggybank, but Henri Robideau, author of *Canada's Gigantic*, has seen both and asserts that Coleman's is the larger one—roughly the size of a railcar.

OFF THE MAP

Vermilion Bay, ON, isn't included on the map because its attraction isn't officially advertised as being the "largest in the world." That attraction is a very large "mutant hitchhiker" built in the 1960s in the town of Waldhof and moved to its present location outside a Vermilion Bay Texaco station in the 1980s. The proprietor of the station used to run out and animate his mutant by making noises into a megaphone when people passed by; when the technology was updated, the hitchhiker got a speaker system. Its costume has been updated, too: once it sported a big pair of floral boxer shorts, but now it wears a green loincloth, more becoming a monster.

WORLD'S LARGEST, AMERICAN-STYLE

Termite—Providence, RI; Boll Weevil—Enterprise, AL; Six-Pack of Beer—La Crosse, WI; Jackalope—Douglas, WY; Frying Pan—Long Beach, WA; Dog Dish—Bloomington, MN; Fruit Cocktail Can—Sunnyvale, CA; Ball of Barbed Wire, Jackson, WY; Rosary Beads—Newport, RI; Stack of Empty Oil Cans—Casselton, ND; Incandescent Light Bulb—Menlo Park, NJ; Porch Swing—Hebron, NE; Office Chair—Anniston, AL; Running Chain Saw and Working Rifle—Ishpeming, MI.

THE WORLD'S LARGEST MAP of CANADA

N

MODIFIED *Geistonic* PROJECTION

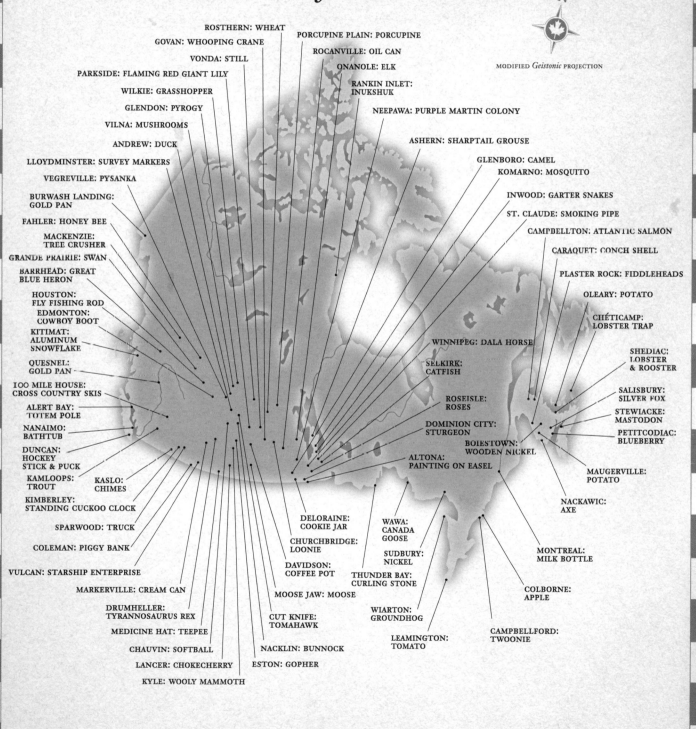

ROSTHERN: WHEAT

GOVAN: WHOOPING CRANE

PORCUPINE PLAIN: PORCUPINE

VONDA: STILL

ROCANVILLE: OIL CAN

PARKSIDE: FLAMING RED GIANT LILY

ONANOLE: ELK

WILKIE: GRASSHOPPER

RANKIN INLET: INUKSHUK

GLENDON: PYROGY

NEEPAWA: PURPLE MARTIN COLONY

VILNA: MUSHROOMS

ANDREW: DUCK

ASHERN: SHARPTAIL GROUSE

LLOYDMINSTER: SURVEY MARKERS

GLENBORO: CAMEL

VEGREVILLE: PYSANKA

KOMARNO: MOSQUITO

BURWASH LANDING: GOLD PAN

INWOOD: GARTER SNAKES

FAHLER: HONEY BEE

ST. CLAUDE: SMOKING PIPE

MACKENZIE: TREE CRUSHER

CAMPBELLTON: ATLANTIC SALMON

GRANDE PRAIRIE: SWAN

CARAQUET: CONCH SHELL

BARRHEAD: GREAT BLUE HERON

PLASTER ROCK: FIDDLEHEADS

HOUSTON: FLY FISHING ROD

OLEARY: POTATO

EDMONTON: COWBOY BOOT

CHÉTICAMP: LOBSTER TRAP

KITIMAT: ALUMINUM SNOWFLAKE

WINNIPEG: DALA HORSE

SHEDIAC: LOBSTER & ROOSTER

QUESNEL: GOLD PAN

SELKIRK: CATFISH

100 MILE HOUSE: CROSS COUNTRY SKIS

SALISBURY: SILVER FOX

ALERT BAY: TOTEM POLE

ROSEISLE: ROSES

STEWIACKE: MASTODON

NANAIMO: BATHTUB

DOMINION CITY: STURGEON

PETITCODIAC: BLUEBERRY

DUNCAN: HOCKEY STICK & PUCK

BOIESTOWN: WOODEN NICKEL

KAMLOOPS: TROUT

KASLO: CHIMES

ALTONA: PAINTING ON EASEL

MAUGERVILLE: POTATO

KIMBERLEY: STANDING CUCKOO CLOCK

NACKAWIC: AXE

SPARWOOD: TRUCK

DELORAINE: COOKIE JAR

WAWA: CANADA GOOSE

COLEMAN: PIGGY BANK

CHURCHBRIDGE: LOONIE

SUDBURY: NICKEL

MONTREAL: MILK BOTTLE

VULCAN: STARSHIP ENTERPRISE

DAVIDSON: COFFEE POT

THUNDER BAY: CURLING STONE

MARKERVILLE: CREAM CAN

MOOSE JAW: MOOSE

COLBORNE: APPLE

DRUMHELLER: TYRANNOSAURUS REX

WIARTON: GROUNDHOG

MEDICINE HAT: TEEPEE

CUT KNIFE: TOMAHAWK

CAMPBELLFORD: TWOONIE

CHAUVIN: SOFTBALL

NACKLIN: BUNNOCK

LEAMINGTON: TOMATO

LANCER: CHOKECHERRY

ESTON: GOPHER

KYLE: WOOLY MAMMOTH

LA TUQUE, QC: Originally a portage named Ushabatshuan, but the voyageurs called it La Tuque because a nearby rock feature resembled their classic Canadian wool headwear (which itself likely got its name from *tuc*, a French word for a high rock—everything comes full circle). In 2003 La Tuque merged with the village of Parent and several other municipalities, making it the largest municipal land area in Quebec and the second largest in Canada, at 29,000 square kilometres (9,266 square miles). La Tuque relies mainly on a pulp-and-paper economy, but it also has a sizable tourist industry, and hosts an annual international canoe race.

DOMINION, NS: The word "dominion," once the definition of the country, has fallen out of use. It took its worst hit in 1982, when July 1 was changed from Dominion Day to Canada Day. About six Canadian towns, a provincial park, and a bunch of hills and wetlands still honour the word in their names, however. Dominion, NS, took its name from the Dominion Coal Company in 1906 (evolving from Dominion Shaft #1).

ZED LAKE, MB: The last in a series of alphabetically named lakes in the region. The "zed" spelling wasn't necessarily a nationalistic act—the phonetic style was used in the entire series: Ex Lake, Wye Lake, and so on. (Wye Lake was originally called Nootutikwayo, Cree for "he hunts caribou"). Those who named A Lake, NB, and Lac Y, QC, opted for the minimalist approach (see notes on the Geographer's Map, p. 82).

MUSHER LAKE, ON: Probably named for the dogsled teams that crossed it in the winter. The word "mush" as a command to sled dogs comes from English explorers in the Yukon who misheard francophone sled operators when they yelled *Marche!* ("Walk!") to their dogs. When the anglophone trappers took up the rigs and started yelling "Mush!," their dogs failed to correct them, so the neologism stuck. In the 1800s and early 1900s the RCMP used dogsleds widely, especially in the Territories. In 1969 the RCMP retired their last dogsled, which had been used on the route between Old Crow, YT, and Fort MacPherson, NT, and replaced it with a snowmobile.

LAKE LABERGE, YT: Named for Michael Laberge, who spent months in the wild surveying the area for the Western Union Telegraph Company in 1867, only to discover that the whole telegraph project had been cancelled. Klondike prospectors who rafted along the lake as a shortcut were taking a risk: a calm day meant an easy journey, a sudden gust of wind down its narrow length meant possible death. The lake became a Canadian legend (spelled as "Lake Lebarge") in Robert Service's poem "The Cremation of Sam McGee," which sold millions of copies around the world.

INSTRUCTIONS FOR AN IGLOO

Find a patch of compact snow, or stamp some down with your feet. Dig out blocks with a spade or saw, refine them with an axe (or a ski), and arrange them in a circle around the area you are excavating. The first row should slant inward, and then subsequent layers of smaller blocks will form a dome. Fill the cracks between the blocks with more snow, cut out a small entrance and smooth the inside walls. Allow the warmth from your body and your camp stove to melt the inside surface a bit—this will refreeze and form a protective and insulating layer of ice. Lay down some furs, put up a picture of your favourite Mountie, and relax!

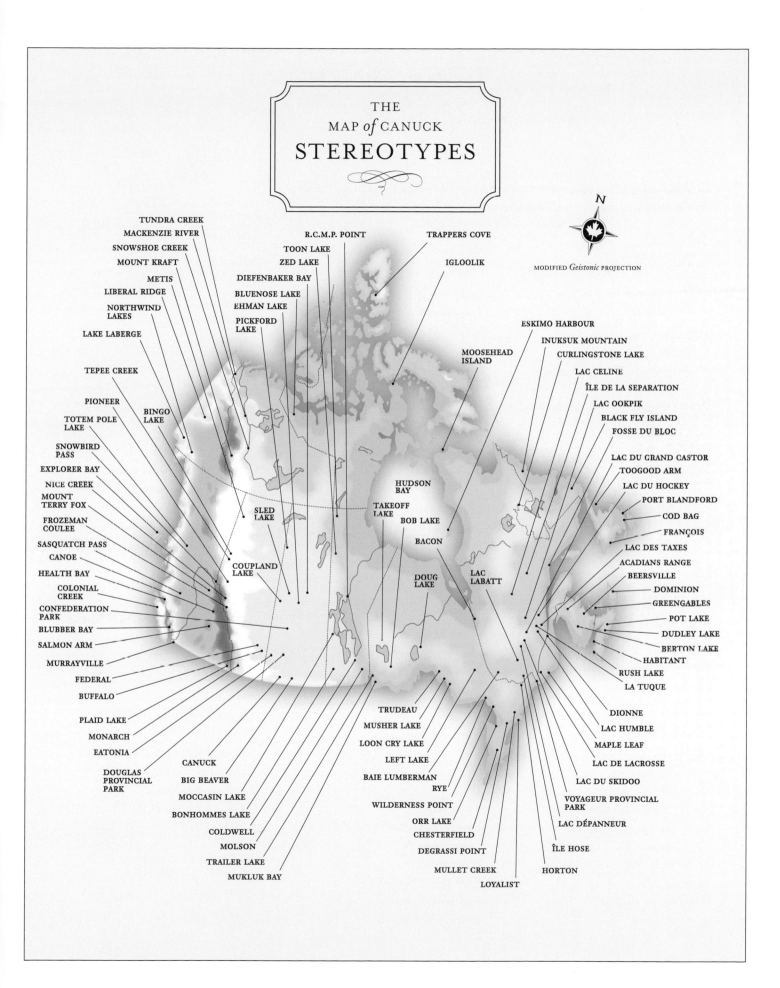

THE MAP *of* CANUCK STEREOTYPES

MODIFIED *Geistonic* PROJECTION

APPENDIX A: ALMOST MAPS
Maps in the Subjunctive

A few maps are still in progress because we can't find enough relevant place names. Suggestions? Send them to maps@geist.com.

HARD ROCK
Moshers Corner, NS
Portage de la Mauvais Musique, QC
Hendrix Lake, BC
Healey Falls, ON
Rock Bay, BC
Altamont, MB
Metal Dome, BC

WOMEN
Chick Lake, NT
Lac Old-Wives, QC
Ladysmith, BC
Ta Ta Creek, BC
Amazon, SK
Biddys Mount, NL
Bitch Lake, ON
Fox Rock, NL

MEN
Hairy Hill, AB
Jock River, ON
Manly, AB
Oddfellow Lake, MB
Tie Creek, MB
Nut Mountain, SK
Lac Agressif, QC

LABOUR
Old Sweat, NS
Anvil Brook, NB
Seven Days Work, NB
Jump Up and Go Down, NL
Good Enough Big Pond, NL
Erg Mountain, BC
Factorydale, NS
Holdfast, SK
Carry the Kettle, NS

AILMENTS
Mono, ON
Cold Lake, AB
Coughlan, NB
Transmission Pond, NL
Languish Lake, NT
Hole in the Head, NL
Coronary Lake, NB
Sick Wife Creek, BC
Lac du Virus, QC
Baie Carbuncle, QC

PRECIOUS STONES
Jewel Lake, BC
Jade City, BC
Little Gem, AB
Jewellville, ON
Bijoux Falls, BC
Diamond, QC
Sapphire Lake, SK

CHRISTMAS
North Pole Stream, NB
St. Nicholas Peak, AB
Christmas Creek, YT
Tiny Tim Lake, BC
Yule Rock, BC
St. Carols, NL
Santy Lake, NT
Christmas Island, ON
Saint-Noël, QC

VINTNERS
Baie du Vin, QC
Brandywine, BC
Champagne, YT
Corkscrew Channel, ON
Red Wine River, NL
Grape Run, ON

Lac du Pinot, QC

MYTHOLOGY
Juno, MB
Jupiter Bay, NT
Avalon Peninsula, NL
Lac Adonis, QC
Pegasus Lake, SK
Mount Sisyphus, BC
Argonaut Pass, BC
Hercules Bank, ON

DRUGS
Stoner, BC
Pusher Lake, ON
Zone, ON
Jones, ON
Crique Pill, QC
Weed Creek, AB
High Level, AB
Trippers Head, NL
Crackers Rocks, NL

INTERROGATIVE
How Lake, NL
Whonnock, BC
Wha Ti, NT
Quand Shoal, NL
Where Lake, ON
Whyac, BC
Lac du Pourquoi, QC
Lac Pourquoi-Pas, QC

APPENDIX B: DEMONYMS

What are you called when you live there?

Banff: Banffite
Belleville: Bellevillian
Bragg Creek: Bragg Cricket
Brandon: Brandonite
Calgary: Calgarian
Charlottetown: Charlottetowner
Chemainus: Chemaniac
Culp: Culprit
Czar: Czardine
Dawson: Dawsonite
Digby: Digbonian
Edmonton: Edmontonian
Egmont: Egg Monster
Faro: Faroite
Fredericton: Frederictonian
Gaspé: Gaspésien
Gravelberg: Gravel Burger
Guelph: Guelphite
Halifax: Haligonian
Hamilton: Hamiltonian
Iqaluit: Iqalummiuq
Jellyby: Jellybite
Kamloops: Kamloopsian
Kelowna: Kelownan
Kenora: Kenoraite
La Tuque: Latuquois
Matsqui: Mat Squealer
Medicine Hat: Hatter
Moncton: Monctonian
Montreal: Montrealais, Montrealer
Moose Jaw: Moose Javian
North Bay: North Bayite
Orangeville: Orange Villain
Ottawa: Ottowan
P.E.I.: Peeler

Penhold: Penholder
Penticton: Pentictonite
Peterborough: Peterburian
Pictou: Pictonian
Regina: Reginaian
St. John: St. Johner
St. John's: St. Johnsians/Townies/Baymen
Sainte-Élizabeth: Bayollais
Sandy Hook: Sandy Hooker
Saskatoon: Saskatonian
Sault Ste. Marie: Sooite
Scarborough: Scarberian
Smithers: Smithereen
Stainer: Abstainer
Stratford: Stratfordian
Sudbury: Sudburian
Summerside: Summersider
Surrey: Surrealist
Swift Current: Speeky Creeker
Sydney: Sydneyite
Terrace: Terracites
Thunder Bay: Lakeheader
Toronto: Torontonian
Trois-Rivières: Trifluvien
Ucluelet: Ucuelily
Vancouver: Vancouverite
Victoria: Victorian
Ville de Québec: Québécoise/Québécois
Vita: Vitaman, Vitawoman
Winnipeg: Winnipegger
Yarmouth: Yarmouthian
Yellowknife: Yellowknifer

Send your own demonyms to maps@geist.com.

The official authorization and recording of toponyms, or place names, began in Canada in 1897 with the creation of the Geographic Board of Canada. The board was established in response to booming immigration and far-reaching resource development, which made it crucial to clarify areas with multiple names, or multiple areas with the same name, and to standardize the spelling of names across different records.

In 1961 the board was reorganized, and the right to decide on most official names was given to the provinces (the naming rights for Native and military reserves and national parks are controlled jointly by the provinces and the respective federal departments). The territories were given the right to authorize their own names in 1984. The board was restructured again in 2000 and now is known as the Geographical Names Board of Canada (GNBC). Natural Resources Canada is responsible for appointing the Chair of the GNBC and for managing the Secretariat, which oversees the day-to-day functions of the organization. The other twenty-six members of the board represent cartography and geomatics, hydrographic charting, translation, archives, parks, defence, linguistics, Native affairs, statistics, and each provincial and territorial government.

The GNBC is responsible for naming standards and guidelines, records, promotion, and lobbying for international standards. It also oversees a complete database of official Canadian place names, which is held by Energy Mines and Resources Canada. Each province and territory generally uses its own researchers to seek out local names and report them to the GNBC. Most names come from residents of the area, local resource industries, and historical records. The names of each region reflect both its history and its sociological priorities. In Newfoundland, for example, many names came from early Portuguese fishers, and the coast of British Columbia is peppered with names given by Spanish explorers. Prairie naming shows a history of pioneering by Ukrainian,

Mennonite, and eastern European immigrants. More modern naming trends honour notable Canadians, reflect pop culture or the post-structuralist whims of outdoor adventurers, or reclaim the original names used by local First Nations and Inuit people. Members of the public can also propose toponyms for unnamed features by sending a report (including coordinates, a marked map, the origins of the name, and the reason it should be adopted) to their appropriate provincial or territorial representative on the board.

Each year thousands of names are brought before the board, and thousands more remain unregistered. When a feature or area does not have an official name and requires one, the board generally adopts the most common local name, except in cases of duplication, bad taste, or spelling that doesn't conform to standard language rules. When there is no local name, the board consults with residents or industry and creates a new one, leaning toward words from regional Native languages, descriptive words, references to regional historic events, or the names of pioneers, explorers, or Canadian soldiers who died in service.

Canadian place names are usually official in either French or English, though there are eighty-one Pan-Canadian sites— places considered significant enough to have two official names (such as Lake Winnipeg/Lac Winnipeg, the Laurentian Mountains/Les Laurentides, the St. Lawrence River/ Fleuve Saint-Laurent, the Beaufort Sea/Mer de Beaufort, and Anticosti Island/Île d'Anticosti). As well, Manitoba, Ontario, and New Brunswick have a few "dual names" where local usage required a name in both official languages. Dual names are also given to features that straddle the Quebec border: the English name is official on one side and the French name is official on the other.

The GNBC database of Canadian place names is available to everyone at geonames.nrcan.gc.ca.

Appendix D: Bibliography

Akrigg, Helen and G.P.V. *British Columbia Place Names.* Victoria: Sono Nis, 1986.

Bowers, Vivien. *Crazy About Canada: Amazing Things Kids Want to Know.* Toronto: Maple Tree Press, 2006.

Brown, Jeremy, and David Ondaatje. *The First Original Unexpurgated Authentic Canadian Book of Lists.* Toronto: Pagurian Press, 1978.

Coupland, Douglas. *Souvenir of Canada.* Vancouver: Douglas & McIntyre, 2002.

Coutts, R. *Yukon Places and Names.* Sidney: Grays Publishing, 1980.

English, L.E.F. *Historic Newfoundland.* St. John's: Newfoundland Department of Tourism, 1979.

Ferguson, Will. *Beauty Tips from Moose Jaw.* Toronto: Vintage Canada, 2004.

Geographical Names of Manitoba. Winnipeg: Manitoba Conservation, 2000.

Gudgeon, Chris. *The Naked Truth: The Untold Story of Sex in Canada.* Vancouver: Greystone, 2003.

———. *Stan Rogers: North West Passage.* Kingston: Fox Music Books, 2004.

Hamilton, William B. *Place Names of Atlantic Canada.* Toronto: University of Toronto Press, 1997.

———. *The Macmillan Book of Canadian Place Names.* Toronto: Macmillan of Canada, 1978.

Hobson, Archie, ed. *The Cambridge Gazetteer of the United States and Canada: A Dictionary of Places.* Cambridge: Cambridge University Press, 1995.

Holmgren, Eric and Patricia. *Over 2000 Place Names of Alberta,* 3rd edition. Saskatoon: Western Producer Prairie Books, 1976.

LM Media Marketing Services. *What's in a Toponym? The Story of Canada's Geographic Names.* Video. Energy Mines and Resources Canada, 1992.

McClure, Robert Le Mesurier. *The Discovery of the North-West Passage.* Edmonton: Hurtig, 1969.

Rayburn, Alan. *Geographical Names of Prince Edward Island.* Ottawa: Canadian Permanent Committee on Geographical Names, 1973.

———. *Naming Canada: Stories about Place Names from Canadian Geographic.* Toronto: University of Toronto Press, 1994.

———. *Place Names of Ontario.* Toronto: University of Toronto Press, 1997.

Robideau, Henri, and Peter Day. *From the Pacific to the Atlantic: Canada's Gigantic!.* Toronto: Summerhill Press, 1988.

Royal Canadian Geographic Society. *The Canadian Atlas.* Montreal: Reader's Digest, 2004.

Russell, E.T. *What's in a Name: Travelling though Saskatchewan with the Story Behind 1600 Place-names.* Saskatoon: Western Producer, 1973.

Searle, Ronald, and Kildare Dobbs. *The Great Fur Opera: Annals of the Hudson's Bay Company 1670–1970.* Toronto: McClelland and Stewart, 1970.

Snider, Janet, and Betty Sherwood. *La Salle and the Rise of New France.* Toronto: Canchron Books, 2005.

Stanford, Quentin H., ed. *Canadian Oxford School Atlas,* 6th edition. Toronto: Oxford University Press, 1992.

Wallechinsky, David, Amy Wallace, Ira Basen and Jane Farrow, eds. *The Book of Lists: Canadian Edition.* Toronto: Knopf Canada, 2005.

Zuehlke, Mark. *The B.C. Fact Book.* Vancouver: Whitecap Books, 1995.

———. *The Yukon Fact Book.* Vancouver: Whitecap Books, 1998.

geonames.nrcan.gc.ca

ilmbwww.gov.bc.ca/bcnames

pwnhc.learnnet.nt.ca/databases/geodb.htm

www.ainc-inac.gc.ca

www.geographynetwork.ca

www.islandregister.com/placenames/pindex.html

www.nsplacenames.ca

www.toponymie.gouv.qc.ca

www.wikipedia.org

www.gnb.ca/0016/Wolastoqiyik/place-e.asp

www.stanrogers.net

www.afn.ca

atlas.gc.ca

Appendix E: Selected Sources for Map Notes

Hockey Map, p. 12
Geographical Names of Manitoba; *Naming Canada: Stories about Place Names from Canadian Geographic*; *The Yukon Fact Book*; gsc.nrcan.gc.ca/beaufort/pingos_e.php; *What's in a Name? Travelling Through Saskatchewan With the Story Behind 1600 Place-names*; *British Columbia Place Names*; www.toponymie.gouv.qc.ca; www.uqo.ca/observer/RegionalOutaouais/Social/Pauv.pdf; www.nhl.com; www.wikipedia.org

Beer Map, p. 14
The Macmillan Book of Canadian Place Names; *The Cambridge Gazetteer of the United States and Canada*; www.mitiq.com; www.thecanadianencyclopedia.com; *Over 2000 Place Names of Alberta*; www.toponymie.gouv.qc.ca; www.foamlake.com; *Geographical Names of Manitoba*; pwnhc.learnnet.nt.ca/databases/geodb.htm; www.nsplacenames.ca; *Souvenir of Canada*; archives.cbc.ca

Entomological Map, p. 16
Geographical Names of Manitoba; *Over 2000 Place Names of Alberta*; pwnhc.learnnet.nt.ca; www.cbif.gc.ca; www.rideau-info.com

Angst Map, p. 18
The Macmillan Book of Canadian Place Names; www.heritage.nf.ca; www.thecanadianencyclopedia.com; www.mun.ca; *Naming Canada*; *Place Names of Atlantic Canada*; *Geographical Names of Manitoba*; *The Macmillan Book of Canadian Place Names*; pwnhc.learnnet.nt.ca; *Place Names of Atlantic Canada*; www.wikipedia.com; www.centralnewfoundland.com

Doughnut Map, p. 20
British Columbia Place Names; www.crowsnest-highway.ca; *Geographical Names of Manitoba*; *Place Names of Ontario*; www.wikipedia.org; *Over 2000 Place Names of Alberta*; www.nsplacenames.ca; www.bakerlake.org; www.cbc.ca; www.reuters.com

Celestial Map, p. 22
What's in a Name: Travelling though Saskatchewan with the Story Behind 1600 Place-names; *Naming Canada*; *Over 2000 Place Names of Alberta*; www.bivouac.com; pwnhc.learnnet.nt.ca; www.wikipedia.org; www.bartleby.com; www.gov.mb.ca; *Geographical Names of Manitoba*; www.toponymie.gouv.qc.ca; www.astro.ubc.ca; www.rasc.ca

Number 1 Map, p. 24
The Cambridge Gazetteer of the United States and Canada; *Place Names of Ontario*; *The Yukon Fact Book*; www.bigriveryukon.ca; www.toponymie.gouv.qc.ca; www.wikipedia.org; www.amazon.com; *The B.C. Fact Book*; *Geographical Names of Manitoba*; *Statistics Canada*; www.canada.gc.ca; nrcan.gc.ca

Confict Map, p. 26
Geographical Names of Manitoba; *The Macmillan Book of Canadian Place Names*; *Place Names of Atlantic Canada*; www.toponymie.gouv.qc.ca; rootsweb.com/~qcchatea/placenames/n.htm; pwnhc.learnnet.nt.ca; *The Cambridge Gazetteer of the United States and Canada*; geonames.nrcan.gc.ca; *What's in a Name: Travelling though Saskatchewan with the Story Behind 1600 Place-names*; *Naming Canada*; www.pc.gc.ca; www.hockeyfights.com

Map of Board Games, p. 28
Yukon Places and Names; *Yukon Fact Book*; *What's in a Name: Travelling though Saskatchewan with the Story Behind 1600 Place-names*; www.toponymie.gouv.qc.ca; *Place Names of Atlantic Canada*; *Naming Canada*; *Over 2000 Place Names of Alberta*; www.abheritage.ca; *British Columbia Place Names*

Map of Kitchen Implements, p. 30
British Columbia Place Names; www.bivouac.com; *Yukon Places and Names*; www.captaincooksociety.com; pwnhc.learnnet.nt.ca; *Place Names of Ontario*; *Macmillan Book of Canadian Place Names*; *Naming Canada*; *Place Names of Ontario*; www.cbc.ca

Map of Toppings, p. 32
The Cambridge Gazetteer of the United States and Canada; *Macmillan Book of Canadian Place Names*; *The Yukon Fact Book*; pwnhc.learnnet.nt.ca; *Geographical Names of Manitoba*; srmwww.gov.bc.ca; *Over 2000 Place Names of Alberta*; www.toponymie.gouv.qc.ca; www.cbc.ca; geonames.nrcan.gc.ca; www.agr.gov.sk.ca

Spooky Map, p. 34
Geographical Names of Prince Edward Island; www.bivouac.com; *Macmillan Book of Canadian Place Names*; *The Yukon Fact Book*; *The Book of Lists, Canadian Edition*; *Geographical Names of Manitoba*; *Over 2000 Place Names of Alberta*; www.env.gov.bc.ca/bcparks; *British Columbia Place Names*; *The B.C. Fact Book*; www.scugogheritage.com; www.pararesearchers.org

MAP OF BODY PARTS, P. 36

Naming Canada; Macmillan Book of Canadian Place Names; The Book of Lists: Canadian Edition; pwnhc.learnnet.nt.ca; *British Columbia Place Names; Geographical Names of Prince Edward Island;* www.islandregister.com; *Over 2000 Place Names of Alberta; Place Names of Ontario*

MAP OF LOUDMOUTHS & OUTBURSTS, P. 38

The B.C. Fact Book; British Columbia Place Names; Place Names of Atlantic Canada; www.env.gov.nl.ca; *Macmillan Book of Canadian Place Names;* www.toponymie.gouv.qc.ca; *Beauty Tips from Moose Jaw; Naming Canada; The Cambridge Gazetteer of the United States and Canada;* www.usscouts.org

MAP OF NICKNAMES, P. 40

Naming Canada; The Macmillan Book of Canadian Place Names; What's in a Name: Travelling though Saskatchewan with the Story Behind 1600 Place-names; The Macmillan Book of Canadian Place Names; www.gnb.ca; www.toponymie.gouv.qc.ca; www.reference.com

IMPOLITE MAP, P. 42

The Macmillan Book of Canadian Place Names; Place Names of Atlantic Canada; www.offdarock.com; www.countycrier.com; *Place Names of Atlantic Canada;* pwnhc.learnnet.nt.ca; *What's in a Name: Travelling though Saskatchewan with the Story Behind 1600 Place-names; Naming Canada;* www.toponymie.gouv.qc.ca; www.alertbay.com; *British Columbia Place Names; Naming Canada*

MAP OF CRIME & PUNISHMENT, P. 44

Geographical Names of Manitoba; collections.ic.gc.ca; www.toponymie.gouv.qc.ca; *Geographical Names of Prince Edward Island; What's in a Name: Travelling though Saskatchewan with the Story Behind 1600 Place-names;* pwnhc.learnnet.nt.ca; *Over 2000 Place Names of Alberta; Place Names of Atlantic Canada;* covered_bridges.tripod.com

MAP OF HEAVEN AND HELL, P. 46

The Cambridge Gazetteer of the United States and Canada; pwnhc.learnnet.nt.ca; *The Discovery of the North-West Passage;* www.collectionscanada.ca; *The Macmillan Book of Canadian Place Names; Geographical Names of Manitoba;*

The Cambridge Gazetteer of the United States and Canada; Place Names of Atlantic Canada; Place Names of Ontario; Naming Canada; What's in a Name: Travelling though Saskatchewan with the Story Behind 1600 Place-names

SARTORIAL MAP, P. 48

Naming Canada; www.canada.com; *Geographical Names of Manitoba;* www.centralcoastbc.com; ilmbwww.gov.bc.ca/bcnames; www.gg.ca; *Place Names of Ontario;* www.hbc.com

MAP OF HOUSE PETS, P. 50

Place Names of Atlantic Canada; Naming Canada; www.pugwash.org; *What's in a Name: Travelling though Saskatchewan with the Story Behind 1600 Place-names; British Columbia Place Names;* pwnhc.learnnet.nt.ca; www.navalmuseum.ab.ca; *The Macmillan Book of Canadian Place Names;* www.toponymie.gouv.qc.ca; *Geographical Names of Manitoba;* www.akc.org

HOLLYWOOD MAP, P. 52

Geographical Names of Manitoba; ilmbwww.gov.bc.ca/bcnames; *British Columbia Place Names; What's in a Name: Travelling though Saskatchewan with the Story Behind 1600 Place-names;* pwnhc.learnnet.nt.ca; *Place Names of Ontario*

MAP OF JOE JOBS, P. 54

n/a

AUTHORITY MAP, P. 56

Place Names of Atlantic Canada; The Cambridge Gazetteer of the United States and Canada; Place Names of Ontario; What's in a Name: Travelling though Saskatchewan with the Story Behind 1600 Place-names; pwnhc.learnnet.nt.ca; *Over 2000 Place Names of Alberta; The Cambridge Gazetteer of the United States and Canada; Geographical Names of Manitoba;* www.cbc.ca

CANADIAN MAP OF THE WORLD, P. 58

The Macmillan Book of Canadian Place Names; The Cambridge Gazetteer of the United States and Canada; Geographical Names of Manitoba; www.islandregister.com; www.virtualsk.com; *What's in a Name: Travelling though Saskatchewan with the Story Behind 1600 Place-names;* www.nsplacenames.ca; www.athensontario.com; *Yukon Places and Names; The Yukon Fact Book:* www.cic.gc.ca

CANADIAN MAP OF THE UNITED STATES, P. 60

www.nps.gov/fova; www.ci.vancouver.wa.us; www.jaspertx.
org; jaspercounty.georgia.gov; www.torontoohio.com;
www.ci.yukon.ok.us; www.census.gov

ORIGINAL MAP OF CANADA, P. 64

geonames.nrcan.gc.ca; www.nunanet.com; pwnhc.learnnet.
nt.ca; www.tuk.ca; *Place Names of Ontario*; www.tolatsga.org;
www.heritage.nf.ca; www.nunatsiavut.com; *What's in a Name:
Travelling though Saskatchewan with the Story Behind 1600 Place-
names*; www.thecanadianencyclopedia.com; www.ainc-inac.
gc.ca; www.afn.ca

CBC MAP, P. 66

collections.ic.gc.ca; *Over 2000 Place Names of Alberta*;
British Columbia Place Names; *The B.C. Fact Book*; www.pc.gc.ca;
Geist No. 53

MAP OF PEGGY'S CANADA, P. 68

n/a

STAN ROGERS MAP, P. 70

www.stanrogers.net; *Stan Rogers: Northwest Passage*

FAIRY TALE MAP, P. 72

www.destination-nfld.com; pwnhc.learnnet.nt.ca;
The Macmillan Book of Canadian Place Names; *British Columbia
Place Names*; www.doukhobor.org; www.civilization.ca;
Place Names of Ontario; archives.cbc.ca

ART-MAKING MAP, P. 74

Geographical Names of Manitoba; *Place Names of Atlantic
Canada*; www.nbm-mnb.ca; www.toponymie.gouv.qc.ca;
pwnhc.learnnet.nt.ca

PHILOSOPHER'S MAP, P. 76

Place Names of Atlantic Canada; www.heritagepursuit.com;
pwnhc.learnnet.nt.ca; *What's in a Name: Travelling though
Saskatchewan with the Story Behind 1600 Place-names*;
www.toponymie.gouv.qc.ca; *Place Names of Ontario*;
www.sixnations.org; *British Columbia Place Names*;
www.edu.gov.on.ca

LITERARY MAP, P. 78

Geographical Names of Manitoba; *Over 2000 Place Names of
Alberta*; *What's in a Name: Travelling though Saskatchewan with
the Story Behind 1600 Place-names*; pwnhc.learnnet.nt.ca;
Yukon Places and Names; *British Columbia Place Names*;
www.thecanadianencyclopedia.com;
www.librairiepantoute.qc.ca

LINGUISTIC MAP, P. 80

Place Names of Ontario; ilmbwww.gov.bc.ca/bcnames;
www.toponymie.gouv.qc.ca; pwnhc.learnnet.nt.ca;
Geographical Names of Prince Edward Island; *Over 2000 Place
Names of Alberta*; www.town.vulcan.ab.ca; Statistics Canada

GEOGRAPHER'S MAP, P. 82

Yukon Places and Names; www.nrcan.gc.ca/inter/trailblazers/
logan_e.html; www.cbc.ca; www.bivouac.com; geonames.
nrcan.gc.ca; www.kiwiherald.com; *What's in a Name: Travelling
though Saskatchewan with the Story Behind 1600 Place-names*; *Western Canada Wilderness Committee*; atlas.gc.ca

HAIRCUTS MAP, P. 84

British Columbia Place Names; www.britishcolumbia.com;
www.rideau-info.co; *Place Names of Ontario*; *Naming Canada*;
The Macmillan Book of Canadian Place Names; pwnhc.learnnet.
nt.ca; www.dogrib.ca; *Over 2000 Place Names of Alberta*;
www. collections.ic.gc.ca

MAP OF MALLS, P. 86

www.wikipedia.org; www.westedmall.com; www.toronto.ca/
path; www.yukonalaska.com; www.icsc.org

RETAIL MAP, P. 88

The Macmillan Book of Canadian Place Names; *The Great Fur
Opera: Annals of the Hudson's Bay Company*; *British Columbia
Place Names*; www.bivouac.com; www.toponymie.gouv.qc.ca;
www.thecanadianencyclopedia.com; www.bonjourquebec.
com; *What's in a Name: Travelling though Saskatchewan with the
Story Behind 1600 Place-names*; Statistics Canada

MONEY MAP, P. 90

Place Names of Atlantic Canada; Historic Newfoundland; Geographical Names of Manitoba; Place Names of Atlantic Canada; What's in a Name: Travelling though Saskatchewan with the Story Behind 1600 Place-names; Place Names of Atlantic Canada; www.wikipedia.org; *British Columbia Place Names;* www.canlit.ca; *Yukon Places and Names; Yukon Fact Book;* www.collections.ic.gc.ca; www.bankofcanada.ca

CHEAP MAP, P. 92

Macmillan Book of Canadian Place Names; Place Names of Atlantic Canada; www.islandregister.com; *The Cambridge Gazetteer of the United States and Canada;* www.canadianencyclopedia.ca; www.collectionscanada.ca; www.wikipedia.org; www2.marianopolis.edu/quebechistory; www.toponymie.gouv.qc.ca; *Yukon Places and Names; Geographical Names of Manitoba;* www.vancouverislandkayak.com; www.pc.gc.ca

GAY MAP, P. 94

The Macmillan Book of Canadian Place Names; www.toponymie.gouv.qc.ca; *Geographical Names of Manitoba;* www.cbif.gc.ca; *What's in a Name: Travelling though Saskatchewan with the Story Behind 1600 Place-names; Place Names of Atlantic Canada;* www.heritage.nf.ca; pwnhc.learnnet.nt.ca; archives.cbc.ca

MEAT MAP, P. 96

www.toponymie.gouv.qc.ca; www.islandregister.com; *Geist* Nos. 49, 50; www.nsplacenames.ca; *Place Names of Atlantic Canada; What's in a Name: Travelling though Saskatchewan with the Story Behind 1600 Place-names; Over 2000 Place Names of Alberta;* www.head-smashed-in.com; *British Columbia Place Names;* www.thecanadianencyclopedia.com; www.ats.agr.gc.ca

EROTIC MAP, P. 98

The Macmillan Book of Canadian Place Names; Place Names of Atlantic Canada; www.aroundthebay.ca; *What's in a Name: Travelling though Saskatchewan with the Story Behind 1600 Place-names; The Yukon Fact Book;* www.toponymie.gouv.qc.ca; *Place Names of Ontario;* www.greycounty.ca; *The Naked Truth: The Untold Story of Sex in Canada*

MENSTRUAL MAP, P. 100

The Macmillan Book of Canadian Place Names; The Cambridge Gazetteer of the United States and Canada; British Columbia Place Names; Place Names of Atlantic Canada; pwnhc.learnnet.nt.ca; *Over 2000 Place Names of Alberta; The Macmillan Book of Canadian Place Names;* www.wikipedia.org; www.collectionscanada.ca; www.hc-sc.gc.ca

AUTOMOTIVE MAP, P. 102

The Macmillan Book of Canadian Place Names; Over 2000 Place Names of Alberta; Place Names of Atlantic Canada; www.littletechshoppe.com; www.northword.ca; *British Columbia Place Names;* www.toponymie.gouv.qc.ca; *Place Names of Ontario;* www.forces.gc.ca; www.bricklin.org

HAPPY MAP, P. 104

The Macmillan Book of Canadian Place Names; Naming Canada; The Cambridge Gazetteer of the United States and Canada; Place Names of Atlantic Canada; pwnhc.learnnet.nt.ca; *Place Names of Ontario; Geographical Names of Prince Edward Island; Geographical Names of Manitoba;* www.legermarketing.com

APOCALYPSE MAP, P. 106

Geographical Names of Manitoba; www.toponymie.gouv.qc.ca; www.nsplacenames.ca; *Over 2000 Place Names of Alberta;* www.crowsnest.bc.ca; pwnhc.learnnet.nt.ca; www.alertbay.com; *British Columbia Place Names;* www.wikipedia.org; archives.cbc.ca

WORLD'S LARGEST MAP, P. 108

www.vegreville.com; www.wlra.us; www.roadsideattractions.ca; *Canada's Gigantic!*

MAP OF CANUCK STEREOTYPES, P. 110

The Macmillan Book of Canadian Place Names; www.toponymie.gouv.qc.ca; *The Cambridge Gazetteer of the United States and Canada; Place Names of Atlantic Canada; Geographical Names of Manitoba; The Yukon Fact Book;* www.rcmp-grc.gc.ca; *Yukon Places and Names; Crazy About Canada;* www.pbs.org

INDEX OF PLACES

Note: Italicized page numbers signify a text entry.

ABOUT GEIST

Geist is a quarterly magazine of ideas and culture with a profound (if offbeat) sense of place, and is home to the Cross-Canada Phrasebook-in-Progress, the Distance Writing Prize, the Honorary Canadian Award, Haiku Night in Canada, and the Literal Literary Postcard Story Contest, among other made-in-Canada cultural endeavours.

In fiction, non-fiction, poetry, comix, photography, and the interactive accumulation of little-known fact—as well as strange cartography—the magazine reflects the cultural landscape as it evolves and registers the sensibility of people in the process of inventing the country we call Canada.

The magazine is published in Vancouver by the Geist Foundation, established in 1990. It is run by a small staff of part-time publishers and volunteers and is overseen by an editorial board of writers, editors, photographers, and educators. *Geist* enjoys a circulation larger than any literary magazine in Canada has ever achieved. Over the years it has been awarded dozens of nominations and prizes by the Western Magazine Awards and by the National Magazine Awards—for Best Column, Travel Writing, Science Essay, One-of-a-Kind Essay, Poem, Photo Essay, Fiction, and Cover, as well as two awards for Magazine of the Year.

Geist is a German word meaning "spirit"—as in mind, intellect, mettle, wit and/or ghost.

To subscribe, or for news, information, and generous samples of writing, art, and photography from *Geist*, stop in at www.geist.com.

If you have suggestions for our cartographic teams, or complaints or compliments, you can write to *Geist* directly at maps@geist.com.